A PRACTICAL GUIDE TO MENTAL HEALTH PROBLEMS IN CHILDREN WITH AUTISTIC SPECTRUM DISORDER

A PRACTICAL GUIDE *to* MENTAL HEALTH PROBLEMS *in* CHILDREN *with* AUTISTIC SPECTRUM DISORDER

It's not just their autism!

KHALID KARIM,
ALVINA ALI *and*
MICHELLE O'REILLY

Jessica Kingsley *Publishers*
London and Philadelphia

Twenty-five per cent of the author's royalties are being donated to local autism charities: Spectrum and Leicestershire Autistic Society.

First published in 2014
by Jessica Kingsley Publishers
73 Collier Street
London N1 9BE, UK
and
400 Market Street, Suite 400
Philadelphia, PA 19106, USA

www.jkp.com

Library of Congress Cataloging in Publication Data
Karim, Khalid.
  A practical guide to mental health problems in children with autistic spectrum disorder : it's not just
their autism! / Khalid Karim, Alvina Ali, and Michelle O'Reilly.
    pages cm
  Includes bibliographical references and index.
  ISBN 978-1-84905-323-5 (alk. paper)
  1. Asperger's syndrome in children. 2. Autism in children. 3. Anxiety in children. 4. Attention-deficit-
disordered children. 5. Asperger's syndrome--Patients--Mental health. 6. Comorbidity. I. Ali, Alvina. II.
O'Reilly, Michelle. III. Title.
  RJ506.A9K36 2014
  618.92'858832--dc23
                          2013015438

British Library Cataloguing in Publication Data
A CIP catalogue record for this book is available from the British Library

ISBN 978 1 84905 323 5
eISBN 978 0 85700 697 4

Printed and bound in Great Britain by Bell & Bain Ltd, Glasgow

For Adam, Omar and Matthew,
the people with ASD in our lives

LIST OF BOXES AND FIGURES
Boxes

Figures

ABBREVIATIONS

ADHD Attention Deficit Hyperactivity Disorder

ASD Autistic Spectrum Disorder

BDI Beck Depression Inventory

CBT Cognitive Behaviour Therapy

DSM Diagnostic and Statistical Manual of mental disorders

EEG Electroencephalogram

FCBT Family Cognitive Behaviour Therapy

ICD International Classification of Diseases

IPT Interpersonal Therapy

OCD Obsessive Compulsive Disorder

ODD Oppositional Defiant Disorder

MRI Magnetic Resonance Imaging

NHS National Health Service

SSRI Selective Serotonin Reuptake Inhibitor

WHO World Health Organization

PREFACE

The need to address the mental health difficulties of children on the autistic spectrum is becoming more evident. There has been an increase in the numbers of children diagnosed with Autistic Spectrum Disorder (ASD) and, while a greater awareness of the condition is positive, it is increasingly apparent that services are recognising an increase of comorbid mental health problems in these children. It is, therefore, important that all those involved in the care of these children are aware of these difficulties and have an understanding of the strategies available to address these problems. Mental health needs have been the subject of increasing research and have also been highlighted by campaigns such as the UK National Autistic Society's 'You Need to Know' (2012). There remains, however, a lack of information and practical guidance to help parents and professionals ameliorate the difficulties these comorbid conditions can give the child with ASD.

This book aims to fill the gap between understanding ASD and its relationship to mental health presentations. While providing basic information about ASD, the book will not serve as an introductory text to the condition as such information can be found elsewhere (e.g. in *The Complete Guide to Asperger's Syndrome* by Tony Attwood). Rather, we propose here to consider the relationship between ASD and mental health presentations in children and young people, and what can help to improve the lives of them and their families.

Although there is an extensive published library on ASD from different perspectives, there are few books available on the subject of mental health and ASD. Although other books have provided an overview of the subject or have considered specific aspects of the condition (such as anxiety), there are very few texts that deliver the entirety of the mental health field in a practical and accessible fashion. This is something we address in this text by providing a clear, accessible and practical guide for parents and professionals to help them in the daily routines of living or working with children with ASD and comorbid mental health problems.

STRUCTURE OF THE BOOK

The introductory chapters of this book focus on a brief overview of ASD and mental health, giving a context for the more practical advice covered in later chapters. The introductory chapters also provide definitions and consider the important aspects of mental health and ASD.

Following chapters focus on the common comorbid (additional) mental health problems experienced by children with ASD, such as Attention Deficit Hyperactivity Disorder (ADHD), anxiety, tics, eating disorders and depression, illustrating these issues with case studies.

In the later part of the book, we provide practical advice and strategies for both parents and professionals. Some of the strategies described will be suitable for home, school and other settings, but there are also descriptions on the more specialist treatments available. The nature of the text will thus help to educate professionals regarding appropriate approaches to treatment and will help parents to demystify the techniques used.

INTENDED AUDIENCE

This book has been written for a diverse audience, and we expect it to be of use to parents or carers of children with ASD, as well as other family members. This is a resource which is designed to help parents and families to better understand mental health and ASD and provide some practical advice for managing these conditions.

We have also written this book to help a wide range of professionals involved in the care of children with ASD, including: teachers, social workers, psychologists, counsellors, psychiatrists, volunteer workers, teaching/learning support assistants, family support workers, family therapists, community psychiatric nurses, occupational therapists, speech therapists, academics and other mental health professionals.

ASD is a global issue, affecting both children and adults. Awareness of mental health difficulties is becoming increasingly recognised internationally, with a wide range of different problems presenting. This book is a useful resource for an international audience as the practical approach to helping these children is relevant to most countries.

TERMINOLOGY

In this book we use a number of terms for general use. As a way of avoiding clumsy sentences and an over-subscription to different terms, we use particular terminology for convenience, rather than to imply that these terms are preferred or better than the possible alternatives.

When appropriate, and referring to children and young people of different ages, up to the age of 18, we use the words 'children' or 'child' to describe them. This saves using multiple terms each time we refer to this group as a whole. When it does become necessary to differentiate different age groups of children, we have used the terms 'young people/person' or 'teenager' to refer to those children in the older age category. We only use the term 'adolescent' when it is part of an institutional name or if a research study we are citing specifically uses this term.

When we make reference to the legal guardians of the children, we use the term 'parents' to encompass all adults who may have primary care of the children. We appreciate that in reality this includes foster parents, adopted parents, biological parents, step-parents, carers, residential carers and many other possible groups. For convenience and space saving, we use the term 'parent' to represent the diversity of this group.

This book refers to children specifically with the condition 'Autistic Spectrum Disorder' (ASD). We provide more detail in Chapter 1 about our use of terms for this condition, but please note here that for consistency we use the more contemporary concept of 'Autistic Spectrum Disorder', which we frequently abbreviate to 'ASD', to cover all possible labels for this condition.

There are occasions in this book where we use personal pronouns to enhance the style of writing. When the pronoun 'we' is used in this book, it means us, the three authors; and when we use the pronoun 'you' in this book, we mean you, the reader.

We hope that this clarifies the main terminology employed throughout the chapters and illustrates that the book is all-inclusive, despite adopting particular terminology to describe things. We acknowledge that, because of the nature of the topic of ASD, some of the language in this book will relate to medicine, health, mental health and pharmacology. We endeavour to provide descriptions of this institutional jargon as each chapter is developed; and, additionally, there is a clear glossary of terms at the back of the book should you require a quick reference point.

INTRODUCTION

We endeavour to keep this introduction as short as possible as we recognise that many people will not read it; but if (as we hope) you do, it will help you to understand our viewpoint on Autistic Spectrum Disorder (ASD). The world of ASD is a rapidly changing environment and it seems that every week some new thing is discovered about autism. There is often considerable media coverage when new ways are suggested about diagnosing and treating children with this condition. There is extensive funding being awarded around the world for research looking at all the different facets of the condition, but at present it is the genetics and biological basis of ASD which continue to generate most interest.

What is understood regarding ASD has changed considerably in recent years. Not too long ago the term 'ASD' did not exist and children were diagnosed with different labels, such as 'childhood autism'. In reality, it was felt to be a fairly well-demarcated condition which affected a small number of children (1 in 10,000). However, the concept has changed, with it now being thought to be a spectrum condition affecting a range of children not previously diagnosed. This has obviously been helpful for parents and families who can now better understand their children. However, the rapid growth in the number of those diagnosed (some studies suggest a prevalence of up to 1 in 60 children), has meant that services have had to expand rapidly to cope with the demand. Although this book focuses on children, due to the background of the authors, it should not be forgotten that this is a life-long condition and for many years adults with ASD have gone unrecognised. Some of the information from this book, while written with children in mind, may therefore be applicable to adults with ASD.

When looking at the field of ASD and the increasing numbers diagnosed, it has been obvious that much of the work in this area (particularly research) has focused on the diagnostic process (i.e. accurately finding those children with ASD), rather than managing the ongoing care. There have been attempts at finding a 'cure' for ASD but, although this continues to be sought, there has been little success to date. This is not to say there has however been considerable work in looking at ways of helping these children over the years, but, with the increasing range of presentations seen in children with ASD, it is difficult to find ways that will suit all children.

In helping children with ASD, it is important to acknowledge that much of the work in looking at the ongoing needs has originated in the field of education. It is normal for children to spend much of their lives at school, and education specialists have sought ways to engage children with ASD in the educational process. There are now programmes available to help children and schools develop a more positive learning environment, and there are specialist schools and professionals who dedicate their lives to this area. Unfortunately, it can be difficult for some schools to know how to manage children with ASD as, while having the same diagnostic label they can present quite differently, and have different needs.

The focus of this book is to look at the relatively new area of comorbid mental health problems in children with ASD. Although many of these problems have been recognised for some time, only recently has there been an increase in research into the prevalence and identification of these problems, with studies now looking at the best ways to help the children. As you probably realise, ASD has certain core features, such as difficulties in social skills and communication and a lack of flexibility in thinking, but there are many other areas of a child's functioning which also appear to be affected. These children are more prone to physical problems, such as epilepsy, bowel and coordination problems; and there may be associated learning difficulties – which might be considerable – in all areas of learning, or more specific, affecting reading (dyslexia) or numeracy (dyscalculia).

An increasing recognition of these difficulties and their consequences, together with the symptoms of ASD, reinforces the idea that children with ASD are vulnerable and are prone to developing further mental health problems. From our perspective, ASD can be seen as the foundation, which in many ways cannot be changed, with the comorbid mental health problem developing on top of this. Therefore, this leads to the importance of recognising the development of these problems and how best to help the child and their family. It can be frustrating for parents to feel that their concerns have been dismissed when they have sought help for particular problems, which leads us to the subtitle of this book: *It's not just their autism!* It is not uncommon to come across families in our clinical practice who have been told by well-meaning professionals that their child's problem was just part of their autism. Now in some cases this can be true, and there are things that cannot be changed easily (if at all). For example, occasionally some parents can have unrealistic expectations of how their child will develop socially, and it is important to have a frank and honest discussion regarding this. However, other problems, although related to the ASD symptoms, cannot be so easily dismissed. These can range from the extreme hyperactivity of Attention Deficit Hyperactive Disorder (ADHD), to a change in the presentation of a teenager who is getting depressed. We talk about how to identify the differences in this book, but – to be honest – it remains quite a challenge.

There are many professionals involved with ASD who appear to have a natural flair for working with these children and who give extremely useful and sensitive advice on many matters. Unfortunately, there have also been experiences which are less positive and which leave families with the feeling that they are being over-dramatic or silly. The authors of this book all have personal experience of a family member with ASD, be it a son or a sibling. This does enable us to have a different perspective on the whole experience of having a child with ASD in the family. We have had very good experiences and also some poor experiences. Unfortunately, the poor experiences often stick with families, and they have stuck with us. Being told that a child was not talking because his mother was not talking enough to him was one of our personal experiences, while another was being told that there was simply nothing wrong with the child and that the mother was being 'melodramatic'. As we are professionals who have an interest in working with children with ASD, and also we have experience of living with it, we can empathise with the difficulties of both professionals and families. We have therefore written this book because we feel that there continues to be a gap in the understanding of ASD.

The area of mental health is very complex and therefore we can only give a basic guide to the field, but we hope this will help people to further their knowledge and reading. We aim this book at a wide range of people – both those who care for and those who work with children with ASD. Parents and carers should find it useful in identifying a new problem and what basic things can be done before they seek specialist help. We also hope that this book will help a number of professionals to expand their understanding of this particular area of need. We have spoken to specialist teachers who want to know at what point a specialist mental health service would say that a child has a particular disorder or what treatments would actually be available.

To this end, the earlier part of the book is only a brief introduction to mental health, followed by sections on mental health conditions. We then move on to developing a framework to help the child in different ways. Included within the chapters are examples of cases which we have come across in our clinical practice, although some details have been changed. In addition, we hope that the inclusion of 'Think points' will help to illustrate certain important messages. The chapters that follow are written in a slightly different format as we attempt to answer the questions that we consider most important in a book of this nature. We hope that this book will be helpful to you and that it may improve your understanding of this complex condition.

CHAPTER 1

AUTISM SPECTRUM DISORDER
AN INTRODUCTION

This chapter will cover:

- Introduction.
- Why are different terms used?
- What is Autistic Spectrum Disorder (ASD)?
- What are the components of ASD and how do they influence mental health?
- Chapter summary.
- Further reading.

INTRODUCTION

Before we consider mental health problems in children with Autistic Spectrum Disorder (ASD), it is essential to have a good understanding of ASD itself. We emphasise to parents and professionals the need to appreciate the subtle and less subtle presentations of ASD, as it is *so* important in helping those children; and this becomes *doubly* important if they have any other conditions. It has been our experience that parents and professionals sometimes do not have sufficient knowledge about ASD to help a child, but considering how complex ASD can be, this is hardly surprising. For families, there is obviously the additional problem of the child's ongoing development, which can lead to unexpected problems. We often describe this as a 'moving target' – just as parents manage one developmental stage, the child reaches another. The problems of a teenager can be very different from those of a toddler, and the onset of puberty opens up a whole new world.

It was always going to be difficult to cover all the aspects of ASD which influence the presentation of a mental health problem in a child with ASD – this would probably require a another book in itself! In this book, we aim to provide information and advice on the additional (known in medical terms as 'comorbid') mental health problems that children with ASD may experience or develop. Therefore, this chapter simply provides a brief overview of the features of ASD and relates some of these to the development of comorbid mental health problems. Unfortunately, although at first glance there appears to be a huge amount of literature and online resources dedicated to ASD, finding relevant information (particularly information relating to teenagers), is often difficult and people frequently feel as though they have to 'muddle through'. If you are trying to understand the additional mental health problems that a child with ASD might be experiencing, we would suggest that it is useful to have a good overall knowledge about ASD first. There are some excellent resources available, some of which we recommend at the end of the chapter. Nonetheless, this chapter will help you to contextualise the additional mental health problems and does provide you with a simple overview of what ASD is and how it presents.

WHY ARE DIFFERENT TERMS USED?

There are a number of different terms that are used in the field of ASD and, although the terminology may improve in the future, these differences have caused some confusion. The rapid changes in the field have led to a number of official and unofficial terms being applied to children in this group, and it is fairly common to see these used interchangeably. We list the main ones in Box 1.1. While there is an ongoing attempt to standardise this terminology, in reality most of these terms will continue to be around for a number of years. For consistency, we will use the term 'Autistic Spectrum Disorder' (ASD) throughout this book as this is becoming the more commonly used phrase and is the term that best describes the wide range of differing presentations.

BOX 1.1 THE VARIETY OF TERMS
- Autism.
- Childhood autism.
- Asperger's Syndrome.
- Autism Spectrum Disorder.
- Atypical autism.
- High-functioning autism.
- Pervasive developmental disorder.

The history of ASD demonstrates how recently it has existed as a modern concept. Although ASD has been a feature of human development from antiquity, the term 'autism' was first used by Paul Bleuler in 1911 to describe schizophrenia. It was then used by Leo Kanner (1943) to describe a group of children who were characterised by extreme aloneness, preservation of sameness, and a variety of behavioural, cognitive and affective symptoms. In the same era, Hans Asperger (1944) described a syndrome (autistic psychopathy) with similar characteristics, which included a lack of empathy, limited ability to form friendships, and clumsy movements, but, notably, often some form of high functioning. Unfortunately, due to historical events (mainly World War II), the work was not widely disseminated. In the post-war era, the difficulties were still recognised, but, tragically, some children were labelled as having problems due to their mothers – the so called 'refrigerator mother' idea (Bettelheim 1967; Kanner 1949). It was argued by Kanner that this condition seemed indicative of a lack of 'maternal warmth', an idea extended by Bettelheim, who promoted the theory that these children were the products of cold and rejecting mothers. Although typically accepted by the medical world at that time, due to the prevailing fashions of the day, the notion was challenged as early as 1964 (Rimland 1964), and, despite occasional reference, the idea has little place in modern thinking.

The more up-to-date name for the condition was coined by Lorna Wing (1981a), who, through interpreting the work of Hans Asperger, developed the term 'Autistic Spectrum Disorder' (ASD) (Wing 1981b; Wing and Gould 1979). Although the term ASD is now more frequently used, it has taken some time for the classification systems to adopt it. The terms 'autism', 'Asperger's Syndrome' and 'pervasive developmental disorder' have been used for some time. There are some differences between these labels, which at a simple level appear to depend upon the child's development of language and the extent of the other features. For example, the main differentiating feature between Asperger's Syndrome and childhood autism is the development of fluent language before the age of three years. However, in reality, many of those children diagnosed with Asperger's Syndrome will also have some sort of speech problems. In addition, terms such as 'high-functioning autism' which is a less well-defined term, have been used. In this group of children there are more significant language problems present before the age of three years than in the children who are diagnosed with Asperger's Syndrome, so they appear much less able. However, over time, once their speech improves their overall functioning appears very similar to those children with Asperger's Syndrome. As can be seen, this is a confusing area for clinicians as well as for parents and other professionals, but these terms should become clearer as the diagnostic systems are updated.

WHAT IS AUTISTIC SPECTRUM DISORDER (ASD)?

Most of you will know, and have experience of, a child with an Autistic Spectrum Disorder. Therefore, some of what we will be saying will not be completely new. Because of this, you will not be surprised when we describe ASD as a complex condition which presents with a number of difficulties in various areas of daily functioning. ASD is called a neuro-developmental condition as it is a condition which indicates impairment in some aspects of the brain or central nervous system, but it has a developmental cause rather than an acquired cause, such as infections or tumours. Another neuro-developmental condition would be Attention Deficit Hyperactivity Disorder (ADHD). This is obviously a very biological way of viewing this condition and is not without its critics. Sometimes a slightly alternative way can be useful when working with these children – just by considering ASD as a different way of viewing the world.

Basically, ASD is a life-long condition which has the potential to present in many different ways at different times in an individual's life. While many believe that individuals can move 'up and down' the spectrum, there are still certain features which are always present. It can be difficult to know how a young child with ASD will develop over time and so it is often difficult to give a long-term prognosis. Some children who appear to have fairly significant ASD when younger can develop skills later on in childhood, while others, who appear to be developing well, can slow down during adolescence. It is important to realise, particularly when working with children with ASDs, that 'ASD' is an umbrella term, which in time may be identified as a number of different conditions. This is potentially the explanation for the different presentations and also explains why it has been difficult to define the exact cause of the disorder. In some ways, our understanding of the brain and the features of ASD is like the understanding of lung symptoms, such as a cough, before the advent of x-ray and modern technology (i.e. not very accurate).

In daily practice we are often asked by parents what causes ASD as this can be a source of worry for them. While in some families there appears to be an apparent genetic link, with multiple members of the family having the condition or traits of it, in other families the child/individual may be the only member affected. Some children have experienced problems before, during or after birth, and there is an increased prevalence in premature babies. In many cases we do not actually know why a child has ASD, and often attempts at identifying a cause are just educated guesses.

The term 'Autistic Spectrum Disorder' is one that encapsulates the huge range of presentations – from those who are apparently high functioning to those with severe learning difficulties and developmental delay. Despite these variations, ASD is defined as having a particular presentation, which is classically defined as the 'triad of impairments' (Wing 1981a, 1996). This triad of impairments can be seen within the diagnostic systems for diagnosing child mental health problems, such as the International Classification of Diseases (ICD) and in the Diagnostic Statistical Manual (DSM). While there may be changes in the diagnostic criteria over time, for ease of understanding the triad remains a good way of describing the problems in these children. While there are variable definitions of the aspects of the condition, and of the symptoms, certain core issues are fundamentally clear (please see Box 1.2).

BOX 1.2 THE TRIAD OF IMPAIRMENTS
1. Qualitative impairments in reciprocal social interaction (difficulties in social interaction/understanding).
2. Qualitative impairments in communication.
3. Restricted, repetitive and stereotyped patterns of behaviour, interests and activities (limited flexibility in thinking).

We will explain the triad in more detail a little later. In addition to these core features, there are other aspects of ASD which are important to those looking after, or working with, these children. In recent years there has been an increased interest in understanding the sensory processing of individuals with ASD. This encapsulates the difficulties which children with ASD have in processing/making sense of all the information they receive through their senses, and how they process this information. However, this is not seen in all children with ASD, so it is not considered by some experts as a core feature. A commonly seen example of this problem is the child who is over-sensitive to noise or smells; this is discussed further in the chapter on sensory issues.

To complicate things further, there are other factors which need to be considered. We need to understand how these children think, and particularly useful for this is the concept 'theory of mind'. This was a theory developed by Simon Baron-Cohen and his colleagues to explain how individuals without ASD understand that other people also have thoughts and feelings of their own (Baron-Cohen, Leslie and Frith 1985). We will come back to this issue later in the chapter.

Additionally, children with ASD can have a number of other difficulties, including learning difficulties, coordination problems and epilepsy. This is the reason why it is so important to find professionals who really understand the different facets of ASD, and why at different times professionals appear to give different advice to parents faced with a problem. It is often easy to attribute a difficult behaviour to one aspect of ASD, rather than consider all the different elements – in reality, most problems are a combination of a number of things. From a professional perspective, it can be complicated at times to provide the correct advice as each child is unique and it can be difficult to account for all the factors. In respect to comorbid mental health problems, we cannot cover all the contributing factors, but we will try to summarise the salient points. For simplicity's sake, we describe each mental health condition in isolation in this book, but it is essential to recognise that often a *combination of factors* is the root cause for any given problem.

THINK POINT!

The development of mental health problems is likely to be caused by a combination of different factors.

WHAT ARE THE COMPONENTS OF ASD AND HOW DO THEY INFLUENCE MENTAL HEALTH?

Rather than laboriously describing each individual difficulty experienced by those with ASD, which are well defined by other sources, we will briefly describe some features of ASD in relation to their impact on mental health.

Social difficulties

Social difficulty is one of the core features of ASD and is something which often distinguishes the child from their peers. There is a huge range of variability in this area, and the social difficulties may range from a complete disinterest and disengagement from the social world, to wishing to engage with others but having problems behaving in a socially appropriate way. Please see Box 1.3 for an overview.

BOX 1.3 SOME EXAMPLES OF SOCIAL DIFFICULTIES
- Difficulties initiating social interaction.
- Difficulties maintaining social interactions.
- Difficulties recognising and responding to social cues.
- Difficulties recognising emotions in others.
- Limited interest in social interactions.
- Difficulties sustaining and maintaining relationships.

As can be seen from the Box 1.3, there are hugely important skills which a child needs to develop as they grow. Developing these skills is essential in order to successfully negotiate the world around them, particularly in school and later in college or work. It should be remembered, however, that the development of mental health problems is not always clearly correlated with the developmental level of social skills in the child; rather it is the situation or context in which the social skills have to be used that is important. Often it appears to be the response of others, such as peers, to the child which is the determining factor.

EXAMPLE
A child in a specialist autism school surrounded by similar children may not feel different to his/her peers and may therefore feel less stressed by the experience.

Our own experiences – both personal and in clinical practice – have reinforced our belief that children with ASD often relate well to other children with ASD and that this can be a source of resilience and comfort (this is not the case for all children though). Children with

ASD who attend mainstream schools have to deal with a complex social environment, particularly during adolescence, and they often find the whole experience challenging. Although not all children with ASD are sensitive to the attitudes of their peers, a child who feels rejected by their peers can often have low self-esteem, and this has the potential to increase anxiety or depression. The need for friendship in many children with ASD can often be very strong, but their difficulties in social skills may lead to an inability to 'fit in', a particular problem among adolescents who can be quite judgemental. Conversely, the self-esteem of those children who do not feel the need to engage with others may actually have a degree of protection (resilience), although in other ways they can be more affected by the ASD.

Communication difficulties

It can sometimes be difficult to separate social and communication difficulties as they are interrelated. Communication forms an essential part of our daily living and permeates all aspects of our interactions with others. It should be remembered that communication is not just language but encompasses all the ways in which a child expresses their needs. This includes non-verbal communication, such as the use of eye contact or the use of gestures, and verbal language, classed as receptive or expressive language. Put simply:

- Receptive language is being able to understand the words of others.
- Expressive language is the ability to talk.

Language, a skill most children develop naturally, is by definition affected to some degree by ASD. While some children do not develop any language, or it is significantly delayed, there are other aspects of language which are typically seen in children with ASD. Common communication problems are summarised in Box 1.4.

BOX 1.4 COMMON COMMUNICATION PROBLEMS

- No development of language.
- Delayed development of language.
- Disordered development of language.
- Poor use and recognition of non-verbal communication.
- Echolalia (repetition of the words of another person) and delayed echolalia.
- Receptive and expressive language difficulties.
- Problems in voice control.
- Problems with reciprocal speech, turn-taking and recognising cues.
- Pedantic use of speech.
- Literal understanding of speech.
- Difficulty initiating and maintaining conversations.

From this list it is easy to see how communication relates to social abilities. Communication and language form an essential way of interacting with the world around us; therefore it is easy to see how difficulties in this area may lead to comorbid mental health problems. Those who have little or no language may struggle to get their needs understood or to communicate distress caused by factors such as cold, hunger or pain, and therefore it can fall to parents to recognise the subtle/less subtle changes in behaviour which indicate those needs.

EXAMPLE

The behaviour of a child with ASD can change dramatically in response to toothache. If the child cannot communicate this, it can cause them a great deal of distress and will probably be expressed in behaviours such as aggression, hitting or biting.

It is clear that expressive language and the thoughts behind this are intrinsically linked (i.e. a child's speech can reflect what they are thinking). To illustrate the link between communication and mental health problems, we provide two examples below.

EXAMPLE 1

A child with ASD is bullied at school and becomes depressed as a result, but they struggle to communicate with teachers regarding these issues. As a consequence, their behaviour deteriorates at home and they refuse to go to school.

■ EXAMPLE 2

A child with ASD becomes anxious due to loud noises within the school environment, but they cannot explain what factors are affecting them, due to their limited communication abilities. Again, this may present as a behaviour problem, with either a withdrawn child, or more commonly, with aggression.

The difficulty with looking after, or working with, children with ASD is that it can be difficult to communicate with them and to understand their needs. Although a child can be very fluent in their speech and appear to understand what is being asked of them, the link between social understanding and communication is so strong that they may not be able to say what is wrong. The two examples above may be due to the child having poor language skills, or may be due to their difficulty in expressing their emotional state.

THINK POINT!

Verbally fluent children may still struggle to express their emotions, and this may be expressed through their behaviour.

Body language, which is part of non-verbal communication, is an important aspect of communication and is used to convey meaning. An example of body language is eye contact, which can often be used to indicate intentions and mood. Therefore, the interpretation of body language is essential in day-to-day living. Children with ASD, however, have difficulties in this area – in the use of communication such as gestures, or the interpretation of the body language of others. This can lead to misinterpretation, which can lead to distress and upset.

Lack of flexibility of thinking

A significant aspect of ASD is the difficulty many individuals have with the need to be flexible in their thinking. This can present itself in a number of ways and can cause significant distress to the child. This factor is often first experienced by the family in terms of the child's poor development of imaginary play. Box 1.5 lists some of the characteristics.

> **BOX 1.5 CHARACTERISTICS OF LACK OF FLEXIBILITY OF THINKING**
> - Rigidity of thinking.
> - Literal thinking.
> - Obsessive thinking style.
> - Poor social imagination.
> - Need for routine.
> - Need for sameness.

Depending upon the situation, this difficulty can impact on mental health. There are enormous expectations in modern society on an individual to cope with constant change, and this is considered to be part of normal life. Changes at school and home are inevitable and require a significant degree of flexibility and adaptability. The lack of this adaptability therefore has potential to create considerable stress for the individual. This problem can sometimes be seen even in people who do not have ASD, and many individuals when stressed become rigid and over-focused in their thinking. How many people have experienced trying to give a driver some directions when they are lost? The stress of being lost appears to disable any rational thought, resulting in arguments. Children with ASD are particularly sensitive to change, and it is this stress which can contribute to a deterioration in their mental health.

Despite our best efforts, for children there are changes which are inherent to their age. They may have to change class and teacher at the end of the school year, experience the transition to a new school, and eventually leave school. The transition between schools can be challenging for any children who are identified as being 'at risk' or vulnerable (Yadav, O'Reilly and Karim 2010), but this is particularly difficult for the child with ASD. It is essential to manage these changes in an ASD-friendly way, in the hope that the stress can be greatly reduced. However, this is not always possible and, unfortunately, change can be singularly stressful to a child with ASD. What is particular to ASD is that the child's response may be significantly out of proportion to the actual change. Interestingly, some children are able to manage large changes (e.g. going on holiday abroad), but if there is a small change (e.g. a change in the packaging of a favourite food), there can be considerable distress and/or anger. Therefore, the significant factor is not our perception of the change but the importance it holds for the child. This is a good example of seeing problems from the child's perspective – something which is so important in our line of work. It is also the personal experience of the authors, who have lived through some of the 'explosions' which have resulted from seemingly small/insignificant changes – for example, the weeks of anger/aggression (throwing chairs) experienced following a change of lunch time from 12.00 to 12.30 at school.

THINK POINT!

Changes which may seem insignificant to you may not be seen that way by the child.

Other skills are essential to the development of friendships, particularly the development of play. Play, however, is linked to the development of an imagination and, unfortunately, imagination in children with ASD can often be limited and underdeveloped. As most children develop, their play tends to become more complex, and the child with ASD can become gradually excluded by their peers as they are unable to keep up.

In addition, many children with ASD like certainty and have a 'literal' interpretation to rules (i.e. school rules). This strict adherence to regulations can be equally frustrating to their peers, and becomes most obvious during adolescence. As part of their development, most teenagers will question and challenge authority, which may be difficult for a teenager with ASD to understand. We have come across many examples in which the child with ASD has innocently informed the teacher of a rule being broken by another child, without considering the consequences of being 'the class policeman'. This obviously does not make them popular.

Sensory processing difficulties

The issue of sensory processing has become an increasingly recognised area of difficulty for children with ASD and, although we cover this in detail in Chapter 12, we introduce it briefly here. Sensory processing difficulties refer to difficulties those with ASD have in interpreting the sensations they receive from the world around them and also from their own body. A classic example of this is the child with ASD who can be overly sensitive to sound and may cover up their ears to cope with noise. There are lots of different sensations that individuals are exposed to on a daily basis, as in Box 1.6 (basically all of them).

BOX 1.6 SENSORY AREAS
- Auditory (hearing).
- Visual (sight).
- Olfactory (smell).
- Proprioceptive (awareness of body posture).
- Vestibular (balance).
- Tactile (light and firm touch).
- Hunger and thirst.
- Taste.

These sensations can be affected independently or in combination, and a child can be over- or under-sensitive to different sensations from the same sense. This may sound strange, but a child may be overly sensitive to sudden loud noises, but then insist on playing their music loudly at home. This area may be best considered as a difficulty in regulating how they perceive the world. As we live in a very active sensory environment (noisy, smelly, bright), it is easy to see how children may feel easily overwhelmed by these sensations.

There is some evidence that as a child gets older these sensory difficulties may improve, but not in all cases. The question is: How does this affect a child's mental health? Typically, a school is an environment which can be very hard on the senses, particularly through sound, smell and sight. You may remember your own experiences of the school dining hall or the smells of the gymnasium. All these stimulating sensory inputs can become overwhelming and thus cause heightened stress and anxiety levels, which in turn will sensitise the child further to other factors which can affect their mental health.

THINK POINT!

The effects of the environment in the development of mental health problems cannot be underestimated.

Other aspects of thinking

When considering the thinking style of individuals with ASD, there are two particular theories which are important in understanding their mental health: 'theory of mind' and 'weak central coherence'. It continues to surprise us how important these ideas are in understanding children with ASD and in helping families and other professionals to work with them.

Theory of mind is a very important concept to grasp and is helpful in explaining how a child thinks about the world. Theory of mind is a psychological term for the ability to recognise and understand the thoughts, beliefs, desires and intentions of other people in order to make sense of their behaviour (Baron-Cohen *et al.* 1999). This theory is also known as 'mind blindness' and is often described as the ability to 'put yourself in someone else's shoes', or see a situation from another's perspective. Theory of mind appears to have a developmental aspect and matures throughout childhood; therefore, this becomes important in helping families. Please see Box 1.7 for the different developmental stages.

BOX 1.7 NORMATIVE DEVELOPMENTAL STAGES OF THEORY OF MIND

- *Age 2–3 years* – Cognitive deception (possibility of deceiving others).
- *Age 4 years* – Recognises the difference between experience and expressed emotion.
- *Age 5 years* – Begins to understand that others may hold different beliefs.
- *Age 6 years* – Starts to distinguish fantasy from reality.
- *Age 7–8 years* – Recognises that one thought may trigger another and events placed in memory may trigger thoughts.
- *Age 8 years* – Another thought or desire potentially lies behind an action or a statement.
- *Age 10⁺ years* – Develops a basic understanding of other cognitive processes, reasoning, attention and so forth.

Information adapted from Dogra *et al.*'s (2009) chapter on child and adolescent development.

Theory of mind has been likened to empathy (Gilberg 2002), which is the ability to relate to others on an emotional level and experience their feelings. This is essential in relating to others and forming relationships, and it is therefore an essential component of friendship. Consequently, impaired theory of mind has the potential to become a very isolating component of ASD as other children may misattribute this difficulty as selfishness, stubbornness or argumentativeness. This impairment affects the child's ability to resolve conflict and to compromise, and the perceived lack of sympathy can be seen as being unpleasant.

▉ EXAMPLE

A child with ASD who fails to sympathise with a friend who has broken up with her boyfriend. The friend may perceive them as being unsympathetic to what is often considered 'traumatic' by teenagers and this may result in conflict.

Additionally, an impaired theory of mind means the child may have difficulty in distinguishing between the accidental or deliberate actions of another person. This can lead to the child misinterpreting the actions of others and becoming increasingly anxious or even paranoid about the actions of others. If not managed well, this can obviously become a precursor for mental health difficulties. For therapeutic interventions in mental health problems, the ability to see things from another perspective, often that of the therapist, is essential for treatment progress, so impaired theory of mind does make some 'talking treatments' very difficult.

Case study

Peter is a 12-year-old boy with ASD. Unfortunately, there has been a recent bereavement in the family with the death of his mother's cousin. Peter did not know this person very well, although they were in regular contact with his mother. This death occurred unexpectedly and his mother is very distressed by the news. Peter struggles to see why his mother is so distressed and is more concerned that his dinner is not being made. He becomes increasingly agitated and distressed on his own behalf, but this is related mostly to his immediate needs not being met.

Reflective activity

This obviously shows a limited theory of mind in Peter as he cannot understand why his mother is upset. What other aspects of ASD do you feel are affecting the situation?

Analysing why a child behaves in a particular way can be complicated and, although Peter is being affected by his limited theory of mind, his difficulty in understanding or interpreting the emotions of others or the changes to his routine are significant contributing factors to his behaviour.

The second theory is that of 'weak central coherence'. This is a psychological term in which children with ASD appear to have a problem determining what is relevant and what is not in any given situation. This is the inability to see 'the bigger picture', and children with ASD have a tendency to focus on the small details (Frith and Happé 1994). The child may have difficulty completing activities in the classroom as they tend to become preoccupied with one small aspect of the task rather than the whole task. This attention to detail may be useful in some aspects of their lives (e.g. in hobbies such as collecting memorabilia), but it may be more of a hindrance overall. It should be added at this point that some types of employment value this sort of attention to detail and it may be useful in later years for those who are able to undertake a job.

For some children there may be an attempt to compensate for this difficulty by using rigid routines and rituals, thus providing a very focused and contained way of managing the world. Again, this lack of flexibility in the thinking process can cause significant stress for the child, who may be overwhelmed by the sheer complexity of the world and the work they are expected to undertake. This, therefore, may contribute to mental health difficulties.

Executive functioning difficulties

Parents of teenagers often complain about the chaos, disorganisation and lack of planning in their children. This can be heightened in many children with ASD. This is related to the difficulties in certain cognitive abilities known as the 'executive functions'. The executive functions are a group of activities which include organisation and planning abilities, attention, mental flexibility, working memory, problem solving, verbal reasoning, inhibition, impulse control and multi-tasking (Chan *et al.* 2008). These executive functions are obviously very important in daily living, becoming increasingly utilised during adolescence, and are essential to independent living.

In younger children, these problems are not so obvious; the most noticeable difficulties with executive functioning in this age group are a lack of impulse control and poor working memory. Working memory is a term used in cognitive psychology to describe an individual's ability to use information when solving a problem. It is not simply the ability to remember facts.

In clinical practice, parents commonly complain about their children's inability to organise themselves, remember sequences of activities/actions, or control their impulses. While this is often forgiven in the younger children, by the teenage years it is seen as very frustrating as parents want their children to be more independent. In the teenage group there is increased pressure from school and home to manage themselves and organise their own work and play. Learning often becomes more complex and self-directed and may involve large amounts of coursework, therefore increased use of the executive functions. The ability to prioritise a task becomes increasingly important when approaching adulthood, and this is another area which depends on the executive functions.

The disorganisation which can ensue from these difficulties may become extremely stressful, and it should not be underestimated how this can influence the mental health of those with ASD. This is especially important for the teenage group, particularly those in mainstream education, who have to submit coursework, organise their revision, and generally manage their time independently.

Learning difficulties

ASD is commonly associated with different types of learning difficulties. Some of these are more global in nature and can be termed 'learning disabilities', in which the child has a delay in all aspects of their development. Others consist of more specific learning difficulties, such as dyslexia (difficulties with reading) and dyscalculia (difficulties with numbers). The variety of learning disabilities can be very wide ranging, with some children having profound learning disabilities and requiring a lot of support. Others may appear less affected by their problems, depending on the context.

Context is especially important for the development of some mental health problems. For example, a child who is receiving a lot of support in school and who is also less aware of their own problems may be less likely to develop a mental health problem as they feel more at ease. However, a child in a mainstream school who is having problems with reading may find the situation very distressing, as they are aware that they are not keeping up with their peers, or possibly they could be teased by others. For some children, feeling different due to their learning problems can have a significant impact on their self-esteem, particularly if they require additional support within the classroom. Although this is more often a problem for children without ASD, it is still commonly expressed by those with ASD who may not want to seem different. Again, this is a reflection of how different children on the spectrum can be, and how an individual's view of the world needs to be taken into account.

Coordination difficulties

Although it does not immediately appear obvious how coordination difficulties can affect a child's mental health, in practical terms this is an important issue. For boys in the UK, the ability to kick a football can determine how they are viewed by their peers and can affect their ability to form friendships. In other countries, other sports will be equally significant (e.g. basketball, baseball and cricket). A child may be judged on their athletic ability, and difficulty with coordination can lead to them feeling excluded if they are not picked for the team. This means that the school playground can feel quite unfriendly. The consequence of not engaging in popular sports is that the child may seek alternative activities, which may lead to further isolation. This issue may be less significant for girls; however, there are still arenas in which coordination can lead to feelings of rejection and potential bullying. For example, dance tends to be a popular out-of-school activity.

Coordination difficulties may also become very apparent within the classroom environment, with the need for the child to write or use a keyboard. Some children with ASD can find the production of written work stressful and challenging, particularly if it requires other skills that they may find difficult, such as the use of imagination or executive functioning. As a consequence, children may become very resistant to these activities, and the issue of homework can become a battleground (author's own experience).

CHAPTER SUMMARY

As stated at the beginning of the chapter, this was never going to be an exhaustive list of the difficulties that children with ASD face and of how these difficulties can affect mental health. However, we have attempted to highlight certain points which parents and professionals need to be aware of when working with, or living with, these children. While we have treated these factors independently for simplicity, in reality there is a great deal of overlap between them, which can make the identification of the cause of any problems challenging. The concept that we wanted to express was that these factors all contribute to stress in children, and it is the build-up of stress which may contribute to mental health problems. Therefore, the more factors the child is finding difficult, the greater the stress. Add to this consequences such as isolation, peer rejection and bullying, and it is fairly obvious that these children are very vulnerable. Although in later chapters, such as Chapter 10, we will discuss a framework to think about these problems, it is essential to reflect on these facets when reading through the book. There are some really useful books on the subject of ASD, and you will find further reading suggestions at the end of this chapter.

(!) IMPORTANT LEARNING POINTS

- ASD is a complex condition for which no singular cause has been identified.
- Classically, ASD has been defined as having a 'triad of impairments' with difficulties in the areas of socialisation, communication and thinking styles.
- There are a number of additional components which can affect these children, including sensory difficulties, problems with executive functioning, learning difficulties and coordination problems.
- Any particular problem identified in a child with ASD often has a number of contributing factors which interplay with each other.

FURTHER READING

Attwood, T. (2007). *The Complete Guide to Asperger's Syndrome*. London: Jessica Kingsley Publishers.

Dogra, N., Parkin A., Gale, F., and Frake, C. (2009). *A Multidisciplinary Handbook of Child and Adolescent Mental Health for Front-Line Professionals* (2nd Edition). London: Jessica Kingsley Publishers.

Nichols, S. (2008). *Girls Growing Up on the Autism Spectrum*. London: Jessica Kingsley Publishers.

Wing, L. (1996). *The Autistic Spectrum*. London: Constable and Company Ltd.

Yau, A. (2012). *Autism: A Practical Guide for Parents*. CreateSpace Independent Publishing Platform.

CHAPTER 2

MENTAL HEALTH
AN INTRODUCTION

This chapter will cover:

- Introduction.
- What defines an illness, disease or disorder?
- What defines mental health, emotions and feelings?
- What defines child mental health?
- What defines mental illness?
- What is the mental health terminology in relation to ASD?
- How are mental health disorders/illnesses categorised?
- What are the diagnostic systems used in mental health problems?
- How common are mental health problems in the population and in children with ASD?
- What are the causes of mental health problems in children?
- Why do children with ASD have a higher incidence of mental health problems?
- What is stigma?
- Chapter summary.
- Further reading.

INTRODUCTION

When reading books which provide practical advice on problems, it is fairly common for people to miss out some of the earlier chapters, particularly if these are not felt to be obviously relevant to the problems they may be facing. However, this chapter, which contains mental health definitions, helps to explain some of the concepts and terms commonly used by mental health professionals and will set some context for the rest of the chapters. It is by no means fully comprehensive but it does allow certain points to be clarified. The term 'mental health', for example, is often thrown around fairly freely, without people fully appreciating its meaning. The difficulty is that some of these terms, including mental health itself, are fairly difficult to define fully, despite many attempts, especially when defining mental health in children. In reality, there is a subjective element to mental health, which results in people experiencing and reporting it differently. This is one of the inherent problems which can lead to mental health disorders remaining hidden.

Unfortunately, without understanding mental health, symptoms and difficulties may be attributed to the child's ASD, rather than viewed as an additional/comorbid entity – 'It's just their autism'. This chapter will address these issues by providing you with a framework in which to explore this field, with signposts for additional reading at the end of the chapter.

WHAT DEFINES AN ILLNESS, DISEASE OR DISORDER?

Before we discuss what defines a mental illness or mental disorder, it is useful first to define what is meant by an illness, disease or disorder. This is actually much more difficult than expected. The terms 'illness', 'disease', and 'disorder' are often used interchangeably, depending on the context within which they are used, but the terms 'disease' and 'illness' can be considered to be different in certain ways. Although these views are not universally held, for simplicity a *disease* is often considered to be the biological aspect of an abnormality in the person's body, where symptoms can be observed and measured, whereas *illness* is the human experience of the disease. Illness is thus more subjective, with the person's experience of ill-health being the defining feature (Idler 1979). The presence of symptoms (the disease), therefore, is experienced differently by different people, having a subjective and social element (the illness). As a consequence, how the problem affects a person depends on the culture surrounding the condition and what is felt to be the most appropriate behaviour. For example, in certain professions such as fishermen or miners, it is perceived to be less acceptable to complain about physical symptoms, while in other groups the same symptoms could lead to people taking a day off work.

A *disorder* is a vaguer term, but is one often employed in a more medical way through the diagnostic classification systems (these are dealt with in more detail later in the chapter). In the diagnostic classification context, a disorder is defined as 'the existence of a clinically recognizable set of symptoms or behaviour associated in most cases with distress and with interference with personal functions' (WHO 2010b, p.11). So in defining a disorder, a doctor will consider both the presence of the symptoms, or the disease, and the patient's experience of the illness.

In reality, when defining an illness, disease or disorder in clinical practice, the assessment and therapeutic process tend to consist of looking for the underlying pathology and/or comparing an individual against a data set which defines the normal range in a population. In physical aspects of health, this tends to be less complicated than in mental health. For example, the definitions of anaemia or abnormal blood pressure are clearly accepted. Professionals define these individual diseases against a benchmark of what is considered 'normal'. The word 'normality', when used in the context of mental health or ASD, can be quite contentious, and is a term that authors (including us) tend to avoid in their work. Regrettably, the word 'normal' stands in direct contrast to the word 'abnormal', and generally people do not want to be considered abnormal. The question in mental health is: What defines normality? In mental health, the notions of normality are vague, due to the vastness of the human experience. The nature of problems, and thus the difficulty in quantifying them, makes this a challenging exercise. Consider the following two examples:

▇ EXAMPLE 1

Children may be described as having hyperactivity. In reality, there are no charts of what defines typical levels of activity, overactivity or hyperactivity, and therefore professionals make a judgement on its presence by comparing a child to others of the same age.

▇ EXAMPLE 2

Anxiety is very common in children and is an experience that most parents can relate to. Deciding whether this anxiety has become an illness or disorder is tricky as it depends on how the child is affected in their day-to-day functioning and if the problem is persistent.

From these examples it should be fairly obvious how the assessment of mental health differs from that of physical health. While the medical professional can check a patient's blood pressure against a normal range, checking a child's anxiety or activity levels is much more complicated.

Children's understanding of health and illness

Given the complexity of defining these terms, it is perhaps unsurprising that children have some difficulty defining illness and disease. Children seem to define illness differently to adults, and their definitions seem to be affected by their developmental maturity (Millstein, Adler and Irwin 1981). It was previously thought that children's understanding of illness was limited, but this was probably underestimated as they actually have a strong understanding of their own health (Myant and Williams 2005).

Young children's definitions of illness typically bear some similarity to those provided by their mothers (Campbell 1975). However, older children, such as teenagers, may not share this perspective, and from our experience we are very clear that children with ASD may have their own views.

■ EXAMPLE

A teenager who, when asked how they are doing, says they are 'alright'. However, their parents have a very different perspective. The teenager may feel they have been brought to see a professional for no reason.

WHAT DEFINES MENTAL HEALTH, EMOTIONS AND FEELINGS?

As stated above, the term 'mental health' is widely used in everyday language, but in reality it is actually quite a difficult concept to define. There have been a number of attempts to define this term over the last few decades, and it is perhaps not surprising that there has been some controversy. Mental health does not mean 'mental illness' or 'mental health problem', and relates more to 'mental well-being'. The definition used by the World Health Organization (WHO) (2011) is probably the most accepted today. This is provided in Box 2.1.

BOX 2.1 WORLD HEALTH ORGANIZATION DEFINITION OF MENTAL HEALTH

'Mental health is defined as a state of well-being in which every individual realizes his or her own potential, can cope with the normal stresses of life, can work productively and fruitfully, and is able to make a contribution to her or his community.'

(WHO 2011)

This is obviously a generalised picture of mental health, but it makes some essential points. It is important to recognise that mental health is a state of 'well-being' and not just the absence of a mental health disorder/illness. This concept has a considerable impact when considering children. It is therefore essential that we consider ways in which we can maintain or improve a child's mental health rather than just treating mental health problems. These are often referred to as 'resilience factors', which are as important as those factors which adversely affect mental health – 'the risk-factors'.

THINK POINT!

In addition to considering the risk-factors which affect mental health, also consider the resilience factors which are protective.

There are obviously many social, psychological and biological factors which can influence mental health at any one time, and it is essential to realise that mental health can vary from day to day, situation to situation and place to place. We will consider these later.

When describing mental health, the terms 'emotion' or 'feelings' are often used. Now is probably a good time to look at these terms to contextualise their usage. As with many other terms we have used in this chapter, there is no agreed definition of 'emotion', and it has to date proved impossible to reach an agreed universal definition (Reisenzein 2007). The notion of what constitutes emotion is something that has long been debated in mental health circles, including clinicians such as Freud, who saw emotion as a central feature of the study of mental health problems (psychopathology). We supply one example of a definition of an emotion (see Box 2.2).

BOX 2.2 DEFINITION OF AN EMOTION

'...a patterned collection of chemical and neural responses that is produced by the brain when it detects the presence of an emotionally competent stimulus – an object or situation.'

(Damasio 2001, p.781)

Basically, emotions are an evolutionary adaptation which allow people to cope with situations – which can be either advantageous or dangerous for them – by developing certain responses in the brain (Damasio 2001).

A simpler definition of emotion is offered by the psychological dictionary as 'feelings about a situation, person, or objects that involves changes in physiological arousal and cognitions' (AllPsych Online 2012). In other words, an emotion causes changes in a physical and psychological way. Physical examples of this are a raised heart beat in anxiety, or blushing when embarrassed. Psychological manifestations are the positive thoughts when happy, or the racing thoughts of excitement. Notably this dictionary definition refers to a person's feelings.

The term 'feeling' is an equally vague term used to represent an individual response to their situation. One attempt to define 'feelings' it is represented in Box 2.3. This definition essentially defines feelings as more privately experienced than emotions. While your emotions are represented by changes in your body, such as blushing, and can be seen by others, feelings are more easily hidden and are in themselves a consequence of the emotions you feel. As you can see, these terms are thrown around fairly freely and are sometimes treated synonymously.

BOX 2.3 DEFINITION OF FEELINGS

'Feelings are the mental representation of the physiological changes that characterize emotions. Unlike emotions, which are scientifically public, feelings are indeed private, although no more subjective than any other aspect of the mind.'

(Damasio 2001, p.781)

WHAT DEFINES CHILD MENTAL HEALTH?

In children the definitions of mental health can be different due to other things, such as taking into consideration their developmental age, the expectations of the family and the culture around them. Child mental health overall relates to mental well-being and means positive child mental health. It is child mental health problems/illnesses/ conditions/disorders that indicate an absence of child mental health. Commonly used definitions of mental health in children are provided in the Health Advisory Service report (1995) and the Mental Health Foundation (1999). These are presented in Box 2.4.

BOX 2.4 DEFINITIONS OF CHILD MENTAL HEALTH

- Developing psychologically, emotionally, creatively, intellectually and spiritually.
- Initiating, developing and sustaining mutually satisfying personal relationships.
- Using and enjoying solitude.
- Becoming aware of others and empathising with them.
- Playing and learning.
- Developing a sense of right and wrong.
- Resolving problems and setbacks and learning from them.

(Mental Health Foundation 1999)

- A capacity to enter into and sustain mutually satisfying personal relationships.
- Continuing progression of psychological development.
- An ability to play and to learn so that attainments are appropriate for age and intellectual level.
- A developing moral sense of right and wrong.
- A degree of psychological distress and maladaptive behaviour being within normal limits for the child's age and context.

(Health Advisory Service 1995)

These definitions attempt to reflect the ongoing developmental aspects of children and their need to adapt to the constant change in their physical and psychological situations. Although these definitions are a good starting point, they have some limitations, such as culture, and do not appear to account for the variation which exists in the human experience, especially for those who experience life a little differently.

WHAT DEFINES MENTAL ILLNESS?

As with many other aspects of this chapter, mental illness is not a clearly defined idea. The lack of an agreed definition for illness and disease, as mentioned earlier, makes it particularly difficult when translating these terms in the concept of exploring the comorbid mental health problems some children with ASD might experience. Commonly, we talk about mental health problems or disorders, in addition to mental illness. Some sources define a mental health problem as being one that encompasses a range of situations and experiences, and can be thought of as a continuum of experience – from being mentally healthy to severe mental illness (Mental Health Foundation 1999; O'Reilly, Ronzoni, and Dogra 2013). Others consider mental health problems to be a range of experiences which are less serious but can develop into mental illnesses (National Mental Health Strategy; Australia 2010). In addition, mental health disorders can be an alternative name for mental illness in some contexts. We explain this further in Box 2.5.

BOX 2.5 DEFINITION OF MENTAL ILLNESS
'Any of various psychiatric conditions, usually characterized by impairment of an individual's normal cognitive, emotional, or behavioral functioning, and caused by physiological or psychosocial factors. Also called mental disease, mental disorder.'

(The American Heritage 2007)

THINK POINT!

Mental health problems/illness/disorder are characterised by an impairment of an individual's typical day-to-day functioning.

This is an extremely important concept to remember when defining whether a child with ASD has developed a comorbid mental health problem, as it depends on what is 'normal' for them.

An important issue to highlight at this point is that many illnesses/disorders have a fluctuating cause and tend to vary over time; and the experience of any of these illnesses/problems has a huge subjective element (personal/human). Different people can describe the experience of the same illness very differently, and the thresholds for seeking help can vary enormously, depending on other things which are happening in their lives. This subjectivity is especially important when looking at mental health problems, as the experience of emotional changes is essentially a personal experience.

■ EXAMPLE

In ASD, parents are often affected quite significantly by sleep deprivation and can be less able to manage the other behaviours of their child. Once they sleep again, they can feel revitalised and less stressed (this is not a mental illness, but an example of a changing situation that can affect the perception of a situation).

WHAT IS THE MENTAL HEALTH TERMINOLOGY IN RELATION TO ASD?

It needs to be recognised that the use of mental health terminology in respect to ASD is a little contentious. While autism is cited in the diagnostic classification manual, in the section on mental disorders, many people do not consider ASD as a mental illness. It is seen by some as an underlying way of thinking and behaving which is different from that of the general population. This is a viewpoint often described by those who are higher functioning.

When considering whether a child with ASD has an additional mental health problem or illness, it is essential that those working with, or caring for, that child have a good understanding of their typical day-to-day functioning and experiences. It is important to recognise that children given the diagnosis of ASD can vary greatly in their presentation and abilities, which need to be accounted for when looking for any additional problems. The nature of ASD is that the children do not think and behave in a manner which is typical of the majority of their peers, and it is these differences which help define the condition. Although these differences define the presence of ASD, at the same time it defines the baseline behaviour of the child (i.e. what is typical for them). This is why it is fair to say that not all children with ASD have a comorbid mental illness. It is true to say that in children with ASD, some emotions are often experienced to a more extreme degree than in other children of the same age, but this may be 'normal' for them.

A good example of this is anxiety. Although we will be exploring this in Chapter 4, anxiety is often experienced by the child with ASD in response to many different things. Changes in routine, loud noises or social situations are frequently described as making the child anxious.

Once these factors are addressed, the anxiety can often be seen to diminish very quickly. A persistent picture of anxiety (or anxiety which is significantly affecting the child's ability to function and therefore changes their behaviour) is much more likely to represent the development of an anxiety disorder. Again, it should be emphasised that to make these diagnoses, a good understanding of the nature of ASD and the typical behaviour of the individual child is essential.

THINK POINT!

It is the 'persistent change' in thinking or behaviour which is one of the take-home points of this chapter (sorry to labour the point!).

HOW ARE MENTAL HEALTH DISORDERS/ ILLNESSES CATEGORISED?

In day-to-day mental health practice, all mental health problems and illnesses are defined using a particular system of categorisation. Unlike physical illnesses, where health services can look for particular signs and symptoms or perform a number of tests to make a diagnosis, mental health problems are much more difficult to define. The categorisation of illnesses follows what is described as the 'medical model', which is an approach that aims to find medical treatments for diagnosable signs and symptoms according to a classification. A considerable issue among professionals is related to the appropriateness of this 'medical model', with claims that although mental health has some synergy with physical illness, it is still distinct from it (Macklin 1972). There is thus some controversy as to whether mental health problems and mental illnesses are medical issues or not, but we will not go into these issues in depth for the purposes of this book.

In physical illness, if a doctor elicits a symptom such as a cough, this may prompt an examination, which can then be followed up by a blood test or chest X-ray to confirm a particular problem. Mental health problems are often assessed through the description an individual provides of their feelings and emotions or the description of their behaviours by others. This has some inherent difficulties, due to dependence upon an accurate description by the person or observers of these factors, and this is particularly difficult when dealing with children and young people. Everybody describes their emotions in subtly different ways, and so the previous experiences of the professional become an essential part of the assessment process.

Eliciting the symptoms can call for significant skill from the diagnosing professional, and requires them to understand children, particularly children with ASD, very well.

■ EXPERIENTIAL EXAMPLE

From our experience working with and living with children with ASD, they can struggle to articulate their emotions. Describing how they are feeling can be extremely difficult, and then explaining why they feel a specific way can be even more difficult. Children with very limited verbal skills tend to express their distress through their behaviour, but this is also fairly common in those who are higher functioning. This may lead to the problem being missed or misinterpreted.

As a way of helping to understand mental health problems and also to develop and utilise effective treatments, symptoms or descriptions of behaviours are grouped together to form the classification of a particular condition. As you are probably aware, ASD is classified using this method with the classical triad of impairments defining it (as discussed in Chapter 1). In reality, as we understand more about mental health and recognise different presentations, some conditions are created while others disappear. A good example of this is post-traumatic stress disorder, which was only described towards the end of the 20th century.

Often, for simplicity, child mental health problems are categorised in three different domains by professionals. These are:

1. *behavioural problems*, such as conduct disorders and oppositional defiant disorders

2. *emotional problems*, such as anxiety, depressive illness and eating disorders

3. *neuro-developmental problems*, such as ASD, ADHD and Tic disorder.

Although these problems are not mutually exclusive, it is sometimes easier to consider their presentation within these groups as it can help to clarify what aspect may need addressing.

WHAT ARE THE DIAGNOSTIC SYSTEMS USED IN MENTAL HEALTH PROBLEMS?

There are two major classification systems which are used in this field. These are the International Classification of Diseases (ICD) and

Diagnostic and Statistical Manual (DSM). At present these are the manuals on which professionals worldwide base their classification of mental health problems and illness, and these are updated to reflect contemporary changes, resulting in different versions over the course of history. These manuals are available online if you wish to look at them further; see the end of the chapter for details.

It needs to be recognised that these documents are seen by some professionals only as guides, due to unique individual differences among children and young people. This is a particular issue when diagnosing mental health problems in children with ASD. They tend not to present in the typical way, and there are no particular guides to diagnosing these problems in this group. In the real world, this has given rise to some difficulty with comorbid mental illnesses being under-diagnosed in this group.

HOW COMMON ARE MENTAL HEALTH PROBLEMS IN THE POPULATION AND IN CHILDREN WITH ASD?

Mental health problems in the general population, and particularly in children, are surprisingly common. People, however, can be reluctant to discuss their mental health problems or even seek help for them. It has been estimated that more that 450 million people at any one point suffer from mental disorders worldwide (World Health Organization 2010a). There have been various studies on children, which have estimated the prevalence as being between 10 per cent (Scottish Needs Assessment Programme 2005) and 20 per cent (National Institute of Mental Health 2012a). This variation is probably due to the criteria used to define what a mental health problem is, rather than any particular social or cultural factors. There may be some differences, however, between cultural groups within and across countries, and this may be due to a number of factors which are beyond the scope of this book.

In children with ASD, the prevalence of comorbid mental health problems is probably significantly higher than in children of comparable age. The picture remains a bit unclear but there has been some research to provide information on this issue. A recent study of a group of 112 10–14-year-old children with ASD, assessed for a range of DSM IV diagnoses, demonstrated raised mental health problems in a number of categories (Simonoff et al. 2008). In this study 70 per cent of the young people had a least one comorbid disorder and 41 per cent had two or more comorbid disorders. Just fewer than 30 per cent had a social anxiety disorder, with 28 per cent having Attention Deficit Hyperactivity Disorder (ADHD) and 28 per cent having Oppositional Defiant Disorder (ODD). From this study, it is fairly clear that anxiety of all types is the most commonly experienced comorbid mental health problem, with other mental health problems being present in various degrees. Other research indicates that 42 per cent of children with ASD have a comorbid mental health disorder with mood (17%), anxiety (12%), adjustment (8%) and disruptive behaviour (12%) being diagnosed (Moseley *et al.* 2011). We will address the prevalence of many of these conditions in later chapters.

WHAT ARE THE CAUSES OF MENTAL HEALTH PROBLEMS IN CHILDREN?

This is a highly complex area and it can be difficult to define a particular cause of a mental health problem. In practice, the factors which influence the development of a mental health problem are broken down into two types:

1. *Risk-factors* – those that increase the likelihood of developing a problem.

2. *Resilience factors* – those that protect.

These factors often do not work in isolation, and it is the interplay between them which defines when and how someone presents with a problem. For example, in child mental health we commonly see a surge in problems before the major exam season, due to the stress young people are feeling; thus, exams operate as a risk-factor and the individual child's coping style and resilience will determine the reactions to that stress.

These factors can be categorised in different ways. Sometimes it is useful to consider the factors in terms of those inherent to the child, those particular to the family, or influences in the environment. Another way is to separate the factors into biological, social, psychological and environmental, with some appearing to be more influential than others, depending on the condition. We will discuss the various influences on specific comorbid problems in more detail throughout the book. To summarise, these broad causal factors can include, but are not limited to, those highlighted in Box 2.6.

In children with ASD, these factors are still very pertinent, but the relationship between these factors and the development of a mental health problem is not so straightforward. In practice, we come across children who are physically aggressive towards their siblings, when in reality it is another issue that is causing them distress (e.g. stress at school). It is therefore important that professionals and parents take a global view of all the potential stressors which may be affecting that child, rather than focusing on those which appear to be the most obvious.

> **BOX 2.6 CAUSAL FACTORS OF MENTAL HEALTH PROBLEMS**
> - *Biological factors* – genetic (inherited), developmental (abnormal brain development), trauma (physical brain damage), metabolic disorders, infections, endocrine or hormonal problems, malnutrition, toxins.
> - *Social factors* – impact of school, peer relations, culture, family influences, community attitudes.
> - *Psychological* – attachment to carers, cognitive ability (e.g. IQ), personality, self-esteem, identity, learned behaviours.
> - *Environmental* – role models, teaching environment, home environment, sensory issues, media influences.

WHY DO CHILDREN WITH ASD HAVE A HIGHER INCIDENCE OF MENTAL HEALTH PROBLEMS?

Unfortunately, it is not entirely clear why children with ASD have a higher incidence of mental health problems. In the subsequent chapters we will attempt to clarify the situation for the different conditions, but in reality the reasons can vary from child to child and from condition to condition. Some conditions, such as anxiety, appear to be inherent to the nature of ASD, so the development of an anxiety disorder is not surprising. The same can be said of ADHD where attention problems and overactivity are often seen. When considering conditions such as depressive illness or psychosis, the link is not so clear. Although there is some evidence that there may be a genetic tendency for teenagers with ASD to develop depressive illness, it is also evident that many of these teenagers struggle with rejection by others of their age or find this period of development very stressful.

In reality, it is probably the interplay of many factors which increases the risk of these children developing a mental illness. In this book, when considering the risk-factors for any presentation of mental illness, it may be useful to separate them into:

- *Predisposing factors* – factors which increase the risks.

- *Precipitation factors* – factors which herald the start of an illness.

- *Perpetuating factors* – factors which keep the illness going.

WHAT IS STIGMA?

When discussing the terms for this area, it is useful to think about stigma. Parents of children with ASD, and the children themselves, often describe the stigma they have felt from those around them. Stigma is commonly described as an issue for those experiencing mental health problems more generally, and there are many terms used to describe these individuals in a negative way (see for example, O'Reilly, Taylor and Vostanis 2009). This is often not helped by the lay perceptions of mental health and the common media portrayals, including the representation of those who are mentally ill as being dangerous – these can induce unwarranted levels of fear, at odds with the true picture (Link *et al.* 1999).

Stigma is defined as an aspect of the individual that sets them apart from others. They are often labelled as being part of a different group, which can lead to negative attitudes, prejudice and discrimination. See Box 2.7 for a formal definition.

> **BOX 2.7: DEFINITION OF STIGMA**
> 'The co-concurrence of its components – labelling, stereotyping, separation, status loss, and discrimination.'
>
> (Link & Phelan 2001, p.363)

Stigma and mental health

Unfortunately, mental illness in particular is stigmatised, and this can be a barrier to accessing help, with individuals being reluctant to admit their problems. The stigma of having a mental health problem or mental illness can therefore be an additional burden for those experiencing the illness and their families (Gaebel, Zaske and Baumann 2006).

Reflective activity

You might want to think about your own attitudes towards those with mental health problems and mental illnesses. Do you see individuals with mental health problems as less threatening than those with mental illness? Why do you think you hold the attitudes that you do?

Unfortunately, stigma has the potential to affect the children themselves with regard to seeking help for their mental health problems. This seems to affect boys more strongly than girls in terms of their willingness to engage with mental health services and of acknowledging their mental health problems (Chandra and Minkovitz 2006).

Stigma and ASD

Parents of children with ASD suffer greatly from the effects of stigma, with mothers more than fathers encountering problems (Gray 2002b). Although parents of children with ASD can use the diagnosis to resist some of the stigma (Farrugia 2009), they typically encounter hostile staring, rude comments and avoidance from others (Gray 2002b). This general public attitude to mental health and the effect of stigma can also be seen in young people with ASD – it can make them reluctant to engage with professionals and make life very difficult for their parents, and in our experience, they may refer to mental health services and illnesses in fairly derogatory ways.

Reflective activity

You might want to think at this point about any barriers you encountered after your child was diagnosed with ASD. If you are a professional, you might want to think about the problems that parents face with stigma and how this might affect their relationships with you.

CHAPTER SUMMARY

Before understanding how comorbid conditions present in children with ASD, it is necessary to understand what defines 'mental health' and other terms such as 'illness' and 'disorder'. As you can see from this chapter, although superficially this appears fairly straightforward, in reality defining these concepts is complex and there are often no universally agreed terms. Diagnostic systems have been developed to help define and determine at what point a child can be diagnosed with a mental health problem, but these remain limited by their subjectivity. Although for many years mental health problems in children were thought to be fairly rare, they are increasingly recognised in all age groups and particularly now in children with ASD. The cause of these mental health problems is often multifactorial and therefore the unique aspect of each child needs to be considered. This chapter has guided you through some of the complexities regarding definitions for key terms and pointed out some of these factors and problems affecting the child with ASD.

ⓘ IMPORTANT LEARNING POINTS

- It remains difficult to define many of the terms used in mental health due to the subjective element and the social and cultural context.
- Diagnostic systems are available to guide the process of identifying a mental health disorder, but they do have limitations.
- ASD is classified in the mental health sections of the diagnostic classification systems, but this is controversial.
- Mental health problems are being increasingly recognised in children, including children with ASD.
- Stigma remains a barrier to seeking and receiving help for mental health problems.

FURTHER READING

Dogra, N. (2010). Culture and child psychiatry. In R. Bhattacharya, S. Cross, and D. Bhugra (Eds) *Clinical Topics in Cultural Psychiatry* (pp. 209–221). London: Royal College of Psychiatrists Press.

Dogra, N., Parkin A., Gale, F., and Frake, C. (2009). *A Multidisciplinary Handbook of Child and Adolescent Mental Health for Front-Line Professionals* (2nd Edition). London: Jessica Kingsley Publishers.

Simonoff, E., Pickles, A., Charman, T., Chandler, S., Loucas, T., and Baird, G. (2008). Psychiatric disorders in children with Autism Spectrum Disorders: Prevalence, comorbidity, and associated factors in a population-derived sample. *Journal of the American Academy of Child and Adolescent Psychiatry, 47*(8), 921–929.

WHO (World Health Organization) (2010). *Mental health: Strengthening our response: Fact sheet.* Available at www.who.int.mediacentre/factsheets/fs220/en/, accessed on 13 May 2013.

FURTHER SUPPORT AND INFORMATION

A website which provides clear aspects of DSM can be found at: http://dsm.psychiatryonline.org/book.aspx?bookid=22

A website which provides clear aspects of ICD can be found at: www.who.int/classifications/icd/en

CHAPTER **3**

ASD AND COMORBID ADHD

This chapter will cover:

- Introduction.
- What is ADHD?
- What causes ADHD?
- Why is ADHD a controversial label?
- How common is ADHD?
- How does ADHD present in individuals with ASD?
- How can ADHD in ASD be diagnosed?
- How do you manage ADHD in the individual with ASD?
- Chapter summary.
- Further reading.

INTRODUCTION

Poor attention levels and overactivity are commonly found in children with ASD, and their coexistence can significantly change how a child behaves. Although for many years it was felt that ASD was a separate condition from Attention Deficit Hyperactivity Disorder (ADHD), there is now recognition that these conditions can occur together. In our clinical practice we often see that ADHD can significantly affect how a child with ASD behaves and presents to professionals, which may be a reason why clinicians sometimes find diagnosing ASD difficult when ASD and ADHD coexist. Living with a child with ASD and ADHD can often be described as 'eventful', with life dominated by a very overly active child who has little impulse control and in whom there appears to be no 'off button'. It is this group of children who can get themselves into difficult situations, such as climbing on roof tops, up trees, getting stuck between railings, getting items stuck on their heads/hands/feet, and they seem to inject an element of chaos into daily life. One young man that we know has an unbelievably good climbing ability and a liking for window sills, roofs and ceiling pipes.

On a more serious note, these children are also more likely to suffer injury, have poor understanding of road safety, and are the ones the educational system may find the most difficult to manage. In reality, they can present quite differently from those children with classical ASD, and in one way can be considered 'predictably unpredictable'. While most children with ASD can be helped effectively by having the same routine every day, it is not unusual for us to be contacted by an exasperated teacher or parent who, after finding a successful way of working with a child, finds that the technique is no longer effective. In this chapter we will explore what is meant by the term 'Attention Deficit Hyperactivity Disorder' (ADHD) and how this can and cannot apply to some children with ASD.

WHAT IS ADHD?

There are some differences in how ADHD is defined clinically according to the different diagnostic classifications, but for the sake of this chapter we will concentrate on the common features. In some classifications, the key features of attention and hyperactivity have had to exist together to make the diagnosis, while in others they could be separate. The key diagnostic symptoms of ADHD are outlined in Box 3.1.

BOX 3.1 KEY CHARACTERISTICS OF ADHD
- Impaired attention/concentration.
- Hyperactivity.
- Impulsivity.

Impaired attention

For children to manage in their daily lives, their ability to pay attention is central. To complete any task, children need to be able to concentrate and focus properly. This can vary quite significantly in all children and is influenced by factors such as their age, understanding of the subject, their interest in the subject, their listening skills and what is happening around them (this is also true for children with ASD). Impairments in attention may be evident in many different ways. For example, the child may move quickly from one activity to another, never really getting immersed in what they are doing; they may look bored, daydream, or be easily distracted. This level of concentration may obviously also vary depending upon the type of activity. It is not unusual for a child with ADHD to be able to concentrate for long periods of time on a computer or console, only to be distracted extremely easily in many other situations. This difference may also be evident in how focused a child with ASD may be with their special interest, compared with activities such as school work. Attention may also be affected by other factors, such as anxiety. We have often seen children who appear to have good levels of concentration when we first meet them, due to their anxiety, and for this to change significantly as they become more comfortable. In some cases, children show either excessive focus or poor focus, with the problem being a difficulty in moderating their attention. Attention problems in ADHD appear to continue throughout childhood and, although in some cases this can improve in later years, in many others it may be the main difficulty during the teenage years.

Clinically, there is a problem in assessing a child's level of attention. This level can be assessed to a certain extent by the history given by the carers or by direct observation, but this can sometimes be difficult. Unfortunately, there are also no 'normal' values for attention for the clinician to judge a child by, and therefore it can become a very subjective judgement.

Hyperactivity

How do you define hyperactivity? This is actually immensely difficult. Activity levels in children vary considerably, depending on their age and what they are doing. The difficulty lies in deciding what a normal level of activity is for that particular child, and hence whether they are actually overactive or hyperactive. This may be one of the reasons why ADHD is not diagnosed before the age of six years due to this enormous variability. Toddlers are notoriously 'busy'. While hyperactivity may be apparent in children below this age, most clinical professionals are fairly reluctant to diagnose it in younger children. Consequently, parents who have their children diagnosed at a later date can feel aggrieved that treatment was not started sooner as in the meantime they have had to cope with the child's difficulties.

Hyperactivity can present as children being very active, and in clinic we often have children running around the room in a fairly chaotic way. In reality, these children can be easier to diagnose, due to the overt nature of their presentation. Other children tend to squirm in their seats; they constantly fidget or play with things with their hands. Teachers can complain that these children have difficulty sitting still in class, or that they constantly wander around the room. Like all aspects of ADHD, hyperactivity is very subjective and is determined from both the parents/carers and the clinical professional's perspective. Some parents are much more comfortable with an overactive child than other parents and so may not feel their child has a problem until it is reported by the school. Additionally, when assessing for hyperactivity, it is a recognised phenomenon that children on their first visit to a clinical professional can be very well behaved and show few signs of overactivity. They may need a few appointments to become comfortable. To those who are new to the field it can be easy to overlook this.

Impulsivity

Impulsivity is basically defined as the inability to control one's impulses, which means the person is likely to act with undue haste and with a lack of thought or deliberation. From a clinical standpoint, this is quite difficult to define or elicit. A clinical professional will ask whether the child acts without thinking, interrupts conversations frequently or appears not to be able to control their excesses.

▉ EXAMPLE

A child in our clinic was unable to stop herself eating any chocolates within the household, even if they did not belong to her. Other children may have poor road sense and run across the road without paying attention to safety.

In the clinic environment these children may interrupt conversations with their own concerns or impulsively run out of the room. Time-keeping is often important when dealing with these children as they may become agitated if left waiting too long in the waiting room. This is probably a consequence of their lack of impulse control and their intolerance of poor timekeeping, which is part of the ASD.

THINK POINT!

Attention, impulsivity and hyperactivity can be difficult to assess and can easily be affected by many factors.

WHAT CAUSES ADHD?

The aetiology of ADHD is not entirely clear – it is probably a combination of many factors. There may be some differences in the biological basis of the condition between children who have ASD and those without ASD, but this remains uncertain in the research literature. In children without ASD, there are some cases where there is a strong genetic link and ADHD can be seen in other members of the family, particularly the fathers or other male relatives. Some research supports the idea that of all mental health conditions, ADHD has the strongest genetic link (Cantwell 1996).

In other situations the causation is less clear, but there may be an association with events which occur around birth or soon afterwards. There are increased levels of ADHD symptoms in children who are premature or of low birth-weight. As stated above, in children with ASD the aetiology is less clear and may be different in certain respects to those children without ASD. For simplicity, we sometimes describe to parents the association between ADHD and ASD as a consequence of roughly the same area of the brain being affected in both conditions. Obviously, it is far more complex than this, and there is further information regarding the neurobiology available in the literature (see for example Amthor (2012) in the Further Reading section).

WHY IS ADHD A CONTROVERSIAL LABEL?

You may be aware that ADHD is a controversial diagnosis, despite the evidence supporting its existence. The validity of ADHD continues to be challenged from many sources including the media, where these children are viewed simply as naughty children. In our practice, some children have behavioural problems, some have ADHD and some have both. To say that ADHD does not exist seems over-simplistic. While there may be instances where the condition is misdiagnosed, the authors have seen the benefit to children who receive a diagnosis and are provided with appropriate interventions. The difficulty continues to be around the diagnostic process and the lack of any definitive diagnostic test. Children are diagnosed on the history families and schools provide and through the filling out of questionnaires such as the 'Conners questionnaire' (Conners 1997). There are developments currently underway to enhance the diagnostic process, but at the time of writing these are only experimental.

In addition to the controversies that surround the diagnostic process and what constitutes ADHD, significant concerns exist regarding the treatment. Often these children require specialist medication, which may raise concern – mostly due to the young age of the children treated. There is little data on the long-term actions of these treatments, and the lay perception is that children are being given strong amphetamine-based drugs. While parents and clinicians need to be cautious when giving any medication to children, there is significant evidence that these forms of medication are effective. There is a considerable bank of literature available now for people to form a balanced opinion.

For a balanced perspective it is important to acknowledge the counter-argument to ADHD. It has been argued that there is vagueness in the diagnostic systems and that the diagnosis absolves parents of their responsibility, excusing what is essentially just a naughty child (McKinstry 2005). While the authors recognise this perspective, the reality of ADHD is that in many cases a correct diagnosis does enhance children's daily living skills and their interactions with the social world. The emphasis, therefore, is on the correct diagnosis, as errors can contribute to the perceptions that it is an over-diagnosed condition or one which excuses bad behaviour.

HOW COMMON IS ADHD?

The studies on ADHD have shown different prevalence rates internationally and cross-culturally. A significant determinant appears to be the attitudes and tolerance of the symptoms within a culture. For example, in the modern era children are expected to sit at a desk and concentrate for significant periods of time at their school work. This can be very difficult for many children, particularly those with a tendency towards ADHD. Some societies tolerate more boisterous behaviour in their children and, again, this moderates how criteria are applied. This is a good example of the subjectivity of mental health conditions, as one condition can apparently appear and disappear in different families and contexts.

ADHD has been estimated as affecting approximately 5 per cent of school-age children (Polanczyk *et al.* 2007) with boys affected to a greater degree than girls (Bauermeister *et al.* 2007). There are concerns, however, that the rates of ADHD in girls is under-diagnosed as they present in a different way, tending to be less disruptive at a younger age. Although there are no absolutes, girls tend to present with less hyperactivity and with problems in the areas of attention and concentration. They are often described as 'daydreamers', and their usually better social skills can sometimes mask the presentation of symptoms.

HOW DOES ADHD PRESENT IN INDIVIDUALS WITH ASD?

Parents and representatives of settings such as schools have become increasingly informed and capable in managing both ASD and ADHD in isolation. However, the presence of ADHD and ASD together can often be much more challenging. While there are certain aspects of children with ASD which are fairly easy to predict and therefore the child can be helped, when ADHD is added it often appears to unsettle this dynamic, and leading, as stated before to the 'predictably unpredictable'. The difficulty lies in deciding whether ADHD exists in the child with ASD as the presentation is sometimes difficult to recognise. Children with ASD can have poor attention and be distractible for a number of reasons, including sensory sensitivities or not feeling the need to follow the social norms (i.e. do what the other children are doing). These factors can also affect their activity levels, particularly their levels of fidgeting and their impulsivity. We discuss this further later in the chapter.

THINK POINT!

ASD with comorbid ADHD can present in many different ways, and behaviour can often be described as 'predictably unpredictable'.

It has been estimated that hyperactivity occurs in approximately 42 per cent of children with ASD (Green *et al.* 2004), but the estimates of comorbid ADHD vary from 25–30 per cent (e.g. Siminoff *et al.* 2008). This is obviously quite substantial, but even from these figures it can be seen that defining ADHD in children with ASD is difficult.

It would be easy to say that all children with ASD who are hyperactive have ADHD, or a form of ADHD; but as there are so many factors which can cause children to be overactive, we need to be cautious with such a conclusion. This obviously adds to the difficulty in making a diagnosis and can potentially lead to being told 'It's just their autism'.

In reality, the presentation of ADHD within ASD can be quite variable. There is some debate as to whether ADHD and ASD actually fall on a continuum – with ASD at one end and ADHD at the other – with a considerable overlap of symptoms, but this is not a universally agreed concept. There is some evidence of ASD symptoms within children diagnosed with ADHD and vice versa. For the sake of simplicity, we provide some examples below in Box 3.2 to demonstrate this point, but this is not an exhaustive list.

BOX 3.2 DIFFERENT TYPES OF CHILDREN WITH ASD

- Children with classical symptoms of ASD who are hyperactive/overactive.
- Children with ASD who have poor concentration and attention skills.
- Children with ADHD who have poor social skills and some rigidity of thinking and who are diagnosed with ASD.
- Children with ASD and ADHD who present with uncontrolled aggression and agitation.
- Children who appear quite manipulative as they tend to push social boundaries in an impulsive way, but do not have the social skills to recognise when they have gone too far.

The profile of children diagnosed with ASD has changed to some degree over the last few years, with a broadening of what categorises ASD. This broadening of the categories has incorporated some children with complex presentations, particularly young men with poor social skills as their predominant characteristic. They will have the other aspects of ASD, but this can be to a lesser degree than in classical ASD. Additionally, it should be remembered that some children with ADHD appear to show difficulties with some aspects of thinking, such as empathy, and poor social skills, but with treatment this can improve as they can consider their actions more carefully.

ADHD presentations do tend to change with increasing age. In the teenage years attention difficulties tend to become more prevalent, compared to hyperactivity. The upshot of this is that in children who present later, such as teenagers, the ADHD can be missed. Other factors may also mask the presentation, particularly if a number of measures have already been put in place to help the child. A good example of this is a learning support assistant moderating the child's attention by keeping them on task. This function is almost replicated by a computer console at home (a common teenage activity), resulting in apparently good levels of concentration.

Case study

Joshua is a nine-year-old boy who has a diagnosis of ASD. His mother is concerned that her understanding of ASD fails to explain all the behaviours her son displays, and school are having problems managing him. He struggles to sit still in class and will often wander around the room. It takes significant effort to keep him on task – he fidgets constantly and it is a struggle to keep his concentration on any activity. If he enjoys something, he appears to have very good concentration and can focus for prolonged periods of time. His mother is concerned about his road sense – a recent episode involved him chasing a cat across a busy road. Joshua gets easily distracted by sensations, such as a ticking clock and strong smells, and he appears to struggle to focus in a busy classroom environment.

Reflective activity

You may want to consider the case above. How would you distinguish if ADHD is present together with the ASD or if there are other causes which account for the child's difficulties? Remember that there can be multiple causes for a child's behaviour, and it may be necessary to think about these causes individually.

Bearing an example in mind, we will now try to address this problem.

HOW CAN ADHD IN ASD BE DIAGNOSED?

One of the difficulties is that in mental health problems we are looking for a notable change in the child. Unfortunately, with ADHD the symptoms can be present from the early years and therefore it forms part of the child's baseline profile. It is important for a diagnosing professional to have a good understanding of the different aspects of ASD and how they particularly apply to the individual child. It is essential that the child's behaviours and actions are analysed to understand their true cause. A good example of this sort of problem is a distractible child with ASD in a classroom setting. The distraction could be for a number of reasons:

1. The child may truly have attention problems.

2. The child may have sensory processing difficulties and be distracted by lights or sounds or smells.

3. The child may not understand the task presented to them and therefore disengages.

4. The child may have difficulties following verbal instructions.

5. The child may be hungry or tired, which can occur in any person.

6. The child may not see the relevance of the task for them.

7. The child may be bored/unmotivated.

As can be seen, there are multiple reasons which need to be considered when looking at this area. The same can be said for the fidgeting child – they may have sensory difficulties or may just be uncomfortable. Diagnosis needs to consist of a careful history of the behaviours in multiple environments as ADHD symptoms should occur in all areas. The only caveat to this is that the anxious child or the child who is experiencing sensory overload may not behave as expected. This tends to result in a suppression of their activity levels and an apparent improvement in their concentration, probably as a result of fear. Direct observation of the child with ASD in different arenas is very useful – in both structured and unstructured settings, such as classrooms and playgrounds. As we mentioned earlier, assessment tools such as the 'Conners questionnaire' may also be useful but may not be as useful as a direct observation.

Unfortunately, there may come a point when the diagnosis continues to be difficult and this is one condition where 'testing out' hypotheses and intuitive thoughts may be the only way forward. Best practice with ADHD is to be clear on the diagnosis before starting medication. Many clinical professionals, however, recognise that a response to treatment does help to clarify the presence of ADHD in children with ASD. One difficulty with this approach, which clinical professionals tend to be aware of, is that many children will respond in some way to the medications used in this condition.

THINK POINT!

A good understanding of ASD is necessary when looking for the presence of comorbid ADHD.

HOW DO YOU MANAGE ADHD IN THE INDIVIDUAL WITH ASD?

How to manage a child with ASD and comorbid ADHD is a question we are often asked by many different groups of people. Although we would like to give a definitive answer to this question, we tend to tell people to try their best as there is often no straight-forward solution. This may sound a little lame, but practice over the years has taught us that ASD with comorbid ADHD can be quite tricky. The management of ADHD in children without ASD depends very much on the severity of their symptoms and the available resources. In all children with ADHD, with or without ASD, symptoms can be divided into mild, moderate and severe in their prevalence and intensity, which can help guide the possible treatment. The management of mild cases of ADHD often utilises a behavioural approach with parental education on how to deal with the child's problems. In moderate to severe cases, parents and children benefit from behavioural modification techniques, but it is often suggested that the child is started on medication. As stated above, the use of medication to change a child's behaviour remains controversial with many unhappy about its application.

Behavioural

Suggested strategies that can help any child with ADHD include the following:

1. Providing structure and routine gives the child a framework for them to know what is expected and helps with their disorganisation as they lack an internal means of focus.

2. Keep instructions clear, short and simple, and repeat as necessary.

3. Break activities, if possible, into smaller activities that work with the short attention span.

4. Make an activity as interesting and stimulating as possible.

5. If it is possible to allow the child to change tasks when they want to, allow them to do so.

6. Make boundaries and rules consistent, fair and easily enforceable.

7. Give positive feedback as many of these children feel that they are constantly in trouble.

8. Keep calm – these children will often respond to irritation with anger.

9. If the child is getting agitated, consider giving them some 'time out', and return to the task when they are calmer.

10. Physical exercise can be used to help the child burn off the extra energy.

In a child with ASD, there is limited evidence for the effectiveness of the behavioural treatments commonly used to treat ADHD. However, it is important to instigate the normal strategies one would use with a child with ASD, which include understanding the reasons for their behaviours, providing structure and routine, addressing environmental issues, dealing with change, and any emotional issues such as anxiety (discussed in Chapter 4). It is still amazing to see how a good school placement, which addresses the ASD components of a child's difficulties, can significantly reduce the hyperactivity and ADHD aspects. Some of these children appear to respond very positively to firm boundaries and structured settings. Unfortunately, others treated with the same framework appear to get worse, becoming more disruptive and difficult to manage. Often any success appears to be short-lived. Reward schemes, such as star charts, may work very well initially but rapidly lose their appeal. We have seen a number of exasperated teachers and parents who feel nothing is working. Problematically, sometimes nothing appears to work behaviourally. This leads on to the use of medication, which can sometimes salvage this position and enhances the behavioural strategies which once failed.

It is important not to underestimate how much is required to be in place to support these children and how difficult it can be to live or work with them on a daily basis. They require an infinite amount of patience and a consistently calm manner. Unfortunately, children with ASD and comorbid ADHD can respond strongly to other people's agitation, irritation or anger and become increasingly agitated themselves. In our experience, once they reach this point, the anger can go on for hours.

THINK POINT!

The management of ADHD typically requires multiple approaches, including behavioural and pharmaceutical.

Medication

We have already noted that the use of drugs for children remains contentious and many people feel uncomfortable in using medication to control the behaviour of young children. In later chapters we will talk about ways in which the behaviour of children with ASD can be helped, but here we focus on the pharmacological management of comorbid ADHD as it is important to have a good understanding of this area in order to provide help.

Medication has been used for a number of years for children with ADHD, and there is a significant quantity of literature available relating to this. Most of the literature, however, relates to children without ASD, while a smaller amount is available on those with comorbid ADHD and ASD. At present there do not appear to be any significant problems with long-term usage, but children do need close monitoring by clinical services. As with all treatments, there can be problems, and professionals need to be vigilant for the side-effects which can occur, and be willing to moderate treatment administrations to obtain the best outcomes. Different medications may be useful at different developmental stages of a young person's life in response to their different needs (e.g. the need to control of symptoms in the later evening for activities such as homework).

The mode of action on the brain of these treatments is only partially understood, with continued research exploring the effects of the drugs. There is significant research exploring the effects of how the drugs interact with the neurones in the brain and also how they affect the functioning of certain aspects of the brain. The difficulty lies in the fact that the brain is a complex organ that is not currently fully understood. To find out further information about the science behind this, we recommend that you look at O'Shea (2005) or Amthor (2012).

The typical medications that have been used for ADHD are methylphenidate, atomoxetine and dexamphetamine, which have different trade names internationally. There are other medications used to treat ADHD, but these tend to be used when the more common treatments have failed to have an effect or the child is experiencing significant side-effects. The medications are produced in different formulations, designed to target particular aspects of the day, and come in either tablet or capsule form. The medication tends to be licensed for usage for children aged six years and over, due to the diagnostic issues described earlier in the chapter.

The choice of medication in children with comorbid ADHD depends on a range of factors, such as the existence of coexisting conditions, the side-effects experienced and patient preference. In addition, specific issues, such as the need to improve adherence to treatment (e.g. avoiding midday treatment) should be considered, together with the potential for 'drug diversion' (i.e. the supplying of medications to others). Prior to giving medication to the child, there are a number of investigations performed.

Investigations prior to medication

- This is dependent upon clinical practice within any given country.

- The assessment should include, at least, a full physical examination (height, weight, heart rate, blood pressure), an assessment for family history of cardiovascular disease, and an electrocardiogram (ECG) if there is any indication of possible heart problems (NICE guidelines 2008). Some authorities also suggest blood tests.

We will describe an outline of the different medications commonly used. Box 3.3 describes methylphenidate, Box 3.4 describes atomoxetine and Box 3.5 describes dexamphetamine.

BOX 3.3 METHYLPHENIDATE

Methylphenidate is described as stimulant medication which is related to the amphetamine group. Dosages are started small and increased until a good control of symptoms is reached or there are significant side-effects. Licensed dosage is up to 60 mg per day but can go higher under specialist supervision. Effectiveness of the treatment can be immediate but is time-limited; therefore, there is little effect in the evenings when the medication has worn off. There is also no effect before the treatment begins in the morning.

Format

- *Short-acting treatments* – dose lasts up to 4 hours.
- *Longer-acting treatments* – dose lasts 8–12 hours.

Caution

- Extra care is required for children with the following problems: anxiety or agitation, severe depression, suicide ideation, tics, drug/alcohol dependency, psychosis, hyperthyroidism, cardiovascular disease.

Possible common/significant side-effects (not an exhaustive list)

- Effect on appetite (decrease).
- Weight loss and effect on growth.
- Cardiovascular problems (increased heart rate and increased blood pressure).
- Effects on sleep.
- Increasing irritability and possible hyperactivity.
- Increasing level of tics.
- Convulsions (fits).
- Psychosis (rare but significant).

BOX 3.4 ATOMOXETINE

Atomoxetine is a noradrenalin reuptake inhibitor, which has a similar mode of action in certain ways to antidepressants. It can take a number of weeks to become fully effective but the mode of action is continuous. Dosages are effective from 1.2 mg/kg to 1.8 mg/kg, therefore it is important to constantly monitor the child's weight to ensure the correct dosage.

Format

- Available as a capsule, which is taken 1–2 times per day.

Caution

- Extra care is required for children with the following problems: cardiovascular disease, history of seizures, glaucoma, liver problems.

Possible common/significant side-effects (not an exhaustive list)

- Gastrointestinal side-effects (nausea, diarrhoea, constipation, weight loss, abdominal pain, dyspepsia, flatulence).
- Cardiovascular (increased blood pressure, increased heart rate, palpitations, postural hypotension).

- Mood-related side-effects (depression, anxiety, irritability; uncommonly, increased suicide ideation).
- Liver problems (very rare).
- Other side-effects (sleep disturbance, dizziness, headaches, fatigue).

BOX 3.5 DEXAMPHETAMINE

Dexamphetamine is a stimulant medication. It is related to the amphetamine class of drugs. Dosages are started small until a good control of symptoms is reached or there are side-effects. The maximum dosage varies with the child's age.

Format
- Short-acting preparations.
- Long-acting preparations.

Caution
- Extra care is required for children with the following problems: cardiovascular disease, tics, glaucoma, hyperthyroidism, drug/ alcohol dependency.

Possible common/significant side-effects (not an exhaustive list)
- Sleep difficulties (insomnia, night terrors).
- Restlessness, irritability and nervousness.
- Gastrointestinal problems (including weight loss).
- Cardiovascular problems (increased heart rate, palpitations, increased blood pressure).
- Increase in tics.
- Convulsions.
- Psychosis (rare).

If there is a poor response to these three treatments, a re-assessment of the child and a more specialist opinion may be necessary. Less commonly used treatments include imipramine, bupropion and clonidine, and new treatments are undergoing development. Ongoing monitoring is needed to maximise the effectiveness of the treatments and to assess adherence and the side-effects.

Medication outcomes in the child with ASD

In our experience, getting the right medication for a child with ASD and comorbid ADHD can be a little more problematic than for those who just have ADHD. There has been some research in this area which supports this view, with many experienced clinicians reporting similar experiences. For reasons which seem to be unclear, these children appear to be more sensitive to the treatment regimes. They can be more sensitive to the side-effects of medication and therefore tolerate smaller doses than other children. This may lead to poorer symptom control. Therefore, it may be best to increase treatment dosages at a slower pace and monitor each dose increase carefully. Unfortunately, this is not consistent across the ASD group, with some children needing a particularly high dose before an effect can be achieved, and so clinical judgement will be required on a case-by-case basis. Good communication with parents and schools should always be encouraged to facilitate this process.

As stated above, children with ASD can be more sensitive to the potential side-effects of medications, which can lead to non-adherence of treatment due to poor tolerance. Additionally, in our clinical practice it has been those children with ASD and comorbid ADHD who have occasionally become extremely hyperactive or, more rarely, psychotic following treatment. Obviously, as practising clinicians, our first guiding principle is 'first do no harm', so making a child ill with a prescription treatment is not a good outcome. Fortunately, in the cases we have seen, the symptoms have rapidly improved on stopping that particular medication.

The outcome of treatment can be unpredictable for this group, due to the apparent delicate balance between ASD and ADHD symptoms. In some children it appears that the ASD symptoms related to the triad of impairments, such as rigidity of thinking, poor communication and social withdrawal, are counterbalanced by the ADHD symptoms, which encourage the child to be more outgoing and social. The clinical experience of ADHD treatment can be very good, with the child concentrating better and thus able to improve their social skills through their interactions with others as they are less agitated. However, commonly seen is the child who has an improvement in their ADHD symptoms but an apparent worsening in their ASD presentation. Parents and schools may complain that these children are now more rigid in their thinking or perhaps more anxious. This can worsen to a point where it is felt that the child was better without medication for the ADHD. Clinical professionals may need to balance the treatment to obtain the optimal outcome.

CHAPTER SUMMARY

The presence of comorbid ADHD is becoming increasingly recognised as occurring in children with ASD. Although ADHD remains a controversial diagnosis, it appears to occur in approximately a quarter of children with ASD. While ADHD can present with the classic features, the signs can sometimes be less clear. Diagnosing ADHD requires a good knowledge of both ADHD and ASD, the influences which affect the presentation and in particular an awareness of the pitfalls. Treatment requires good management of both the ASD and ADHD problems and can utilise a number of approaches, including behavioural and drug interventions. Medication can be used successfully, but caution needs to be exercised to achieve optimal care.

ⓘ IMPORTANT LEARNING POINTS

- ADHD can be diagnosed in approximately 25–30 per cent of children with ASD.
- ADHD can present with problems in the areas of attention, concentration, hyperactivity and impulsivity.
- The presentation of ADHD in children with ASD can be quite variable and difficult to diagnose.
- Management requires a multi-modal approach, using a number of different strategies and treatments to achieve the best result.

FURTHER READING

Amthor, F. (2012). *Neuroscience for Dummies*. Ontario: John Wiley and Sons Ltd.

Blakemore-Brown, L. (2002). *Re-weaving the Autistic Tapestry: Autism, Asperger Syndrome and ADHD*. London: Jessica Kingsley Publishers.

Conners, C.K. (1997) *Conner's Rating Scales – Revised; technical manual*. North Tonawanda, NY: Multi-Health Systems.

Green, C., and Chee, K. (1997) *Understanding ADHD: A Parent's Guide to Attention Deficit Hyperactivity Disorder in Children*. London: Vermilion.

O'Shea, M. (2005). *The Brain: A Very Short Introduction*. Oxford: Oxford University Press.

Simonoff, E., Pickles, A., Charman, T., Chandler, S., Loucas, T., and Baird, G. (2008). Psychiatric disorders in children with autism spectrum disorders: Prevalence, comorbidity, and associated factors in a population-derived sample. *Journal of the American Academy of Child and Adolescent Psychiatry, 47*(8), 921–929.

CHAPTER 4

ASD AND COMORBID ANXIETY DISORDERS

This chapter will cover:

- Introduction.
- What is anxiety?
- How does anxiety present in children with ASD?
- What defines an anxiety disorder and what are the different types?
- When does 'normal' anxiety become an anxiety disorder in children with ASD that needs treatment?
- How common are anxiety disorders in children with ASD?
- How can you help children with their anxiety?
- When should you seek specialist help?
- Chapter summary.
- Further reading.

INTRODUCTION

We have significant personal and professional experience of managing anxious children with ASD in its many forms. It cannot be underestimated how difficult it is to work or live with a stressed and anxious child, and how draining this can be for all involved (definitely so!). It is an incredibly common occurrence to find anxiety of one form or another in a child with ASD, and in some ways it does appear to be one of the defining features. There are also some authors who feel that some of the features of ASD are better attributed to anxiety rather than being features on their own, therefore managing the child's anxiety forms an essential part of their treatment plan. It could be surmised that the need for routines, predictability and sameness is, in fact, a way of reducing anxiety in a child who is struggling to understand the world. In this chapter we will be exploring what is meant by stress and anxiety, and the point at which a comorbid anxiety disorder may appear.

WHAT IS ANXIETY?

Anxiety is a normal feeling experienced by all of us at some stage of our lives – in reality, probably on a daily basis. It is an evolutionary aspect of our development and was essential in order to keep us alive. The function of this emotion is to prepare us when we are under threat so we can deal with the danger in an appropriate way; it has different components that include preparing the body and mind to react. This preparation can mean either to fight, face the threat, or to flee – hence it is called the 'fight or flight' phenomenon (Cannon 1929). In more contemporary thinking, there is an additional component, that of 'freezing' in response to danger. Anyone who has any experience of children with ASD will be familiar with all these phenomena.

The words 'anxiety', 'fearfulness', 'worry' or 'stress' are used interchangeably in everyday language, but in the context of mental health some of these words have a specific meaning. Stress is a widely used, but ill-defined concept, and one that is typically described as a negative influence on both physical and mental well-being, characterised by an inability to cope with certain aspects of the environment. Stress can be experienced intensely over a short period of time and can lead to an acute stress reaction (e.g. following a car accident), or it can be experienced over a longer period of time (e.g. the ongoing pressures in the school environment).

The word 'anxiety' is often used to describe an emotional state, but it can also describe a state which in medical terms could be defined as an 'anxiety disorder'. (We will discuss what defines an anxiety disorder later in the chapter.) Anxiety has different components that are felt and experienced by everyone. Broadly speaking, these can be divided into:

- physical
- emotional
- cognitive
- behavioural.

An understanding of the normal anxiety reaction helps to explain what is happening, and we often go into this when educating families about anxiety. It is important to recognise that all these symptoms do not have to occur at the same time and people react differently. When we explain these symptoms to children, we make it clear that each symptom actually makes sense when someone is dealing with danger. A good example is an increased breathing rate, which will increase oxygen to the body. Please see Box 4.1 for a description of these four main components.

BOX 4.1 THE FOUR MAIN COMPONENTS OF ANXIETY

- *Physical Symptoms* – may include tachycardia (irregular/increased heart beats), palpitations, muscle aches and tension, fatigue, nausea, chest pain, shortness of breath, stomach aches, breathing quickly, blurred vision, sweaty palms, dry mouth, shaking, headaches.
- *Emotional symptoms* – may include feelings of apprehension or dread, trouble concentrating, feeling tense or jumpy, irritability, restlessness, paranoia, anticipating the worst.
- *Cognitive effects* – can affect the ability to focus and attend to things (becoming hyperfocused or unfocused), and the ability to recall or not recall information; can lead to obsessive thinking and feeling overwhelmed; can also lead to negative thinking patterns (e.g. that chest pains are a heart attack).
- *Behavioural expressions* – includes difficulty sleeping, irritability, isolation, tiredness, poor appetite and even avoidance.

The reality is that an individual can express a wide range of anxiety symptoms, from a simple raised heart beat and sweating to panic attacks. Unfortunately, the individual may misinterpret these symptoms as a physical illness and worry that they have a medical condition. For the child with ASD, given their thinking style and sensory issues, interpreting anxiety may be very difficult, and their reactions to sensations of panic may become more extreme. If they become severely anxious in a situation, they may choose the 'flight' reaction, leaving you as a parent/professional running after them.

HOW DOES ANXIETY PRESENT IN CHILDREN WITH ASD?

The way in which anxiety presents in children with ASD can result in problems for both the child and those looking after them. In children without ASD, many of the signs of anxiety are fairly easy to see, due to the behavioural changes of the child and also what they say. However, the presentation in children with ASD can be quite different. Although some of them present with identical symptoms to the ones we have already described, unfortunately some children with ASD are unable to express their emotions adequately. Consequently, this difficulty presents with either a change in behaviour or a failure to even indicate its presence at all. Most commonly, anxiety in this setting presents itself with agitation, aggression, running off or extreme distress. Familiar to most parents of a child with ASD is the 'meltdown', when the stress of a particular situation overwhelms the child and their behaviour becomes uncontrollable.

Everybody who has experienced a child in meltdown can recognise the difficulty in salvaging the situation at this point, and it is usually a case of coping as best as possible. The presentation of anxiety can be fairly wide ranging, with both verbal and behavioural ways of expressing stress and distress. This is what makes the recognition of anxiety so difficult, particularly for those unfamiliar with the child, who may interpret the behaviours as being caused by something else. For example, in our experience we see children who we believe to be anxious, but the response from parents or schools, might be 'I can't see it'. It is probably useful here to provide a list of different presentations to show the broad range of signs. Please see Box 4.2 for the classic signs of anxiety.

The cause of increases in anxiety can be multifactorial and it can sometimes be difficult to understand why the child is anxious. It may be useful to consider anxiety as a response to different stressors. In some children with ASD the anxiety may be secondary to a single stressor (e.g. a change in routine or staff member, or changes within the family environment). Although these changes may seem insignificant to us, they can have considerable meaning to the child. They can range from something as small as changes in food packaging to something more profound, such as a change of teacher. Additionally, it should be recognised that these children can see the world in a very different way. For example, parents often tell us of episodes when someone in the family has been very ill and needed hospitalisation, but the child becomes anxious about where their dinner is coming from.

THINK POINT!

When considering what makes a child anxious, try to look at it from their point of view.

BOX 4.2 SIGNS OF ANXIETY IN CHILDREN WITH ASD

Verbal indications include:
- saying they are anxious but cannot explain why
- using different terms such as 'unsettled', 'tired', 'ill' or 'bored'
- constantly seeking reassurance
- becoming more talkative (talking to their personal agenda)
- becoming less talkative.

Behavioural indications include:
- becoming more aggressive than typical (hitting, biting and kicking)
- becoming more obsessive than typical
- withdrawing into their own world (shutting down)
- becoming more rigid or less flexible in their routines and thinking
- refusing to do things such as getting out of bed, showering or doing homework
- affected sleep, concentration and appetite
- becoming more hyperactive
- increasing stereotypical movements, such as flapping the arms, rocking, banging the head, screaming and so forth
- fidgeting, picking at the skin, picking at clothes (loose threads)
- becoming more tearful.

Alternatively, for some children with ASD there is a build-up of stress that is more subtle and difficult to recognise. This may explain why some children with ASD appear to go from '0–60' instantaneously, with no obvious cause for the explosion! This is commonly a consequence of dealing with factors such as the complex social environment or sensory issues, in addition to the normal stresses of timekeeping and schoolwork. Also, some children with ASD appear not to display any distress in the school environment, but by the evening they are completely fried by the stress of the outside world and can be quite difficult to manage – this is referred to as 'masquerading' (Carrington, Templeton and Papinczak 2003). At this point it is useful to talk to children who are anxious but also show little or no overt changes in behaviour until they reach crisis point. In our experience, children who have more of a passive form of ASD, or who are more socially aloof, appear to be more prone to this presentation of anxiety and they have significant problems expressing how they feel. In these cases it is important to be vigilant for any subtle changes of behaviour. Obviously, in children who are non-verbal it can be particularly difficult to identify what is causing the distress. Again, it is about looking at the changes in behaviour which would support the identification of these problems.

Case study

Daniel is a 14-year-old boy who has had a diagnosis of ASD for six years. He is in a specialist educational provision for children with ASD as he has significant outbursts of agitation and aggression. He struggles with change and needs a predictable routine each day. Daniel's parents appear to understand his needs and have adapted their lifestyle. It is recognised that Daniel becomes angry when his routines are changed, which can result in physical aggression towards others. The school reports that the level of aggression has increased significantly over the last two months and they are struggling to manage him. There have been no significant changes in the school setting but they have noticed that Daniel has a reduced appetite, and he struggles to focus on his work. The school then discover that his parents have separated and are now living in different homes; Daniel is living with his mother and there is no opportunity for reconciliation.

Reflective activity

Do you think Daniel has an anxiety disorder? What makes you think he has or has not? What do you think needs to be done to help Daniel?

To be able to answer this question, you need to understand what defines an anxiety disorder. Therefore we now address what defines an anxiety disorder and provide ways of helping children with their anxiety.

WHAT DEFINES AN ANXIETY DISORDER AND WHAT ARE THE DIFFERENT TYPES?

The purpose of this chapter is to define when anxiety becomes an anxiety disorder. As we have already shown, anxiety is a normal component of existence, but not everybody has an anxiety disorder. As outlined in Chapter 2, where we explained what defines a disorder, it remains a challenge to decide when somebody has anxiety and when this changes to an anxiety disorder. Despite attempts at assessing the level of anxiety, which in adults may involve the use of rating scales, it often comes down to a subjective decision on the part of the practising clinician to decide if it is an actual treatable mental illness. What is looked for is the change in a child's mental state and behaviour from what is described as their usual self. This is particularly important for children with ASD, who often have naturally higher levels of anxiety. There are a number of strategies that can be used to reduce the levels of stress and anxiety in these children, and there are also books that are useful in providing approaches, some of which we recommend at the end of this chapter. Our discussion relates mainly to anxiety disorders and their treatments, but we will discuss some ways of reducing anxiety and stress at different points in this book.

How do I recognise an anxiety disorder?

Generally, anxiety is considered to be a disorder if the symptoms start to cause distress in the child and have a significant impact on the young person's day-to-day functioning. Classically, an anxiety disorder is an exaggeration of the normal anxiety response. For example, the increased heart rate becomes palpitations, the increased breathing rate becomes hyperventilation, nausea becomes vomiting, and there are very intense emotional responses, such as fear and paranoia. The most common behaviour seen is that of running away from the cause of the anxiety and avoiding the fear object in future. This last factor, which we term 'avoidance', is a very powerful behaviour that can affect someone's life severely as well as their ability to manage a treatment. For example, in an extreme version of agoraphobia, an individual can become housebound by their anxiety. Another concept to consider at this point is that of generalisation, which can significantly affect the progress of an anxiety problem. In this situation the anxiety which is provoked by one situation is generalised (i.e. spread) to another similar situation and therefore the anxiety can slowly worsen. An example of this is a child who starts avoiding school and eventually stops going out of the front door due to the anxiety of meeting anybody.

THINK POINT!

Anxiety is considered to be a disorder if the symptoms start to cause significant distress and impact on the young person's daily functioning.

The specific disorders of anxiety appear to be more common during specific stages of development of all children. For example, separation anxiety disorders and specific phobias are more common in early childhood, while social phobias, panic disorders and Obsessive Compulsive Disorder (OCD) are more common in the teenage years. This appears to relate to the developmental stages that children go through and the normal fears experienced at different ages. Younger children develop phobias in response to their fear of the unknown or to a situation (e.g. a dog jumping up and startling them). In the teenage years, when individuals become more self-aware and image becomes more important, social phobias may develop. The exception to this is generalised anxiety disorder, which can affect all ages. Despite there being a number of different anxiety disorders, the general symptoms of anxiety are the same in each, with some specific differences in the cause, presentation and treatment. Unfortunately, we cannot include all the anxiety disorders but will focus on the more common ones encountered. We outline these in Box 4.3 (drawing from Goodman and Scott 2005).

BOX 4.3 ANXIETY DIFFERENCES

- *Specific phobia* – excessive fear of an object or a situation, resulting in distress and avoidance with anticipatory anxiety.
- *Separation anxiety disorder* – developmentally inappropriate anxiety on separation from carers.
- *Generalised anxiety disorder* – symptoms of anxiety present on most days and most of the time.
- *Social phobia* – marked fear of scrutiny and embarrassment on exposure to social situation.
- *Social anxiety disorder* – good social relationship with family members but marked avoidance of contact with unfamiliar people.
- *Panic disorder* – recurrent unexpected attacks of severe anxiety and discrete fear of dying.
- *Stress reactions and adjustment disorders* – expressions of anxiety in relation to a specific event which is time-limited and tends to result spontaneously.
- *Post-Traumatic Stress Disorder* – intense expressions of anxiety after a traumatic event, with experiences of reliving the event, avoidance, and nightmares.

From Box 4.3 it can be seen that there are diagnosable conditions for many aspects of anxiety. These are described in the diagnostic classifications with particular definitions, but we have attempted to summarise the core features.

What are the causes of anxiety disorders?

There are some organic causes of anxiety (e.g. hyperthyroidism, heart problems, neurological conditions, drugs and alcohol abuse), but there appear to be a number of factors which affect the development of an anxiety disorder. These are outlined in Box 4.4.

BOX 4.4 THE CAUSES OF ANXIETY DISORDERS

- *Genetic* – anxiety affects other members of the family.
- *Psychological* – The development of unhelpful thinking styles which can be learned by the observation of other's reactions to certain situation. For example, watching a parent's fear of spiders which leads to thinking that spiders are dangerous.
- *Psychodynamic* – a response to threat of separation from primary caregivers, based on theory of attachment.
- *Response to severe life events* – for example, relationship breakdown, parental separation, natural disasters.
- *Temperament* – shy children are more prone.

In practice, anxiety disorders are caused by multiple factors, and it is the interplay of these factors that appears to define the severity of the anxiety disorder and how it presents in any child. Children with ASD already have sensitivity to anxiety, and the challenges they face sensitise them to even higher levels of stress and anxiety. Over time this may lead to the development of a more recognisable and distinct comorbid anxiety disorder.

At this point it may be useful to describe how anxiety normally presents in children at different ages. The typical phases of anxiety that children go through are outlined as follows:

- *Separation anxiety* – 6 months–1 year.
- *Stranger anxiety* – 8 months–3 years.
- *Fear of animals* – 2–4 years.
- *Fear of dark or imaginary creatures* – 4–6 years.
- *Fear of death or war* – adolescence.

What this indicates is that the presence of some anxiety in children is nothing to be concerned about. Children at particular developmental stages will experience some levels of anxiety, and this is also the case for children with ASD.

WHEN DOES 'NORMAL' ANXIETY BECOME AN ANXIETY DISORDER IN CHILDREN WITH ASD THAT NEEDS TREATMENT?

We are commonly asked this question. Anxiety, as stated earlier in the chapter, is a prevalent feature of ASD and therefore the boundaries between what is 'normal' anxiety for the child and what is an anxiety disorder do become blurred. Again, it is not the level of the anxiety in the child, but the change in the level of anxiety that seems to be the most important thing in defining whether the child has an anxiety disorder. Obviously, higher levels of constant anxiety are not pleasant and attempts should be made to reduce this at all times. While at first glance this can appear to be a strange view of the situation, the function of most treatments in mental health services is to return a child to their premorbid state (i.e. what they were like before the illness/disorder). If a child has been anxious long term and it appears to be their 'normal' state, then treating them would return them to this state. Strangely, you can therefore have anxiety and an anxiety disorder together. The child can show their normal level of anxiety in certain situations but much more elevated levels in others.

HOW COMMON ARE ANXIETY DISORDERS IN CHILDREN WITH ASD?

With anxiety being such a common feature in children with ASD, it is difficult to say with complete confidence how commonly anxiety disorders occur. Using assessment tools with a particular cut-off point which defines the presence or absence of a disorder can be useful in research; these are not so commonly used in clinical practice. However, in research this does give a fairly good idea of the prevalence. There is considerable evidence that children and young people with ASD are at increased risk of anxiety and anxiety disorders (van Steensel, Bogels and Perrin 2011). This research indicates that 39.6 per cent of young people with ASD had at least one comorbid DSM-IV anxiety disorder, the most frequent being specific phobia (29.8%) followed by OCD (17.4%) and social anxiety disorder (16.6%). It is also known that the young people who self-reported elevated levels of anxiety reported greater feelings of social loneliness (White *et al.* 2009).

Looking at these conditions, it is not that difficult to see why they are more common in ASD. They appear to reflect some aspects of the core features of ASD, particularly social difficulties, leading to social phobia, obsessive/rigid thinking, leading to OCD, and the insecurity that children with ASD can sometimes feel understanding environments, which may lead to phobias.

Phobias can reflect the common fears present in the general population, such as spiders, snakes, heights and the dark; but there may be some unusual presentations. The authors have experience of children with ASD suffering from strange phobias, such as a fear of clouds, buttons or zips. The fear of clouds initially seems very irrational, but the young person in question initially thought the clouds were chasing him on a windy day, which developed into a fear that the sky was going to fall down. This resulted in great difficulty in getting the young person to leave the house. Phobias may seem fairly innocuous, but for some they can be debilitating. Phobias can develop from the difficulties children have in predicting behaviour, and although it is suggested that a lot of children benefit from being around animals, some children are extremely fearful of their unpredictable behaviour. For example, one younger child with ASD ran from a cat, believing it to be chasing him – 'He's coming to get me!' – a good demonstration of poor theory of mind.

HOW CAN YOU HELP CHILDREN WITH THEIR ANXIETY?

It is beyond the scope of this chapter to describe all the ways in which anxiety can be managed in a child with ASD. There are other books and resources that deal with this issue and we recommend some of these at the end of the chapter; but also we discuss the identification and management of stress more generally later in the book in Chapter 10. Some of the suggestions we make in that chapter for managing stress levels or mental health problems may actually be useful for managing anxiety. What we do emphasise now, and throughout the book as a whole, is that the best way to work with a child with ASD is to understand the nuances of the condition, specifically for a particular child. The interplay between all the different facets of ASD often needs to be picked apart to help the child. There can be multiple reasons why a child with ASD becomes anxious, related to many parts of the triad of impairments. When working with comorbid anxiety, it is important to work systematically through the possible causes (again covered in Chapter 10). We refer you to Box 4.5 for a framework in managing anxiety before specialist help is needed.

BOX 4.5 HOW TO MANAGE ANXIETY

1. Think about the ABC (antecedent, behaviour, consequences) so you can plan the best response:
   a) Antecedents cover the situations/events or factors which lead up to a particular episode of anxiety (e.g. a change in routine).
   b) Behaviour covers what the child does as a response to the antecedent (e.g. becomes agitated or withdrawn).
   c) Consequences cover what the response of others has been to the behaviour. This is important as it can shape what the child may do in a similar situation in future (e.g. they then go back to the original routine, which reduces anxiety but may make it more difficult to change in future).
2. Concentrate efforts on dealing with the situation which is causing the most anxiety. (It may be difficult to deal with everything.)
3. Keep instructions simple and clear.
4. Children with ASD like predictability, therefore explain to the child what is going to happen. This depends on their level of communication, so use visual cues if necessary.
5. Make any changes to the child's routine slowly, where possible, and explain to the child why things are being changed. This may help to gauge the child's future responses.
6. Avoid making unnecessary changes.
7. Be aware of the development of new rigid routines as they may be more difficult to change later.
8. Use meaningful rewards/incentives as a way of positively managing the anxiety as this may help to shape further behaviour. For example, the child may become stressed by a change of routine, but rewarding them for coping with the change may reduce the anxiety.

Reducing stimulation within an environment and allowing personal space are both useful strategies to reduce anxiety and to understand behaviour change in simple cases. When that change in behaviour starts to impact on the day-to-day functioning of the child, affecting their performance in school and at home, then it is time to seek specialist help. You can use the indicators in this chapter to help you make the decision about when and who to seek this help from.

WHEN SHOULD YOU SEEK SPECIALIST HELP?

This depends to some extent on the resources in your area and within your country, but it is useful to know at what point it may be fruitful to seek additional support and advice. Basically, this is contingent upon certain factors, such as how badly the child is being affected by the anxiety, the change in their behaviour that is noticeable and persistent, and how much of this change in behaviour can be managed by parents/carers/schools. For example, a specialist autism school may manage quite extreme behaviour quite effectively, but seek help when the child is a danger to themself or others, while non-specialist environments may seek help sooner.

A particular sticking point for seeking help is often the different presentation a child with ASD can display at home and school. The child may hold it together during school hours, but then get very distressed when they come home. The problem may be a school-based issue, which is manifested at home, so the specialist help actually needs to be focused at school rather than home. Problematically, this situation may lead to inconsistent reporting from teachers and parents, which may delay access to services. Unfortunately, it does sometimes come down to how a parent feels about their child rather than anything more scientific.

What are the different specialist treatments available?

Because anxiety disorders worsen the social difficulties and other functional impairments caused by ASD, there is a need for treatments to address the clinical needs of children with this comorbid presentation. It is important for a professional to be experienced in diagnosing and working with children with ASD and to be familiar with the psychiatric presentations. In order to come up with the correct conclusions, the professional will need to make a comprehensive assessment of the core features of ASD in the child and, more importantly, how the child has changed more recently. It is also useful for the assessments to take place in other environments, such as school or home, and it is essential that there is liaison between all the professionals involved with the child. The management of these behavioural changes often requires a multidisciplinary approach by a range of professionals. There are a number of specialist treatment modalities and these are outlined in Box 4.6. We talk about the advantages and disadvantages of a formal therapy in Chapter 14.

BOX 4.6 SPECIALIST TREATMENT MODALITIES
Psychological

- *Cognitive Behavioural Therapy (CBT)* techniques are used to identify and treat certain thoughts (cognitions) that are thought to be unhelpful for the child (Beck 1991). The study by Drahota *et al.* (2011) provides preliminary evidence that CBT may promote increased independence and daily living skills among children with ASD. The therapy needs to be personalised for the child.

- *Family Cognitive Behavioural Therapy* (FCBT) is linked to more at-home exposures and greater child involvement. FCBT outperformed individual CBT for children with moderate ASD symptoms, though both treatments reduced anxiety (Puleo & Kendall 2011).

- *Psychotherapy* (psychodynamic psychotherapy, psychoanalysis). See chapter 14 for a detailed explanation.

Pharmacological

- *Selective Serotonin Reuptake Inhibitors (SSRIs)* – fluoxetine and sertraline are the most commonly used – belong to the group of antidepressants that selectively inhibit the reuptake of serotonin. Specialists may sometimes decide to use these drugs in response to individual clinical risk. Children require careful monitoring and a balanced approach towards risks and benefits while on the treatment.

- *Other medication to reduce anxiety* includes tricyclic antidepressants or antipsychotic medication, such as risperidone.

When using a specialist treatment, it is important to select the right one for the child and family rather than use a standardised approach. The variety of presentations of ASD requires a flexible and adaptable method for addressing anxiety problems which can take into account issues such as the verbal ability of the child, but also their thinking style. When applying a CBT approach, it is essential to assess the motivation of the child to change and also their own insight into their anxiety. Unfortunately, families and schools can be more motivated than the child in dealing with their anxiety – a fairly common situation in outpatients. As a clinician it is not uncommon for the child to be resistant and older children may use colourful language when they feel forced into doing something.

THINK POINT!

Motivation to get better is essential for finding a successful treatment.

CBT in anxiety can be a useful treatment modality, but it does require modification for these young people in respect to their age, in addition to the ASD. Behavioural aspects of CBT may be especially useful in some cases (e.g. desensitisation of a child to a phobic object by increasingly exposing them over a period of time to what they fear).

In many places psychotherapy is still used for anxiety problems in children with ASD, but it tends to be used less commonly than in the past. There is limited evidence that it is effective on the core features of ASD, which includes anxiety, but it may be useful in helping the family to understand the child.

Pharmacological treatments for children with anxiety disorders can be used to reduce some of the features of anxiety. While they can be used alone, they are probably better used in conjunction with another type of work such as CBT, as there is some evidence that the integration of the modalities is more effective than in isolation (Walkup *et al.* 2008). The use of medication such as fluoxetine (an SSRI) can be very effective in reducing many of the features of an anxiety disorder and can significantly improve quality of life for the child and family members. There has been some controversy around the use of SSRIs, particularly around the increased rates of suicide in young people under the age of 18 years (without ASD), and, although guidance does vary internationally, in some countries there are restrictions on what types of SSRI can be used.

Other medications have been used to down-regulate the anxiety features in children with ASD. These include the tricyclic antidepressants, which are an older class of medication but can still be used if a child is intolerant of SSRIs. Risperidone is classified as an antipsychotic medication, and can be used at low dosage to moderate aggression in some children with ASD, but it can also be used to reduce anxiety in more extreme cases. Care has to be exercised in the use of medication, due to the possibility of affecting blood sugars or fat levels within the blood, and also long-term side-effects, such as unusual movement disorders.

Case study

Jayne is a 12-year-old girl with ASD and is in mainstream education. Her parents take her to a show for her birthday, during which she starts becoming extremely anxious so they have to leave prematurely. Jayne says that it was the noise and lights that upset her. Later in the week the school contact home saying that Jayne has experienced a 'panic attack' during the school assembly and wants to go home. Over the next few weeks Jayne becomes more reluctant to leave the family home and refuses to go to school. She is not sleeping or eating well and is disappearing into her obsessions, spending more and more time alone in her bedroom.

Reflective activity

It is obvious that Jayne is struggling with anxiety. What would make you think that this is now a comorbid anxiety disorder, and what can be done to help her and her family?

In this example, it seems that Jayne has developed a comorbid anxiety disorder, due to the significant change in her presentation. There was an initial episode in which she showed some obvious anxiety, probably related to sensory overload among other things. This episode has sensitised her to other anxiety-inducing situations such as group gatherings – in this case the school assembly. Her response to anxiety has now become to avoid the situation, hence her refusal to go to school. Unfortunately, anxiety in this situation can worsen, leading to isolation. In this case, the mainstay of treatment is to get Jayne back to school and to re-establish her normal routine. This may be done gradually with support, avoiding the most anxiety-provoking situations. This may be facilitated by rewards (this may not always work), but will need patience and firmness from the parents. Her natural response will be to avoid the anxiety feelings and this avoidance needs to be challenged. School will be very important to her recovery, but if there is no improvement, she will need a specialist referral. In cases such as this, modified CBT and/or medication may be required.

CHAPTER SUMMARY

Anxiety is a common feature in all children with ASD. Anxiety disorders are also fairly common and can develop rapidly. When identifying anxiety disorders, it is essential to recognise the changes in a child's behaviour, and the anxiety may not be demonstrated in an obvious way. Early identification and treatment, however, are essential to prevent longer-term disability. Milder cases can be managed effectively by understanding the cause and through the application of simple behavioural strategies. More complicated cases may require a specialist, multidisciplinary assessment, and the treatments should be tailored for the specific needs of the child. When using therapies it is important to assess the child's motivation to engage with the treatment and to modify the therapies if necessary. There is a role for medication, which should be taken under specialist guidance.

ⓘ IMPORTANT LEARNING POINTS

- Anxiety is a normal experience but is seen to a greater degree in children with ASD.

- Anxiety manifests through physical, emotional, behavioural and cognitive symptoms, but in children with ASD these can present differently than in other children.

- An anxiety disorder is difficult to define but it is usually diagnosed when anxiety causes a change in the child's mental state and behaviour and affects their daily functioning.

- Treatment for anxiety disorders requires a comprehensive understanding of ASD and the implementation of simple strategies to reduce stress, but may require specialist intervention.

- Interventions for anxiety disorders require modification and adaptation to the child's particular needs.

FURTHER READING

Chalfant, A. (2011). *Managing Anxiety in People with Autism: A Guide for Parents, Teachers and Mental Health Professionals.* Bethesda, MD: Woodbine House.

Dubin, N. (2009). *Asperger Syndrome and Anxiety: A Guide to Successful Stress Management.* London: Jessica Kingsley Publishers.

Lipsky, D. (2011). *From Anxiety to Meltdown: How Individuals on the Autistic Spectrum Deal with Anxiety, Experience Meltdown, Manifest Tantrums and How You Can Intervene Effectively.* London: Jessica Kingsley Publishers.

Reaven, J., Blakely-Smith, A., Nichols, S., and Hepburn, S. (2011). *Facing your Fears: Parent Workbook Pack: Group Therapy for Managing Anxiety in Children with High-Functioning Autism Spectrum Disorders.* Baltimore, MD: Paul Brookes Publishing Co.

CHAPTER 5

ASD AND COMORBID DEPRESSION

The chapter will cover:

- Introduction.
- What is depression?
- What are the common features of depression?
- What is the prevalence of depression in children and young people?
- How does depression present in the child with ASD?
- Why is there an increased prevalence of depression in children with ASD?
- What is the treatment for depression in the child with ASD?
- When should you seek specialist help?
- What are the specialist treatments available?
- Chapter summary.
- Further reading.

INTRODUCTION

Every person will have an episode during their lives when they feel sad and low. This is part of normal life and is often in response to some particular upset. Some individuals will go on to develop a depressive illness and seek help from professionals. Why some people develop an illness as a consequence of becoming sad, is unclear but it has enormous consequences on their lives. Children with ASD are increasingly recognised as having an elevated risk of developing a depressive illness, particularly during their late teenage years and adulthood, which has huge implications for their lives. As our service has developed, we have increasingly identified depressive illness in children with ASD and have had to adapt treatments to suit their needs. Health services are recognising that this problem is having a significant effect on how the young person functions both at school and in their home, and how it is so important that this is identified and treated early. Parents and professionals need to have the skills to distinguish the development of a diagnosable mental illness, such as depressive illness, from the normal mood fluctuations which can occur in these young people.

In this chapter we will discuss the current views around what constitutes a depressive illness and possible treatments, and move on to explore how this can present in children with ASD. It is important to recognise that there are similarities but also differences.

WHAT IS DEPRESSION?

Internationally and in everyday clinical practice, there are different terms commonly used for the illness depression. They include 'depressive illness', 'depressive episode', 'major depressive disorder' or 'unipolar depression', but in reality these terms generally mean the same thing. For consistency, we will use the terms 'depression' or 'depressive illness' in this chapter, to mean any of the different labels applied. It is important to be able to differentiate depression as an illness/disorder from feeling low or miserable, which is a common occurrence for everyone. Generally, everybody has episodes in their lives, their week or even their day when they feel low in mood. This is often in response to stressful situations or bad news and can lead to a general feeling of unhappiness. This unhappiness can last for some time without being classed as an illness, particularly if the situation does not significantly change.

EXAMPLE
When a teenager fails an important exam, they can feel miserable about it. These feelings may go on for days or even weeks, but eventually they improve of their own accord.

In clinical practice it is important to differentiate these feelings of low mood, linked to a particular life situation or event, from depression. It is understandable that someone living under considerable financial strain, in poor housing or in a difficult relationship may feel unhappy, but this does not mean that they are depressed. Many people in these situations do not develop depression, but some do. The different reactions people have to similar conditions and events are wide ranging and it can be difficult to predict how someone will respond. In reality, we only have a limited understanding of how exactly depression develops and the biology behind it. In classification terms there is a label for a change in mood in response to a new situation. This is called an 'adjustment disorder' and is the mind's way of dealing with a significant change.

What do we understand by 'adjustment disorders'?

An adjustment disorders is a feeling of distress which can affect how somebody functions on a day-to-day basis during the time it takes for them to mentally adapt to a significant life event. The onset is usually within one month of the occurrence of the stressful event, and the duration of symptoms does not usually exceed six months.

The features of this distress are similar to the reactions in those with mood and anxiety disorders so it can be difficult to differentiate from the other conditions. Often the diagnosis is made on the existence of a link between a major change and the intensity of symptoms – sometimes retrospectively. Although the symptoms can last up to six months, in many cases they resolve much sooner. The most common changes which affect children are parental separation, bereavement, coping with illness and school-based issues.

■ EXAMPLE

A child who experiences his/her parents separating will need to adjust to changes in their environment, parental mood, and possible anxiety. Additionally, they may need to adjust to potential new partners, step-siblings, and visiting or staying in different homes.

THINK POINT!

Adjustment disorders are very common in children and relate to a significant change in their lives.

WHAT ARE THE COMMON FEATURES OF DEPRESSION?

Unfortunately, mental health remains fairly stigmatised and some people still think that depression is trivial or not a genuine health condition, as evident in the phrase 'Pull yourself together'. Depression is, however, a real and recognised illness, and can have a profound effect on the individual.

Depression affects people in many different ways and can cause a wide variety of symptoms. It is the persistent nature of the mood problem that tends to define the presence of depression, and this is often called 'pervasive low mood'. There are three common symptoms and other associated symptoms, which we outline in Box 5.1.

BOX 5.1 THREE COMMON SYMPTOMS OF DEPRESSION

Common symptoms

- Depressed mood.
- Loss of interest and enjoyment (anhedonia).
- Reduced energy and fatigue.

Associated symptoms

- Biological symptoms:
  - disturbed sleep
  - change in appetite
  - decreased motivation
  - reduced concentration and attention
  - somatic symptoms.
- Changes in thinking:
  - feelings of worthlessness
  - feelings of guilt
  - negative feelings about the future, past and present
  - hypochondriacal thoughts
  - obsessive thoughts.
- Irritability and anger.
- Ideas of self-harm and suicide.
- Occasional psychotic episodes.

The thinking style of someone with depression can change quite dramatically. Everything can feel colourless, grey and muted, and the thought processes can be very negative. Feelings of guilt and worthlessness are fairly commonplace, with individuals describing aspects of their lives – past, present and future – with a negative edge. This, in clinical practice, is called 'cognitive distortion'.

In adults, the low mood tends not to change significantly on a daily basis or in response to different circumstances, but can vary during the day (called the 'diurnal variation'), with an improvement in mood as the day progresses. This is not entirely the picture for children. Clinically, children describe their mood as varying from situation to situation, particularly improving when they are with their friends, but overall the mood is lower than before they became unwell. Unfortunately, this means that depression can be missed in these young populations. It is often useful to ask the child if they are enjoying things as much as they did previously as this can be a good guide to their mood.

THINK POINT!

A child with depression does not need to have a low mood all of the time, but their overall mood is lower.

How does depression differ in children?

Some of the other features of depression in children also vary from those seen in adults. Children may not appear so fatigued, or they may sleep more (rather than having the decreased sleep seen in adults), and they may have an increased appetite (rather than decreased appetite). This may be related to their development, particularly during puberty, as unaffected teenagers can also be notoriously difficult to get out of bed, or have huge appetites. Therefore, the depressive illness may reflect an exaggeration in these behaviours, but often a change in the child is the clue.

The severity of the symptoms can vary. At its mildest, depression may make a child simply feel persistently low in spirit, while at its most severe, depression can make the child feel suicidal with the thoughts that life is no longer worth living. Some severely depressed people lose touch with reality, developing delusions (a false but firm belief which is not true), or hallucinations – a state called 'psychosis'.

In younger children, low mood can present with other symptoms, such as withdrawal, crying excessively or being clingy, and it should be remembered that the age of the child also affects how they can express their emotions. A younger child may say they are feeling bored when they mean they are feeling miserable.

The signs of depression in a child's behaviour can be quite variable, depending on their age and situation. In teenagers depression can present as a decline in functioning at school, socially or at home. It may even masquerade as a worsening in behaviour, particularly in boys, who may display anger and aggression. The fact that children appear to enjoy some aspects of their life should not preclude the diagnosis of depression. Anyone working with children needs to be vigilant for signs of depression or low mood as these will need monitoring or possibly treating. The signs that a child (without ASD) has depression can sometimes be difficult to see, particularly if the child is attempting to hide it. Unfortunately, in clinical practice often the first sign that a child is depressed is an attempted suicide or self-harming behaviour, which can be traumatic for all those involved with the child. The use of alcohol or other substances are sometimes used to 'numb' the feelings and can mask some of the symptoms of depression so this possibility may need to be explored. We put some of the other possible signs in Box 5.2 but this can only be a limited list and, again, it should be emphasised that a change in the child is the important factor.

BOX 5.2 POSSIBLE SIGNS OF DEPRESSION IN CHILDREN
- Separation anxiety and possibly school refusal.
- Complaints of boredom.
- Poor school performance.
- Antisocial behaviour.
- Self-harm/suicide attempts.
- Tearfulness.
- Withdrawal/isolation.
- Aggression/agitation.

Obviously, these behaviours can be due to other factors and therefore an assessment needs to be clear regarding their cause. Not everybody who self-harms, for example, has a depressive illness and care needs to be taken in drawing the correct conclusions. The descriptions of many of these behaviours appear vague and it is the combination and collection of signs and symptoms of depression which is important. Building up a picture of the child in their daily life is essential.

Case study

Sarah is a 14-year-old girl who has always been quiet and reserved. However, she has a good group of friends and enjoys being part of a school hockey team. She has been in her first serious relationship, which lasted six months, but this ended rather abruptly. Subsequent to this Sarah has not been herself. Her parents describe her as 'moody', shouting at her siblings, and being reluctant to attend hockey matches. They initially treated this as normal teenage angst but have been growing more concerned as she appears to be getting worse. She is spending an increasing amount of time alone in her bedroom and has not been eating well. Her school work has deteriorated; she is often tearful and uncommunicative. Her parents seek help when they notice superficial cuts on her forearm.

Reflective activity

Do you think that this is adjustment disorder or depression, or both?

From the description there is clear evidence of a causative event for Sarah's low mood, and the cause of a rapid onset of low mood in the teenage group most often cited is a relationship breakup. With Sarah's symptoms, therefore, we would initially class her as having an adjustment disorder. However, since her symptoms go on for a long period of time and worsen, she appears to be experiencing a depressive illness. Following the self-harm, she needs assessing formally by a professional, who will look for signs of depression.

WHAT IS THE PREVALENCE OF DEPRESSION IN CHILDREN AND YOUNG PEOPLE?

The prevalence of depression in children and young people appears to be increasing. The exact reason for this is unclear but may be in part due to greater awareness and improved diagnosis. The prevalence of childhood depression in the general population has been estimated to be 1 per cent in pre-pubertal children and about 1–5 per cent in post-pubertal young people (Goodman and Scott 2005), with depression being experienced by twice as many teenage girls as boys.

The likelihood of developing depression increases as the child gets older, ranging from 0.5 per cent at the age of 9–10 years old, increasing to over 3 per cent at the age of 15–16 years old (Costello *et al.* 2003). This in some ways mirrors the increasing rates of self-harm, thus demonstrating the link between the two.

What causes depression?

Although depression is a very common experience throughout life, it can be difficult to say what exactly causes a depressive illness. Two people can experience the same stress or trauma, but only one may become depressed. There are obviously a number of factors which influence this process and, as stated earlier in this chapter, depression needs to be differentiated from feeling sad or adjusting to a change in circumstances. There has been a lot of research into the causes of depression, covering genetics, neurobiology, the effect of life events and other factors such as early childhood attachments.

There is strong evidence for genetic susceptibility to depression (Sullivan, Neale and Kendler 2000), with the symptoms being present from generation to generation. Caution is needed in these studies to differentiate those factors which are genetic (inherited) from those which may be due to family or social factors. Related to the genetic studies, there has been extensive research on neurobiology, particularly the neurotransmitters (chemicals which transmit information across brain cells), such as serotonin and noradrenaline (Nutt 2002). Although the studies have sometimes given conflicting information, the prevailing theory is based on the need to raise serotonin transmission across neurones. This is the basis of the drugs called Selective Serotonin Reuptake Inhibitors (SSRIs), of which fluoxetine is the one most commonly prescribed to those under the age of 18 years.

It does appear, therefore, that some individuals have a genetic susceptibility to developing a depressive illness, with other factors then triggering the depressive response. These factors can be almost anything! Many things can cause a build-up of stress which can overwhelm the individual and these adversities come from different areas of life. For children, the main stressors are school-based issues, family relationships and peer relations. In addition, there appear to be psychological influences which predispose people to becoming depressed. Some individuals/children have a particular mind-set which leads them to think negatively about events/situations or feel that everything is out of their control. One of these models is called 'locus of control' (Rotter 1954). This simple but well-established model suggests that individuals who feel that they have more control over their life (internally) are less susceptible to low mood. Another good example is Beck's 'cognitive theory of depression', which states that depression is a result of faulty (maladaptive) cognitive processes (Beck 1987). In this model, people with depression are argued to have negative, unrealistic ways of thinking about themselves, their experiences and their future.

HOW DOES DEPRESSION PRESENT IN THE CHILD WITH ASD?

The presentation of depression in a child with ASD can sometimes be very similar to that in children without ASD, and therefore it is important to reflect on the previous sections in this chapter. However, it is sometimes difficult to recognise the development of depressive symptoms in children with ASD. Obviously, they often have problems in expressing emotions, both verbally and non-verbally (especially facial expressions). Interestingly, some children with ASD have been referred to our service for an assessment of depression when the ASD symptoms have been misinterpreted as low mood. Again, this may be a consequence of limited understanding of the condition. Nevertheless, children with ASD have a greater comorbidity with depressive disorders, and it is important that they are provided with the right levels of support (Mukaddes, Herguner and Tanidir 2010).

As stated above, some children with ASD have fairly limited facial expression (also known as 'flat affect') and appear to demonstrate little emotional response to their feelings. It can be easy to misinterpret this as depression, but the presence of depression needs to be assessed through the child's other coexisting behaviours. It is rare to get only a few symptoms in a depressive illness as depression affects so many areas of the child's life and functioning. It may be particularly useful to review changes in their sleep cycle, appetite, concentration and motivation. They may be more irritable than usual, become more withdrawn, or suffer from insomnia. The sleep problems can often be at the start of the night, rather than the early morning awakening often experienced by depressed adults.

In about half of children with ASD who have comorbid depression, anxiety is also present (Mayes *et al.* 2011) and therefore children should also be screened for anxiety symptoms. Additionally, self-harm is a potential issue and can be present with depression in the child with ASD; because of this, it is important that trained professionals conduct a risk assessment of the severity of the depression to explore any suicidal intent.

THINK POINT!

When dealing with depression, look for symptoms of anxiety and ask about self-harm.

WHY IS THERE AN INCREASED PREVALENCE OF DEPRESSION IN CHILDREN WITH ASD?

The answer to this question is not really known. In the first few chapters we discussed the fact that the risks of developing mental health problems are high in children with ASD in comparison to the general population. The risk of developing depression in such groups is two to three times greater than that experienced by individuals in the general population. It seems especially difficult for individuals with ASD to master everyday challenges (Bakken *et al.* 2010), and this leads to them feeling more isolated and low in mood. Although the increased risk is understood, there is also a lot of variability in reported prevalence in different studies. For example, a recent study reported that 17 per cent of autistic individuals had a range of mood disorders, while 8 per cent had adjustment problems (Moseley *et al.* 2011). However, another study by Lugnegard, Hallerback and Gillberg (2011) reported depression to be as high as 70 per cent, in terms of experiencing at least one episode of major depression, while 50 per cent had suffered from recurrent depressive episodes in their lives. It is essential to realise that depressive symptoms can also occur as part of many other mental health conditions. They can present alongside anxiety, as part of bipolar disorder and as part of adjustment disorders.

Alongside understanding the prevalence of depressive illness in those with ASD, there have also been some attempts at estimating the prevalence of adjustment disorders, as they are clinically significant. Although adjustment disorders have been diagnosed as occurring in 8–9 per cent of individuals with autism at any given moment (Moseley *et al.* 2011), this is a relatively poorly researched area. It seems highly likely, considering the nature of ASD, that this percentage could be even higher than estimated, due to the difficulties individuals with ASD have on a daily basis. There are considerable differences in the methods used across research studies, and these are likely to account for the inconsistencies in reported prevalence findings. Virtually all individuals with ASD have difficulty with transitioning between activities and environments, and therefore the experience of an adjustment disorder over time would be fairly universal. It is important to consider adjustment disorders as they can lead to other problems (as we demonstrated earlier) in children with ASD, and the presentation can coexist with behavioural problems, anxiety or low mood (Ghaziuddin 2005; Ghaziuddin, Tsai and Ghaziuddin 1992).

WHAT IS THE TREATMENT FOR DEPRESSION IN THE CHILD WITH ASD?

There is limited evidence specific to treating children with ASD who are experiencing comorbid depression. Much of the treatment for depression in all children without ASD has been based on the research for treating adults, although the evidence is increasing. Treating depression in children requires an overview of all the factors which are affecting the child, and finding a treatment most suitable for the individual and situation. This also depends on the severity of the depressive illness, which is often classed as mild, moderate or severe, and the associated risk noted during the assessment. Obviously, in those who are severely depressed there is a very real risk of self-harm, which will need specialist interventions (this is discussed in more detail in the following chapters). Many of the treatments for depression in children are also utilised for children with ASD.

Treating depression in children with ASD

In some of the milder forms of depression an attitude of watchful waiting is all that is required. This allows for the situation to be monitored and in some cases it will resolve by itself or by listening to the child. Time has to be made available for this as many children with ASD may be reluctant to talk about their emotions or what is upsetting them. It may be useful in some cases to find alternative ways to communicate with the child (e.g. emailing or texting).

EXAMPLE

A child with ASD who was miserable at school found that the best way to communicate with the teacher was to use email while sitting side by side. This child revealed they were being bullied but would not have been able to express this verbally and face-to-face.

Educating the child and their family about depression can help in early detection and appropriate support for all of them. This not only enhances understanding of the disorder but can also improve patient adherence with therapy. It can decrease the tendencies of the parents to blame themselves or their child for the disorder and may alert parents to depressive tendencies in themselves or other family members.

It is crucial that any professional involved is fully informed about the individual's usual style of communication, both verbal and non-verbal, along with any recent changes from the normal pattern of behaviour. A lot of strategies are helpful to lift mood, and for many young people just following simple steps may result in improvement. For example, some useful suggestions to help a young person to tackle their depressed mood in the early phases could be self-help, alternative and complementary therapies or counselling. We now discuss each of these in turn.

Self-help

There are a number of things that you can do to help your child without necessarily seeking specialist help, and sometimes these things work on their own. We provide you with some possibilities below:

1. Improve physical activity. Encourage the young person to engage in any pleasurable activity on a regular basis. This could range from simple walks to playing a sport. Activity is good for the mind.

2. Pay attention to the physical aspects of good health, such as food and fluid intake, and sleep.

3. Establish a good routine for daily living.

    a) Continue encouraging the child to get out of bed at a regular time each morning and to go to bed at a sensible hour each evening.

    b) Encourage the child to attend school/educational setting as normal (as long as appropriate support is available).

    c) Build leisure time and activities into the day when the child is at home.

4. Encourage the child to talk about their feelings and listen to their concerns.

5. Contact some of the many organisations which provide useful written information and guidance.

Many things, such as good sleep hygiene, eating well or exercising, deteriorate during an episode of depression and it is important to get the child back into a normal routine. This encourages structure, which is obviously beneficial for children with ASD, and keeps them healthy. Aside from all other treatments discussed in the next few pages, we always emphasise these basic strategies.

Alternative and complementary therapies

If it is felt appropriate by a parent, alternative and complementary therapies/medicines can be included in any treatment package. This area of practice for children with ASD can be contentious among professionals (O'Reilly, Cook and Karim 2012), but families may find certain practices beneficial. Alternative and complementary therapies/medicines cover a huge range of different approaches and it is impossible to give guidance here about individual interventions. Practitioners may offer treatments such as acupuncture, massage, homeopathy, aromatherapy and herbal medicine, which many people with depression have found helpful. Our only caution with this group of treatments is to be wary of particularly expensive treatments, overly inflated claims related to effectiveness, and anything that carries extensive physical risk.

THINK POINT!

When using alternative practices, it is important that you inform the healthcare professionals involved in your child's care.

The role of stress in comorbid depression in the child with ASD

After recognising that a child with ASD has a low mood, it is important to look at the factors which are causing the child significant stress or distress. The most important element in this process is being open to examining the stress from different angles. It may be a build-up of these stresses which have resulted in low mood. It is essential to consider the different facets of ASD when trying to help. This is highlighted by the following case example.

Case study

David is a 17-year-old boy with ASD who is usually quite talkative. He has recently appeared quite low and withdrawn and this coincides with taking some major exams. The school are concerned by his appearance as he has lost weight and looks tired. He has been a lot less communicative and tends to isolate himself in the library, where it is quieter. The school want to know what can be done to help. They have discussed the situation with David's parents, who have also noticed a recent change in him. He is spending all his time in his bedroom and his appetite is reduced. The school and his parents have a meeting, and exams appear to be the only significant factor at present which is causing him any stress. The school are worried that he is getting stressed by the number of exams he has to take, but on speaking to David it is apparent that it is the change in the timetable, particularly the increased amount of 'free' time, which is causing him the most distress.

Reflective activity

Is this depressive illness, adjustment disorder or just stress? What do you think can be done to help David with his low mood?

This is a good example of the pitfalls of looking at something from a 'normo-typical' perspective (i.e. seeing things without understanding how a child with ASD views the world). The school were worried about the amount of work, but for David the problem was a lack of routine and structure, which he found unsettling. His only way of coping with this problem was to withdraw into himself. This could be a sign of anxiety or depression, or even an adjustment disorder – it is actually quite difficult to tell. Sometimes depression can only be diagnosed in these cases once the main stress has been removed and the symptoms still remain. In this case we would help the school to support David during this time and encourage as much structure as possible both at school and home. Unfortunately, the school cannot change the timetable back to its previous form so we may be fairly restricted in the practical strategies available. Obviously, we would want to continue to monitor David's mental health for some time after the exams, but the problem is that the post-exam period often coincides with a major transition and school holidays. These are unstructured in themselves and may cause additional stress or low mood.

WHEN SHOULD YOU SEEK SPECIALIST HELP?

The question about when to seek specialist help depends on numerous factors. It is not only the severity of depression, but also the presence of other illnesses, the levels of support available within the home environment, the developmental age of the child and the use of drugs and alcohol that could all lead to increased risk and require prompt assessment by a trained professional or team. It is the level of risk and the level of functioning of the child that help to determine when additional help is sought, but our attitude would be that if there were any concerns, then help should be sought sooner rather than later. These problems often improve more quickly if early help is sought. This in some ways can be compared to many physical complaints (e.g. a swollen knee joint, which would tend to get worse with continued exercise rather than rest, the most common treatment).

How is the child with ASD assessed for depressive illness?

Like all aspects of clinical work, the assessment of low mood in children with ASD needs to be made after a careful consideration of the history of the child, particularly looking at any recent changes in mood and behaviour. As we stated earlier in this book, the diagnosis of mental health problems is difficult and it is especially difficult for these children. Again, it is necessary to look at the overall behaviour. In children without ASD, structured questionnaires can sometimes be helpful in assessing the severity of the problem, but these are used less often in children with ASD. An example of the questionnaires being used is the 'Beck Depression Inventory' (BDI), which has proved to be an adequate screening instrument for depression in that it correctly identified the vast majority of cases with clinical depression in the ASD group (Cederlund, Hagberg and Gillberg 2010). These questionnaires are not used in our practice as a good, thorough assessment is often sufficient.

WHAT ARE THE SPECIALIST TREATMENTS AVAILABLE?

We will discuss briefly here the treatments that can sometimes be used for depressive illness or particularly for children with ASD, but we recommend that you review Chapter 14 on treatments for a more comprehensive coverage. In children it is suggested that 'talking therapies' are the first step in the treatment of depressive illness. When looking at any talking therapy it is important to determine the child's cognitive and emotional development level along with their ability and motivation to engage in the therapy. Talking therapies are most often done by specialist mental health services, but there are examples of this sort of work undertaken in other institutional settings, such as schools, particularly by school counsellors. However, for depressive illness it is more typical to seek a referral to a specialist child mental health service, due to the potential risks involved. While talking therapies tend to be the first step, there are other options, depending on the severity of the illness but also on the difficulty of accessing talking therapies. This is a particular problem for children with ASD, who may struggle with verbal communication. Other options include medication, and if the risk is high, hospital admission.

Counselling and therapy

There are often many professionals involved in schools, health settings or the voluntary sector who provide opportunities for the young person to talk about their problems/low mood, without them having to be referred to a specialist mental health service. Counselling is about talking to somebody who is trained to listen empathically and to provide emotional support when an individual is feeling low. Depending on the level of communication and learning difficulties, this could be a very useful way for children to share their worries and distress. This active listening approach can be very helpful for many children who have milder forms of depression, and can be used quite effectively for children with ASD who are more verbal. This may be an opportunity for them to describe in a secure and comfortable environment what is making them feel stressed.

There are multitudes of talking therapy approaches that have been used in the treatment of depression, and these are outlined in Box 5.3. These approaches are sometimes suitable for children with ASD but may require significant adaptation for the mind-set of these young people. The most commonly studied therapy for depression is Cognitive Behaviour Therapy (CBT), which will be discussed in greater detail in Chapter 14. This form of treatment has been used successfully but requires a therapist who is flexible in their approach and who can take account of the different ways of thinking and communicating in children with ASD. Children with ASD may have difficulty recognising their emotions and how this links to their behaviours.

BOX 5.3 APPROACHES TO TREATING DEPRESSION IN CHILDREN WITH ASD

Type of therapy	What it involves	Duration
Supportive Therapy Often used for children with ASD.	Indicated in milder forms. It enables the young person to think about their problems and how they could work through them.	At least 3 months
Cognitive Behavioural Therapy (CBT) Needs to be adapted for children with ASD.	This approach addresses the emotions, behaviours and cognitive states which are affected in depressed individuals and uses a goal-oriented approach to address these negative aspects.	At least 3 months
Interpersonal Therapy (IPT) Little research available regarding the efficacy with children with ASD.	Interpersonal therapy aims to treat the individual with depression by exploring their interpersonal relationships.	At least 3 months
Family Therapy Can be useful with some families.	This involves looking at the dynamics within the whole family and how this may be contributing to the individual's low mood.	At least 3 months
Psychodynamic Psychotherapy Sometimes utilised but not universally applied in children with ASD.	This involves working with a healthcare professional to look at the ways in which difficult things that happened to a young person in the past are still having an impact on their mood.	At least 30 sessions
Play Therapy Useful in younger age groups and in those who are less able.	Play therapy is based upon the fact that play is the child's natural medium of self-expression. It is an opportunity which is given to the child to 'play out' their feelings and problems.	At least 3 months

When to use medication?

There is always controversy about the use of medication in children. It is very evident that there is an increasing use of medication such as antidepressants in children worldwide, and there has been some concern that these are being over-prescribed. In our clinical practice medication only tends to be used when other therapies have not been successful or the child is felt to be unsuitable for another therapy – for example, children with limited insight, or those who will struggle with the verbal aspects of any talking therapy. Also, medication tends to be used in those individuals whose depression is so severe that they are unable to engage in therapy or who pose significant risk to themselves.

When used appropriately, medications such as antidepressants may be very effective. The use of medications to treat depression depends on the age of the child, comorbidity and if there are problems for them accessing other therapies. Most of the time it's the combination of the medication and other therapies which have been proven to be most effective. Drug treatment should only be initiated by trained professionals, such as psychiatrists, as it requires close monitoring of side-effects and any increase in suicidal thoughts.

There are different medications which can be prescribed. In the past, *tricyclic* antidepressants were the first available pharmacotherapy for depression in children. However, because of the concern about side-effects, especially in the case of overdose, these antidepressants have become second-line medical therapy. A more utilised medication is therefore, SSRIs. We outline these in detail in Box 5.4.

BOX 5.4 SELECTIVE SEROTONIN REUPTAKE INHIBITORS (SSRIs)

SSRIs are more of a new generation of antidepressants. There are different types of SSRI available but the one most commonly used is called fluoxetine. Fluoxetine is generally considered the first choice of medication because of less potential toxicity, especially in the case of overdose, when compared with tricyclic antidepressants. Fluoxetine is now the only SSRI for which the Committee on Safety of Medicines (UK) considers the balance of risks and benefits to be favourable, although it cautions that the drug is likely to be beneficial in only a minority of patients.

Format
- Available in liquid or capsule form.

Possible common/significant side-effects (not an exhaustive list)
- Gastrointestinal upset.
- Sedation.
- Activation symptoms (irritability, sleep problems).
- May induce hypomanic or manic symptoms in vulnerable persons.
- Possible increase of self-harm/suicidal ideas.

Once a child has been diagnosed with depression, they are at greater risk of it reoccurring. If your child has had depression and has been successfully treated for it, then it is important that you keep an eye out for returning signs and symptoms. Furthermore, a greater severity of the first episode, earlier onset, and longer duration of illness before treatment are associated with a longer time to remission.

CHAPTER SUMMARY

In summary, depression is a common illness which can affect children of all ages. It is difficult to acknowledge depression in children with ASD, due to their own difficulties with social interaction and communication. Depression varies in range from milder to more severe forms. As milder degrees respond well to self-help and activity rescheduling, they often do not require too much intervention, but the more severe forms of depression require specialist assessment and treatment with psychotherapy and/or medications.

ⓘ IMPORTANT LEARNING POINTS

- Depression/depressive illness is different from just feeling sad or low.
- Adjustment disorders are seen more commonly and are a normal response to a significant change in circumstances.
- Depressive illness is increasingly recognised as occurring in children, particularly those with ASD.
- It can sometimes be difficult to recognise depressive illness in children with ASD but it may be responsible for a change in their behaviour.
- Depressive illness can be treated and may require a combination of stress reduction, therapy and medication.

FURTHER READING

Massey, A. (2007). *Happy Kids: Understanding Childhood Depression and How to Nurture a Happy, Well-Balanced Child.* London: Virgin Books.

National Institute for Health and Clinical Excellence. (2005). *Depression in Children and Young People.* Available at www.nice.org.uk/CG28, accessed on 1 May, 2013.

CHAPTER 6

ASD AND TICS OR TOURETTE'S SYNDROME

This chapter will cover:

- Introduction.
- What are tics?
- What is Tourette's syndrome?
- How common are tics and Tourette's syndrome?
- What causes tics and Tourette's syndrome?
- How do you differentiate tics and Tourette's syndrome from other conditions?
- How do tics and Tourette's syndrome present in ASD?
- How are tics and Tourette's syndrome treated in the child with ASD?
- What do we do if the child has ASD, ADHD and tics?
- Chapter summary.
- Further reading.

INTRODUCTION

Sometimes we see children with ASD making unusual rapid movements or sudden utterances which they appear to be unable to control. These movements can be distressing to the child or they may not even notice them. However, the parents are usually very concerned about them and often worry that it is a sign of something sinister. We call these rapid involuntary movements 'tics' and in this chapter we will discuss them in more detail.

Tics are surprisingly common in children with ASD. They are very variable in their presentation and it is virtually impossible to say which children will develop tics during their childhood. Some of these tics can be fairly short-lived, while others are more persistent. Tics have been described throughout history, but have been examined more formally from the 19th century, initially by Jean-Marc Gaspard Itard, who described the first case, and Georges Gilles de la Tourette, who described the symptoms in a number of patients (Leckman and Cohen 2005). Although some children with ASD have obvious coexisting tics, tics in others only become obvious due to the side-effects of certain medications which appear to exacerbate the condition. This can make their treatment complicated. Fortunately, most tics improve towards adulthood. Some children and families cope well with the tics and can adjust their lifestyle to accommodate them, but in others the tics can cause considerable distress or embarrassment, and active treatment is sought from specialist services.

WHAT ARE TICS?

Tics can present in hugely variable ways, but, generally speaking, a tic is an involuntary action which is sudden, repetitive, and can either be a movement or a vocal utterance.

Tics tend to be fairly brief, with each tic being very short-lived; they can occur either singularly or in groups. These actions do not appear to serve any apparent purpose and can be described as 'uncontrollable' by the child.

■ EXAMPLE
A child may shout out uncontrollably, which can include obscene language, or they may have an obvious jerky movement of their head and shoulders.

When describing tics, we can describe them as 'simple' or 'complex'. Simple tics include actions such as eye blinking, neck jerking, or grimacing. Complex tics involve more complicated actions, such as hitting oneself or jumping. Vocal tics, which can occur either by themselves or with motor tics, may include the repetition of certain words and socially unacceptable language, such as swearing or cursing. In clinical terms this is referred to as 'coprolalia'. This can be very embarrassing for the young person and their family, and can have considerable social consequences. In most individuals there will be an awareness of when the tic is about to occur, due to a localised feeling in the affected area or general bodily sensation (Leckman, Walker and Cohen 1993), and there can be a sense of relief after the tic has finished. Interestingly, children may not actually be aware that the tic is occurring, and in some clinical cases we have surprised the children by pointing it out. This is a great example of children adapting to their situation and of how they accept these things as being normal.

It is important to remember that tics are a neurological condition, and this forms the basis of the discussion with families. It is helpful to differentiate tics from other neurological conditions, and one way to tell the difference is that tics can be suppressed temporarily by the child. Unfortunately, the sensation of needing to express the tic can become unpleasant and, following the suppression, the tics may return in greater numbers. It is important for those looking after the child to recognise the action or speech as a tic; otherwise it may be believed that such behaviour is a habit which the child can easily stop doing at any point, and so the child may get into trouble. It can also help the families to cope with the tics if they realise that the child is not doing this deliberately, particularly in cases where the child is swearing and parents may feel desperate for the child to stop. Additional features of tics which are important to consider are that they usually disappear during sleep and are fairly well defined by a particular action. Tics can develop at any point in childhood, but most typically develop in middle childhood; however, they may follow a fluctuating course and can improve significantly by adulthood.

THINK POINT!

A tic is an involuntary action which is sudden, repetitive and can either be a movement or a vocal utterance. It serves no apparent purpose and can only be temporarily controlled.

WHAT IS TOURETTE'S SYNDROME?

The terms 'tics' and 'Tourette's syndrome' are often used interchangeably by the general public and sometimes by professionals. Tourette's syndrome is named after Georges Gilles de le Tourette, a French physician in the 19th century, who described nine cases of individuals who had both motor and vocal tics. It is sometimes difficult to define which children have tics and which children have Tourette's syndrome, but Tourette's syndrome tends to be diagnosed if the individual is displaying multiple motor tics and one or more vocal tics, not necessarily occurring at the same time.

The vocal tics in Tourette's syndrome can often be described as fairly explosive and may include obscene words or phrases. These tics may also be associated with certain gestures which can include those of an obscene nature (known as 'copropraxia').

Tourette's syndrome typically begins around the age of six or seven, and starts with simple tics which become more complex with age (Baron-Cohen *et al.* 1999). Over time the tics can become very diverse in their presentation, and, while initially the tics can come and go, many become persistent. In reality, most vocal tics can be described as being fairly simple (e.g. coughing), with the more obscene utterances actually being much rarer. The frequency of the tics can be extremely variable, ranging from occasional occurrences during the week up to multiple tics each minute.

While Tourette's syndrome can occur in isolation, it is also associated with a number of other conditions. Although we do see it alongside ASD, more commonly it is seen in association with ADHD and Obsessive Compulsive Disorder (OCD). The connection, however, remains unclear. We will talk about OCD in Chapter 7, but a high number of individuals with Tourette's syndrome experience some obsessive compulsive symptoms (Bloch and Leckman 2009). However, there is some evidence that the presentation of OCD symptoms in individuals with tics may be different to the symptoms of OCD in individuals without tics (Miguel *et al.* 2001). Although it is clear that Tourette's syndrome is seen in children with ADHD, it is unclear from research how often Tourette's syndrome and ADHD coexist. Unfortunately, the coexistence of these conditions can cause a child considerable difficulties. It is often a reality in the world of a child with Tourette's syndrome that they are teased by their peers, and unfortunately, any social difficulties that are a consequence of ADHD (the difficulties in making friends for some children) can make this problem worse. Children with ADHD are more likely to react aggressively to taunting and therefore get into trouble. In addition, these children are also at higher risk of suffering with anxiety, and mood and behavioural problems, which may be related to the responses of others to the tics. Children typically do not like to feel too different from others.

THINK POINT!

Tourette's syndrome is the occurrence of multiple motor tics and one or more vocal tics, which can occur together but not necessarily concurrently.

HOW COMMON ARE TICS AND TOURETTE'S SYNDROME?

Tics can be fairly common in childhood but many of these are only transient. It is estimated that approximately 5 per cent of children have a transient tic, with persistent tics being less common (Khalifa and von Knorring 2007), but the actual prevalence rates appear to vary quite significantly in the published research. The research of Khalifa and von Knorring (2007) appears to support the prevalence of Tourette's syndrome at approximately 0.6 per cent of the population, although again figures tend to vary. More boys are affected with tics than girls, and there appears to be no difference across cultural or socioeconomic groups.

WHAT CAUSES TICS AND TOURETTE'S SYNDROME?

Although tics do appear to have a strong neurological basis, the aetiology is actually more complex, with genetic, neurobiological and environmental factors playing a role. It is clearly evident from studies of identical twins that if one twin has tics, there is a 50 per cent chance that the other twin will develop tics too (Price *et al.* 1985). The fact that it does not occur equally in identical twins demonstrates that other factors must also play a part. This is a commonly found situation in mental health, with identical twins being affected differently – a demonstration of the complexity of identifying single causes to these problems. Research illustrates that the risk of developing tics is also increased by having a first-degree family member with the condition, particularly for boys (Comings 1994). Medical research has identified a number of brain regions and neurotransmitters which are implicated in the development of tic disorders, but the underlying pathology remains unclear.

In addition to these genetic factors, there appears to be an increased instance of tics associated with some pregnancy and labour difficulties, and the studies indicate associations with maternal stress during the first trimester of pregnancy, premature birth, low birth-weight and difficulty during delivery. Although these factors are associated with tic disorders, the exact nature of the risk of developing the condition remains unknown, and sorting out what factors may have caused the problem can be complicated. This is yet another condition where we are asked in clinical practice what the cause is, and if a particular event, such as problems during labour, are responsible. Unfortunately, in most cases we just cannot be sure and have to say this to families.

In addition to these more biologically based factors, it is also well recognised that tic disorders appear to be exacerbated by increased levels of stress (Silva *et al.* 1995). Symptoms may worsen during episodes of increased stress, as is commonly seen in children at exam times, and tics can also occur more frequently in certain settings where the child feels more anxious (commonly school). In general, the process of interacting with other children is more stressful than being at home with their families. This becomes a negative cycle as the child associates the worsening of the tics with certain social situations and therefore the tics become more frequent.

HOW DO YOU DIFFERENTIATE TICS AND TOURETTE'S SYNDROME FROM OTHER CONDITIONS?

In clinical practice it is necessary to differentiate tics and Tourette's syndrome from other conditions to be in a position to reassure families and children about the nature of the condition. In the world of medicine there are a number of conditions which present with abnormal movements and they can be associated with a variety of different causes. Conditions which cause movement problems are sometimes confused with a tic disorder. It is important, therefore, for us to be able to recognise these other movements. While it is not essential to this book, it is useful to distinguish what the other movements are and we summarise these in Box 6.1.

Conditions which present with these movement problems can be diverse, ranging from those that have a genetic basis to those with a direct neurological or pharmacological cause. We present some of these in Box 6.2 to illustrate this point.

BOX 6.1 DIFFERENT TYPES OF MOVEMENT DISORDERS (NOT AN EXHAUSTIVE LIST)

- *Stereotypies* – simple movements such as body rocking, marching, crossing and uncrossing of the legs.
- *Tremors* – involuntary fine movements (rhythmic muscle contractions).
- *Chorea* – involuntary movements of the limbs, face and body.
- *Athetosis* – involuntary writhing movements of the fingers, arms, legs and neck.
- *Myoclonus* – involuntary twitching of the muscles.
- *Dystonia* – muscle contractions causing repetitive movements or abnormal postures.
- *Akathisia* – restless leg syndrome.

BOX 6.2 CAUSES OF MOVEMENT DISORDERS

- *Genetic conditions*, such as Huntington's disease, which presents with motor symptoms including tremor and chorea (involuntary movements of the limbs, face and body).
- *Neurological conditions*, such as brain tumours or infections, can result in unusual movements, including athetosis (involuntary writhing movements of the fingers, arms, legs and neck) myoclonus (involuntary twitching of the muscles), or dystonia (muscle contractions causing repetitive movements or abnormal postures).
- *Pharmacological causes*, such as side-effects of antipsychotic medication, which can cause dystonia or akathisia (restless leg syndrome).

In clinical practice the diagnosis of tics and Tourette's syndrome is often made on the clinical presentation. This is done by observing the tics carefully and taking a history, which includes the development of the movements, whether the child can control those movements, and what increases or decreases their presence. Practice does differ internationally, with some practitioners keen to absolutely exclude a neurological cause; however, there is no definitive diagnostic test for these conditions. In some clinics children may be given an Electroencephalogram (EEG) to exclude epilepsy, a scan using neurological imaging such as Magnetic Resonance Imaging (MRI), or blood tests. However, in our practice the diagnosis is given on the overall clinical picture.

HOW DO TICS AND TOURETTE'S SYNDROME PRESENT IN ASD?

Although it is clear that tics do occur in children with ASD, it is sometimes difficult to distinguish some of the movements which present in tics, from other abnormal movements which can sometimes also occur. Some children with ASD can have coexisting repetitive movements which tend to be rhythmic and are called 'stereotypies' (referred to earlier). This differentiates them from tics, which do not have this rhythmic quality.

■ EXAMPLE
A child with ASD who rocks repetitively; but this does not mean they have a tic disorder.

Interestingly, it is not uncommon for a child with ASD to be unaware of their tics, and for the families to be the most concerned. We mentioned this earlier in the chapter, and in our experience it appears that this is more common in children who have ASD as they are less aware of their bodies and the social reactions of others.

The frequency of comorbid tic disorders or Tourette's syndrome in these children is not fully known as tics can vary with age. However, tics are reported to occur in approximately 11 per cent of children with ASD (Canitano and Vivanti 2007), with Tourette's syndrome occurring in approximately 8.1 per cent (Baron-Cohen *et al.* 1999). Therefore, the rates are far higher than for those children from the general population, illustrating that this is a condition that needs to be considered in those who have ASD. Furthermore, there may be an increased incidence of tics in those children with ASD who are treated for comorbid ADHD, and this may have an effect on the choices of treatments.

Case study

Blake is a ten-year-old boy with ASD, who was diagnosed at the age of five. Things have been fairly stable for Blake for the last few years. He is settled in school and has support to help him with his school work; he even has a couple of friends. His parents have read extensively about ASD and have put strategies in place which help manage his behaviour. Over the last few months his parents have noticed some unusual movements. Initially there was an increase in blinking, which got worse for a few weeks and then improved. Blake was not aware that he was doing this. This then changed to clearing his throat regularly and a slight cough, which his parents found annoying. This has also improved but has been replaced by a rapid twitching of his head, which Blake is now finding distressing. He tries to stop doing it, but although this works for a while, the twitching then returns more aggressively. Both Blake and his parents want to know exactly what is going on and how he can be helped.

Blake obviously has symptoms consistent with a tic disorder. He has rapid, frequent movements that wax and wane over time, which he can temporarily suspend. We will now go on to describing the ways in which a child can be helped.

HOW ARE TICS AND TOURETTE'S SYNDROME TREATED IN THE CHILD WITH ASD?

Treatment is very similar to that in children without ASD. The first thing to remember is that tics generally have a natural lifespan. Although it is not true in all cases, a significant number of tics will improve or disappear in late adolescence, with a number of people becoming free from them altogether. Another consideration is that tic disorders have a very fluctuating course, with times of worsening symptoms and times when the child can be virtually tic free. This variation in presentation needs to be considered when determining the types of treatment, particularly as some of the pharmacological treatments may have side-effects.

Educational/supportive treatments

Before we consider medication to help with the symptoms, we always consider educational and supportive treatments to be an essential approach for children and families. Due to the expressive and obvious nature of tics, it is important to explain to families the aetiology, presentation and natural progression of tics/Tourette's syndrome to reassure them that it is not a more sinister condition. It is also particularly important to emphasise the likelihood of improvement with age. This may be especially important when some of the tics are socially inappropriate. Like anything else, when people are uncertain about a health condition, it may provoke anxiety, and this is particularly true for parents concerned about their children.

Earlier we mentioned that tic disorders are worsened by stress and anxiety. In children with ASD, anxiety is a part of their daily life and it becomes doubly important to help to minimise stress levels. Sometimes addressing the particular areas of stress in these children can have considerable effects at reducing the frequency of the tics, so although tics are often still present they appear to cause less of a problem. Families will often like this approach as it reduces the need for any medical interventions.

It is, therefore, important that children with ASD and comorbid tic disorders or Tourette's syndrome are adequately supported in their social worlds (such as school), as tics can be seen very negatively by their peers. The overt nature of tics can exacerbate the social exclusion possibly felt already by the child with ASD, with classmates finding tics a target for their amusement. In many situations it may be useful for peers and classmates to have some education regarding tics and Tourette's syndrome, although this needs to be done sensitively, in order to avoid exacerbating the problem. There are also a number of groups and organisations which can provide information and support, and we recommend you source these locally.

THINK POINT!

Before starting any treatment approach, it is important to look at areas that may be causing the child stress and to implement stress reduction strategies to see if there is a positive effect.

Psychological treatments

The psychological treatments for tic disorders and Tourette's syndrome aim to reduce the anxiety which can aggravate the condition and also to manage the tic directly through processes such as 'habit reversal training'. Habit reversal training uses techniques which include raising awareness of the tic, encouraging self-monitoring, relaxation training and 'competing response training', where a movement is performed that is opposite to the tic (King et al. 1998).

The outcomes of these psychological methods are variable but have good responses in some cases. Unfortunately, the nature of ASD can make psychological approaches to treatment more difficult, due to the cognitive rigidity and complex nature of therapy. While it is not impossible to use these treatments, they need to be adapted for this group. The main limitation to accessing this treatment is often the lack of local availability.

Pharmacological treatments

Sometimes, because the tics are so severe in their frequency and intensity, or if there has been a failure to respond to other treatments, pharmacological treatments are necessary. Using medication for tic disorders and Tourette's syndrome may, however, create some anxiety for both professionals and parents. In clinical practice the medications can turn out to be very effective but they need to be monitored closely for side-effects (both in the short and long term), as some are associated with significant health conditions. Initiating these pharmacological interventions needs to be determined on a case-by-case basis, aiming for the best possible outcome for the individual child. This can obviously vary from family to family, with some wanting the complete elimination of the tics while others just wanting a reduction. This may affect the level of medication prescribed and tolerated. Some individuals will take treatments all the time to manage their tics, whereas others will only take medication during more severe episodes. This should be entirely patient led.

Different pharmacological treatments have been utilised over the years for tic disorders. The drugs used for tics were all initially developed for other conditions but were found to be effective for tic disorders and Tourette's syndrome. One of the oldest and best-known treatments is haloperidol (Haldol), one of the original antipsychotic agents used for treating schizophrenia. Although this is still used in some settings, its use has generally been superseded by newer medications due to the problem of side-effects. Newer agents such as risperidone or aripiprazole (called 'atypical antipsychotics') are commonly used, but there are concerns regarding longer-term side-effects.

Side-effects of atypical antipsychotics do vary according to which drug is used, but generally they can have gastrointestinal effects, such as nausea or bowel upset, or they may affect weight and cause drowsiness. Less commonly, they can affect blood glucose or lipids, and this needs monitoring. Other agents – particularly clonidine, which was originally developed to treat hypertension – can also be used effectively. Possible side-effects of this treatment include dry mouth, fluid retention, sedation, headaches and dizziness, and it may also affect mood. Importantly, care has to be taken when this medication is withdrawn; this should be done gradually to avoid a hypertensive crisis in which blood pressure rapidly rises. Choosing these treatments should be a joint decision between the professional and the family, with the family being made aware of all the available treatments, possible benefits and shortcomings. It is worth pointing out that the treatments for tics in children with ASD are the same as those without.

THINK POINT!

Medication can be useful for the treatment of tic disorders but it is best used in conjunction with other supportive and psychological treatments.

WHAT DO WE DO IF THE CHILD HAS ASD, ADHD AND TICS?

In an earlier chapter we explored the frequency in which ADHD can occur in children with ASD. In some cases the child with ASD can have comorbid ADHD and comorbid tic disorder/Tourette's syndrome. There is always the concern that certain treatments for ADHD will exacerbate tics; indeed this does appear to happen in some cases. In some children stimulant medication used to treat ADHD such as methylphenidate, appears to be associated with the onset of tics, while in others it can worsen existing tics. Conversely, in some children the tics actually appear to improve with these treatments and therefore this can cause some confusion for families and professionals. There are other classes of medications available for this combination of disorders, but many should only be given by experienced medical professionals. This again demonstrates how little we really know about the neurology and neuroscience of these conditions, and how the treatments need to be tailored to the individual child. Again, we recommend that families seek the advice and support from professionals who are familiar with ASD and this area, and who have experience of working with these children.

Reflective activity

Consider a child you may know with both ASD and tic disorder. With this in mind, what could you do to help this young person? Make a list of the effects of the tics on the child and/or the family and how they can be helped in the home, in school and more generally. Are there any stress factors that you can identify which cause the tics to worsen?

CHAPTER SUMMARY

Tics are commonly found in children who have ASD. When a child is first assessed for the diagnosis of ASD, it is important that the professional looks for evidence of tic disorders and how they may be affecting the child. It is necessary to recognise what tends to exacerbate the presence of the tics in the child with ASD as this can have an impact on their social interactions. The child with ASD, who already may be socially excluded, could find the presence of comorbid tics a further social barrier as their peers may become more aware of their differences. However, not all children with ASD are actually bothered by their tics, and families may be more concerned.

There are a number of interventions which can be utilised to help with the tics, the most obvious being a reduction in the child's environmental stress levels, which thus reduces their anxiety. It is important for families and other important figures (including peers) to be educated about the nature of tics and how they can change over time. There are other more specialised treatments, both psychological and pharmacological, and these should be used whenever necessary.

① IMPORTANT LEARNING POINTS

- Tics are involuntary, sudden, repetitive movements or vocal utterances that serve no apparent purpose and are difficult to control.
- Although tics can occur in the general population of children, they are more common in children with ASD.
- Tourette's syndrome is diagnosed in those children who have multiple motor tics and one or more vocal tics.
- Treatment for children with ASD and any tic disorder can involve psycho-education, stress-reducing support, psychological and pharmacological interventions.
- Tics often have a natural history and they can improve significantly by the late teenage years.

FURTHER READING

Buffalano, S. (2012). *Coping with Tourette Syndrome: A Workbook for Kids with Tic Disorders.* Oakland, CA: New Harbinger.

Leckman, J. F., and Cohen, D. J. (2005). Tic disorders. In M. Rutter and E. Taylor (Eds). *Rutter's Child and Adolescent Psychiatry* (4th Edition) (pp. 593–611). Oxford: Blackwell Publishing.

CHAPTER 7

ASD AND OBSESSIVE COMPULSIVE DISORDER (OCD)

What this chapter will cover:

- Introduction.
- What is Obsessive Compulsive Disorder (OCD)?
- How common is OCD in the general population of children?
- Why does OCD develop?
- How do we differentiate the behaviours in ASD from OCD?
- What are the challenges in identifying OCD in ASD?
- How would you work with these children?
- What help is available?
- Chapter summary.
- Further reading.

INTRODUCTION

It is obvious to those who live or work with children who have ASD that these children think differently. They seem to have a mind-set which tends to focus intensely and think repeatedly about certain things. This can be seen in how they approach problems or situations in their lives or in the pursuit of their special interests. For example, we have worked with children who, having lost a possession, cannot stop looking for it until it is found – this may take days and can even interfere with sleep. This type of obsessional behaviour, which we commonly see in children with ASD, can sometimes blur with the behaviour which is seen in Obsessive Compulsive Disorder (OCD). Sometimes it is difficult to differentiate between the two and they can actually exist together. This situation can be so complex that some children are actually misdiagnosed as having OCD when they have undiagnosed ASD, and even many health professionals can struggle to tell the difference.

Obsessions and compulsions in children and young people generally are surprisingly common and tend to occur for a short period of time before phasing out. Good examples of these are the bedtime rituals which are common at ages two and three, or the collecting of things that often begins around age seven. This type of thinking can also commonly occur in adults who, for example, may have worries that lead them to do things such as checking locks repeatedly; but as long as they are able to stop after a few times, it is considered normal. How many of you have not done this?

This chapter will help you to understand what we actually mean by OCD as a comorbid disorder and how common it is in the general population. It will also help you to gain a better understanding of how to differentiate between the two types of behaviours when co-occurring in a young person with ASD. We will also look at how it can affect young people with ASD and what you need to look out for in order to ensure that the young person gets appropriate help at the right time.

WHAT IS OBSESSIVE COMPULSIVE DISORDER (OCD)?

It is essential to understand what OCD is. It is defined as a disorder of repetitive behaviour (also known as 'compulsions'), in response to 'obsessions' (recurrent and persistent thoughts), in response to anxiety, to the extent that it interferes with day-to-day living. OCD therefore involves exaggerated or excessive worry about threatening and non-threatening situations coupled with behaviours/actions which are believed by the individual to reduce the anxiety. We use an example below to illustrate this point.

EXAMPLE

Children who learn about germs can become excessively worried about contamination of their hands. These worries about germs will dominate their thinking. They then seek relief from these worries by washing their hands repeatedly, which immediately reduces the anxiety. Unfortunately, this relief is often short-lived and they can get into a cycle in which they wash their hands more and more to relieve the anxiety. This can actually result in the child getting sore hands but they are unable to resist the need to continue washing.

THINK POINT!

OCD is characterised by excessive worry linked to behaviours/actions which are used by the individual to reduce the anxiety.

The extent to which OCD affects the child varies but symptoms can impact greatly on some children's lives (e.g. by impairing social relationships, the ability to complete tasks like schoolwork, hygiene and relationships within the family).

It is important to be able to differentiate this condition from the repetitive activities, special interests and ruminating thoughts which exist in children with ASD. It is those factors that pose the biggest challenge in differentiating OCD from ASD, as the OCD may require specialist help, while the other behaviours need to be understood as part of ASD.

Key characteristics of OCD

Although from the description above it can be seen that OCD is a response to anxiety, there are key characteristics for defining OCD. In current practice a definite diagnosis requires obsessional symptoms, or compulsive acts or both to be present on most days for at least two consecutive weeks. The OCD symptoms must be a source of distress or must interfere with daily activities (WHO 2010b). The symptoms should have the following characteristics:

1. The worries must be recognised as individuals' own thoughts or impulses.

2. There must be at least one thought or act that is still resisted unsuccessfully, even though others may be present which the sufferer no longer resists.

3. The thought of carrying out the act must not itself be pleasurable.

4. The thoughts, images or impulses must be unpleasantly repetitive.

These characteristics help to differentiate the thinking in OCD from other mental health conditions, such as psychosis, as the individual is aware that the thought is their own and not from an apparently external source. The important thing to recognise is that the child tries to resist the unpleasant thought and that they carry out the action to reduce the anxiety of the thought, rather than getting pleasure from the action. Resisting thoughts tends to make them more intrusive. For example, if we say to you, 'Don't think of pink elephants!' most of you will find it impossible not to conjure up an image of a pink elephant.

It is important to get a clear idea of what an obsession and a compulsion are in OCD before discussing the behaviours which have a similar quality in ASD. Much of the literature in the past has described the collecting and thinking styles in ASD as 'obsessions'. This can result in some confusion when working with these children. Some commentators do not like the term 'obsessions' and prefer terms such as 'special interests'. At present there is probably no good term which covers the thinking style in ASD adequately. Now would be a good time to discuss what constitutes obsessions and compulsions so that we can be as clear as possible on the nature of the problem.

What are obsessions in OCD?

Obsessional thoughts are ideas, images or impulses that enter an individual's mind again and again. These can be distressing and as a consequence the individual tries to resist them (i.e. they try to stop thinking the thought). The most common obsessive worries centre on contamination, fear of disasters, symmetry and, in some cultures, religious issues (Goodman and Scott 2005). These worries can be about the individual themselves, family members or even the broader society. In reality, the worry can ostensibly seem to be logical, but excessive in the quantity. It is the constant rumination which can be the problem. The fears can take any form, and can include activities not being completed properly (even after countless repetitions) and a need for certain objects (or even people) to be in 'correct' positions.

When thinking about the obsessions in OCD, it is important to discuss intrusive thoughts. These can be the origin of some of the obsessions. Basically, everybody has a stream of consciousness all the time – we have many thoughts about many different things, most of which we are unaware of or they are fleeting. Some of these thoughts are pleasant and some are unpleasant. On occasion, an unpleasant thought appears to 'pop' into one's head. The unpleasant thought may cause some anxiety and, in an attempt to cope with this anxiety, there is an attempt to suppress it. Unfortunately, this can make the mind concentrate on this thought further and it becomes more intrusive. This can lead to a vicious cycle as the intrusive thought becomes even more intrusive. This is an entirely normal phenomenon which most people cope with on a daily basis. However, this thought process can sometimes be seen causing a lot of distress in children with ASD who have difficulty differentiating reality from fantasy and therefore feel that the intrusive thought must be true.

▄ EXAMPLE

The classic example of this is somebody holding a carving knife in the kitchen who suddenly thinks, 'What if I stabbed this into …? ' The thought tends to come into the mind and then leave fairly quickly with no further attention paid to it. If, however, the individual worries that they might actually stab somebody and fears a loss of control, this is called 'thought–action fusion' – they may worry that they will carry out the action, and this can become obsessive.

What are compulsions?

Compulsive acts or rituals are behaviours or mental acts that are repetitive. The child feels compelled to perform these actions in order to manage the anxiety. The most common compulsions are:

- checking
- cleaning
- repeating
- excessive hand-washing
- bathing or showering
- tapping
- counting
- touching.

The compulsion can even be in a thought process, rather than a physical action (i.e. in the form of repeated phrases or words in the mind).

▄ EXAMPLE

A young girl who has to count to five in her mind before doing any household chores or school work, and therefore struggles to get the work finished in time.

Compulsions can take the form of excessive cleaning of household equipment or furniture, or avoiding 'contaminated' or 'dangerous' objects or substances, such as dog faeces, knives, asbestos and so forth. The child may check doors and windows to make sure they are safe, and many seek repeated reassurance from their parents. In some cases the reassurance itself can become the action which reduces anxiety and it is therefore sought repeatedly and excessively. While some of these compulsions can seem sensible, others appear to be quite unusual or bizarre, but they all have the same function.

Case study

Hannah is a 14-year-old girl who is worried about her forthcoming exams. She worries that she will fail them despite being a grade-'A' student, and she becomes increasingly distressed. The worries increase in their frequency, thus becoming obsessional. As a way of reducing her distress, Hannah starts counting up to seven and developing ritualistic behaviour (compulsions) by opening and closing doors seven times, or tapping the telephone seven times before making a call. The compulsions increase to a point where she is unable to study, and at this point she confides in her mother.

HOW COMMON IS OCD IN THE GENERAL POPULATION OF CHILDREN?

OCD has been increasingly recognised in children and adolescents (Robinson 1998). A third to half of adults with OCD had their first symptoms before the age of 15, and the prevalence is approximately 0.5–2 per cent in adolescents (Goodman and Scott 2005). OCD can occur in children as young as seven, where it predominantly affects boys, but the male/female ratio is otherwise equal in late adolescence and adulthood (Geller 2006). Generally, OCD appears to have two peak ages of onset. The first peak tends to occur around puberty, with the second occurring in early adulthood (Zohar 1999).

WHY DOES OCD DEVELOP?

So far, the actual mechanism is not clear, but there appear to be some biological factors which may predispose some people to developing the condition. There seems to be a genetic element, with the disorder running in families; however, at present this mechanism is not fully clear. Experts have identified structural abnormalities in certain parts of the brain – particularly the basal ganglia and frontal lobe – and the neurotransmitter serotonin has been implicated. There is an unusual condition, Paediatric Autoimmune Neuropsychiatric Disorder Associated with Streptococcal infection (PANDAS), in which children can develop OCD symptoms after having a streptococcal bacterial infection (bacteria which cause sore throats, scarlet fever and tonsillitis). There may be a number of different causes of OCD, but for clinical purposes the treatment at present is the same.

HOW DO WE DIFFERENTIATE THE BEHAVIOURS IN ASD FROM OCD?

It is common to see repetitive and ritualised behaviour in children with ASD. As stated earlier, these children are also described as having 'obsessions' and they have a particular way of thinking which leads to them often ruminating on a particular action or event. It is essential for us to discuss these behaviours to be able to differentiate them from the thoughts and behaviours associated with OCD. This will help in recognising what could be treated as a comorbid disorder and what could not be. It is not unknown for a therapist to have tried Cognitive Behavioural Therapy (CBT) for OCD and to then realise that the obsession is part of the ASD and therefore resistant to change.

It is important to distinguish a special interest from the obsessions in OCD. Special interests of children with ASD can be thought of as excessively intensive interests in a particular activity or subject. These interests can be infinitely variable and can seem at first view to be quite unusual. We have experience of children collecting spare bicycle parts or stones, but often special interests can reflect more normative children's hobbies (e.g. collecting football cards or toy trains), but to a more extensive degree. It is interesting to note that in those children who collect objects (such as football cards) the collecting appears to be more important than the ownership, and once the set is collected the child moves on. What drives the child forward is the need to finish the collection. While special interests do reflect a particular mind-set in these children, the interest also can serve more than one purpose, depending on the child. The functions can be quite varied and we outline these in Box 7.1.

As can be seen, the special interests can take the form of collecting actual objects, or collecting information and knowledge, but both can have the same function. Obviously, if the special interest becomes too overwhelming and domineering, it may no longer feel pleasurable or valuable; and if it is affecting the child's well-being, then the obsessions are much more similar to those in OCD. This obviously poses some difficulty for diagnosis, and it can often be a subjective judgement by carers or professionals when this line has been crossed. In addition, children can have some special interests while concurrently also having comorbid OCD – analysing these behaviours can be a diagnostic nightmare! To complicate matters further, the variation from day to day in the intensity of the special interests can be clinically confusing. Like all matters in mental health, there is a huge subjective element to a behaviour or feeling. Some children who appear to be getting distressed or overwhelmed by their special interest will actually say that they are not feeling that way and that they are enjoying themselves, which can be difficult. A child will not want to engage in therapy if they do not see a problem.

BOX 7.1 FUNCTIONS OF SPECIAL INTERESTS

- *Overcoming anxiety* – the interest develops as a consequence of reducing anxiety (e.g. a fear of spiders leads to a developed interest and a knowledge acquired to reduce the fear).
- *A source of pleasure* – the interest itself provides intense enjoyment (e.g. jumping on trampolines can be fun for the child).
- *Means of relaxation* – reduction of stress, as a form of escapism (e.g. playing computer games for extended periods).
- *Attempt to achieve coherence* – the interest provides security, and the child will put things in order (e.g. putting their DVDs in alphabetical order).
- *Understanding the physical world* – the child develops interests in science and the natural world because the physical world is easier to understand than the social one.
- *Creation of an alternative world* – a contemporary example of this is social gaming, where interactions are easier when virtual than in person.
- *Sense of identity* – an interest can help the child find out who they are and helps them to create an identity as the special interest defines who they are.
- *Occupying time, facilitating conversation and indicating intelligence* – for those with social difficulties, having a special interest can facilitate interaction with others which they feel is safe.

(Attwood 2007)

In addition to special interests, there are other aspects of the behaviour of children with ASD which are similar to the behaviours seen in OCD, such as repetitive behaviour. Repetitive behaviour has been considered as a core component of autism and Asperger syndrome (AS) since the earliest conceptions (Asperger 1991; Kanner 1943). Many children who have ASD engage in a significant number of repetitive motor mannerisms, behaviours and thought patterns – for example, hand and finger flapping, lining up toys, arranging things in a particular order, an obsessive desire for sameness, negative reactions to change, and a narrow range of interests that are pursued in an obsessional manner (Smith, Magyar and Arnold-Saritepe 2002). It is important to distinguish the compulsions in OCD from the repetitive behaviours of ASD in order to provide the appropriate help. Box 7.2 provides some helpful pointers for differentiating between compulsions in OCD and repetitive behaviours in ASD.

BOX 7.2 DIFFERENCE BETWEEN COMPULSIONS IN OCD AND REPETITIVE BEHAVIOURS IN ASD

Compulsions

- Purposeful.
- Aim to prevent some negative event or anxiety.
- Reduce stress but are themselves distressing to young person.
- Unrealistic connection to the anxiety provoking thought.
- Can be associated with a need for perfection.

Repetitive behaviour

- Can be apparently purposeless.
- Consistent and persistent.
- Self-soothing.
- No particular connection to a positive or negative event.

WHAT ARE THE CHALLENGES IN IDENTIFYING OCD IN ASD?

The prevalence of OCD in young people with ASD is around 17 per cent (van Steensel, Bogels and Perrin 2011). As already shown, it can be challenging to diagnose OCD in children who have ASD, due to the difficulty in discerning repetitive behaviours typically found in ASD from the obsessions and compulsions associated with OCD; that is, it can be difficult to demonstrate that the symptoms are 'ego dystonic' (thoughts/behaviours which are in conflict with their actual feelings) to the child (Baron-Cohen 1989). There is some evidence that the content and quality of the repetitive behaviours differs in these groups

(McDougle *et al.* 1995), and children with ASD may develop a similar level of impairment if they develop OCD along with ASD. There may be slight differences with regards to the nature of their obsessions and compulsions; for example, the ASD group present significantly higher frequencies of hoarding obsessions and repeating, ordering and hoarding compulsions, compared to a young person with OCD only. While a child with OCD is typically very upset and embarrassed about their obsessions and compulsions, there is a qualitative difference in children with ASD as they may lack insight into their difficulties. There are, however, some phenomenological differences which could help in identifying OCD from ASD, as listed in Box 7.3.

BOX 7.3 HOW TO DIFFERENTIATE BETWEEN ASD AND OCD

Behaviours in ASD

- Are present in infancy.
- Can vary in form over time but course is unlikely to fluctuate.
- May reduce in the teenage years.
- May be pleasurable.

Childhood OCD

- Mean age of onset is approximately 10 years.
- Symptoms peak at puberty and during young adulthood.
- Often fluctuates but runs a chronic course.
- Provokes anxiety.

Case study

Toby is a 12-year-old boy with ASD. He has always been keen on collecting science-fiction comics. He has them carefully catalogued and put in date order, and they are protected by plastic covers. It is important for him to collect the comics in order of release, and over the years he has enjoyed reading through them. This hobby can take up a lot of Toby's time but tends not to interfere with his daily life. Unfortunately, one comic was lost in the post and he has struggled to get another copy of it. This has made Toby increasingly anxious his collection of comics and he is spending more and more time checking that he has all the others. Despite repeated checking, he feels compelled to check on a daily and more frequent basis. This is taking up so much of his time that his parents struggle to get him to school.

Reflective activity

Do you think that Toby has OCD? What makes you think this? What do you think could be done to help Toby?

It is fairly obvious that Toby has a special interest in collecting comics and this has been with him for some time. The problem has arisen as he is unable to feel the collection is complete. There is obviously now increasing anxiety about the comic collection; the thoughts do have an obsessive feel about them and Toby is developing a behaviour (checking) to reassure himself. This is worsening and therefore, on balance, his special interest is evolving into OCD.

HOW WOULD YOU WORK WITH THESE CHILDREN?

A careful and detailed assessment is essential in order to ensure that appropriate management is in place for a child with ASD in cases where OCD is suspected. It is necessary to understand the functions of the presenting behaviours to determine whether the thoughts and behaviours are part of the ASD or rather have an OCD origin.

▮ EXAMPLE

A child with ASD may display obsessive behaviours, such as lining up all their toys, but may now be engaging in new behaviours, such as washing their hands repeatedly, due to fear of contamination.

It is important, therefore, to ask about the normal day-to-day routine and any distress new behaviours are causing. Standard questions for children with suspected OCD would include: 'If you couldn't do that, how would you feel?' 'What would you do then?' 'Do you dislike your routine?' However, this is more difficult with children who have ASD as it requires a description of their feelings and/or hypothetical situations. It is helpful to use visual cues where communication is difficult verbally. Assessment may require careful observation of the child's behaviours, or descriptions of their behaviours from parents/carers, indicating if there is associated distress.

Another important point to keep in mind is that children with ASD are at high risk of developing comorbid conditions (e.g. depression and other anxiety disorders), which can affect their functioning and also make obsessional thinking worse. Additionally, OCD can be associated with Tourette's syndrome (disorder of repeated tics).

Self-help

There are many ways in which parents and carers can help children with ASD and comorbid OCD to learn to deal with their anxiety and distress (e.g. by adopting very simple strategies within the home environment). Some of them are listed below:

- Refocusing attention.
- Writing down obsessive thoughts or worries.
- Anticipating OCD urges and helping the child to manage them in a practical way.
- Practising relaxation techniques with them.
- Adopting healthy eating habits.
- Exercising regularly.
- Making sure the child is getting enough sleep.
- Giving them assurance that they have support from their family and friends.

WHAT HELP IS AVAILABLE?

Just having obsessions and compulsions does not mean that the child requires treatment. As with many mental health problems, it is important to seek help when the problem affects a child's ability to function, is causing a lot of distress and is interfering with life and relationships.

The different types of treatment available to treat comorbid OCD depend on the severity of the symptoms. The most common treatment for OCD from specialist mental health services for the general population is a combination of CBT and medication. These treatments are also used for comorbid OCD in children with ASD, but the effectiveness is more variable. We discuss modes of therapy, particularly CBT, in Chapter 14, but provide a general overview of its relevance to OCD here.

Cognitive Behaviour Therapy (CBT)

CBT is the next logical step in getting help for comorbid OCD and is a well-established treatment for this condition. The therapy consists of two components: first, behavioural therapy, which tries to change behaviour by gradual exposure to the feared situation; and second, helping children to understand their thinking patterns, and the errors they make when processing information in their minds (cognitive therapy). The aim of this is to get the child to recognise the obsessive thought and the anxiety it causes, and then to modify their behaviour so the compulsion is reduced. By doing this, they demonstrate for themself that the obsessional thought is irrational and that the compulsion has been perpetuating the problem.

▊ EXAMPLE 1
A child who has been compulsively hand-washing needs to wash their hands fewer times in each hour to show that the 'germs' will not cause any harm. This in turn will reduce their anxiety and therefore the need to wash their hands.

▊ EXAMPLE 2
A child who constantly seeks reassurance that a burglar will not break into the house is using the reassurance as their compulsion. The carers will need to offer reassurance less frequently as this is reinforcing the fear.

There are limitations to using this therapy with children who have ASD, and there are many factors which can reduce the effectiveness of this treatment for comorbid OCD: the children's rigid thinking styles can prevent them from trying the 'experiments' as they have difficulty predicting what will happen; they struggle to face the anxiety-provoking actions; they may struggle to understand the therapeutic process and explanations of the treatment; and they may lack the motivation to fully engage; in addition, the children need insight to their problems.

Medication
With very young children and others who have little insight into the irrationality of their thinking, medication may be considered the best possible treatment option.

Medications are helpful when the symptoms are causing so much distress that it is extremely difficult for the young person to focus on talking therapy, or symptoms are so severe they could lead to significant harm to the child or carer. However, medications used alone are not as effective as when combined with a talking therapy.

The most commonly used medications are from a class of antidepressants called SSRIs and we provided you with detailed information in Chapter 4. Other medications in the form of older antidepressants (e.g. clomipramine) have also been used. In children with ASD these medications may be particularly useful due to the limitations of CBT, but they can also be useful in reducing the overall anxiety levels in these children before attempting any other mode of treatment.

CHAPTER SUMMARY

In this chapter we have considered the presentations of OCD and OCD in children who have ASD. It is important to reflect on the nature of OCD and its symptoms to be able to recognise its presentation when co-occurring with ASD. As we have discussed, this is not always simple and there appears to be a grey area between identifying the special interests and the thinking behind this in children with ASD and the obsessive thinking in individuals with OCD. Fundamentally, it appears to come down to the distress and effect the behaviour and thinking have on how a child is able to function on a daily basis. Trying to make this distinction is essential to finding the right management and care for a child, as attempting to treat the special interests as OCD in these children may just cause unnecessary distress. Unfortunately, treatment is not that straightforward and it is best managed under specialist care.

ⓘ IMPORTANT LEARNING POINTS

- Obsessive Compulsive Disorder (OCD) is a mental health problem defined as a disorder of repetitive behaviour (compulsions) in response to obsessions.
- OCD is distressing and can impact significantly on the individual's daily functioning.
- The obsessions in OCD are different from the obsessive thinking/special interests typically found in children with ASD but there can be some overlap.
- Recognising the presence of comorbid OCD in ASD can be difficult and tends to be identified through the levels of distress experienced by the child.
- The standard treatments for OCD need to be adapted for children with ASD to take into consideration their way of thinking and motivation. Medication may be necessary.

FURTHER READING

Robinson, R. (1998). Obsessive-compulsive disorder in children and adolescents. *Bulletin of the Menninger Clinic, 62*(4), A49–A64.

WHO (World Health Organization) (2010). *The ICD-10 for Mental and Behavioural Disorders: Clinical descriptions and diagnostic guidelines.* Available at www.who.int/classifications/icd/en/bluebook.pdf, accessed on 13 May 2013.

Further support and information on OCD

There are a growing number of organisations providing support for sufferers of OCD. The most well known are:

- *OCD-UK* – www.ocduk.org

- *OCD Action* – www.ocdaction.org.uk

You may also be interested in reading the draft proposed guidelines for the treatment of OCD on the National Institute for Health and Clinical Excellence (www.nice.org.uk) website.

CHAPTER 8

ASD AND COMORBID EATING DISORDERS

This chapter will cover:

- Introduction.
- Why is eating so important?
- What are the common eating problems in children with ASD?
- Why do children with ASD develop eating problems?
- What treatments are available for the child with ASD and eating problems?
- How do you differentiate disordered eating from eating disorders?
- What are the eating disorders?
- How do eating disorders occur in ASD?
- What are the treatments for the child with ASD and comorbid eating disorders?
- Chapter summary.
- Further reading.

INTRODUCTION

Feeding and eating problems are a very common feature in children with ASD. In our clinics we have seen faddy eaters, picky eaters, under-eaters, over-eaters and food refusers. Obviously, this causes quite a lot of stress in families and can be a source of conflict with the child. There is a huge range of eating problems and causes of eating problems in children, which we will attempt to discuss in this chapter in respect to their mental health. There is not enough space to give details of all eating problems and practical solutions. What we will describe are the common eating problems which occur in children with ASD and differentiate these from the definitions and presentation of eating disorders as it is important to distinguish comorbid eating disorders, from disordered eating.

WHY IS EATING SO IMPORTANT?

This may sound like a silly question, but it is important to know some of the facts behind eating and food in order to understand how to work with eating problems. First, eating is a biological necessity for normal growth and development. Normal eating means having a healthy relationship with food (Berg 2001). The normal eating pattern consists of eating food when hungry and then stopping when feeling full (i.e. responding to internal sensations). The normal infant dietary experience is shaped by infant-feeding decisions (i.e. breast-feeding/formula and weaning) and the dietary patterns of the mother. It provides the basis for food acceptance and patterns of intake in infancy.

Second, normal eating patterns tend to develop in the first year of a child's life in response to guidance and rules imposed generally by their parents. This has a strong social component as the child tends to mimic the behaviour of those around them. Most children can be seen to copy their family's behaviour about eating. In some way this can explain some of the difficulties for children with ASD as they struggle in this area, tending not to conform to this typical pattern. The food environment the parent provides shapes children's preferences and food acceptance patterns. There is some evidence that parents who over-eat tend to have children who also develop this attitude towards food (see, for example, Francis et al. 2012) and that the parents' dietary choices influence the food a child will eat and find acceptable. In significant parts of the world the eating of insects and larvae is considered culturally normal but this would not be acceptable to most Western European palates. Although this is a more extreme example, the concept can equally be applied to vegetable consumption. While all children can make a choice regarding what they eat, some of the behaviours do appear to represent natural innate fears which have an evolutionary basis. Theories exist on why children do not like to eat their 'greens' (i.e. they resemble leaves and shoots, which in the wild may be poisonous). It is through the modelling of their parents and the need to conform that children learn to eat a variety of foods (i.e. recognising what is safe to eat). There is some evidence that children need to be exposed to a wide variety of different foods as early as possible in their lives so they develop the appropriate responses to taste.

Third, the whole process of eating is a multisensory experience utilising most of the senses. When we eat food, we do not just taste it on the tongue; we also smell it as it is cooking; or when it is presented to us on a plate or in a wrapper, we make judgements about how it might taste, and we appraise its texture. For us to eat something, therefore, the food needs to look appetising, smell nice, have an appealing taste and acceptable textures. (Many people find the sensation of chocolate melting in the mouth exceptionally pleasant for a multitude of reasons.)

There are also some additional reasons why eating is so important:

- Eating is associated with feelings of hunger and the sensation of feeling full and is obviously a biological necessity to maintain the body and growth.

- Food generally has a huge social element, from eating at home with friends or family to dining out.

- Eating also has a significant cultural dimension, and in many settings it forms the central focus for interpersonal interactions.

THINK POINT!

Feeding and eating is a complex behaviour, which is influenced by many factors including biological ones (taste, hunger and other senses), parenting, culture and social environment.

Given the extensive importance of food and eating, any difficulties in this area can raise anxiety in parents. Some issues are rather common. For example, feeding difficulties may occur in any child during the early years of their life although most tend to grow out of these difficulties as they reach school age. It is not uncommon for young children to be selective about their diet ('fussy eating'), or they may refuse to eat in certain situations. Often, refusal to eat is seen as an attempt by children to get attention but this tends to resolve when they are ignored or distracted or the eventual hunger overcomes their behaviour. It is interesting to note that the social and cultural aspects and the biology of eating can be a complex process and that attempts to improve a child's diet can often be detrimental. There is some evidence that child-feeding strategies that encourage children to consume a particular food actually increase their dislike of that food, and are therefore obviously unhelpful (Birch and Fisher 1998).

THINK POINT!

Feeding problems are very common in all young children but most tend to resolve over time.

The reality is often different for children with ASD and their families. In this group such problems are not only very common but tend to be more longstanding. Both parents and professionals working with these children may at times find this anxiety-provoking and often frustrating. In our clinical practice many children present with eating as one of their problems, which can at times seem unchangeable and insurmountable. It is only when we follow these children over a longer period of time that some of these difficulties appear to resolve to a certain degree.

WHAT ARE THE COMMON EATING PROBLEMS IN CHILDREN WITH ASD?

Rather than discuss eating problems in typically developing children and the difference between those and children with ASD, it is more useful to focus on the common eating problems which children with ASD experience. However, it is important to recognise that approximately 25 per cent of all children experience feeding problems in their early life (Manikam and Perman 2000). This prevalence increases to 80 per cent in children with developmental delay (Burklow *et al.* 1998). These problems can be varied. Some examples can be found in Box 8.1, but note that there is some overlap between these difficulties.

It is important to recognise that the eating problems in children with ASD can be fairly unusual and almost unique to the condition. The following examples are cited from our own experiences.

EXAMPLE 1

A child who refuses to have more than one colour on their plate. The child requires that foods of different colours cannot be mixed and therefore multiple plates have to be used for serving. Sauces and so forth cannot be poured over food if they are a different colour. White sauce could be used on white fish but not gravy over vegetables.

EXAMPLE 2

A child who had a fairly selective diet at home and refused to eat certain foods. However, when on holiday he ate anything put in front of him but on returning home he went back to his original eating pattern, to the frustration of his parents.

BOX 8.1 DIFFERENT TYPES OF EATING PROBLEM

- Only eating certain types of food (restricted eating).
- Only eating foods in a particular way (e.g. same plate or fork).
- Eating certain foods in a particular situation (e.g. at home but not in school).
- Avoiding foods of certain tastes, textures or smells.
- Foods not being allowed to mix, either on the plate or in the mouth.
- Not eating solid food.
- Not eating with other people.
- Eating to an exact routine (e.g. same time of day).
- Over-eating or under-eating.
- Eating messily.
- Food refusal.

Most commonly, children with ASD fall into the category of 'selective eaters', meaning they eat only selected types, textures, colours or varieties of food. Research indicates that 57 per cent of these children refused to eat certain foods, indicating that refusals were primarily related to food presentation (48.6%), such as using particular utensils or different food items touching on a plate (Schreck and Williams 2006). A common problem seen in clinic can result in the changes a company has made to the packaging of a particular product and how the child now sees it as different. This disruption to their routine can be quite stressful for them and their families.

WHY DO CHILDREN WITH ASD DEVELOP EATING PROBLEMS?

The reasons why children with ASD develop eating problems is often not entirely clear. It can be complex and may be related to how the environment interacted with their development at an early age. It is often difficult to know what was the original trigger for a particular behaviour and in reality it is probably a multitude of factors. Unfortunately, this can make any treatment of eating problems particularly difficult, and because it often starts at such a young age, the problems can be fairly entrenched by the time professionals become involved with the family. The factors related to the development of eating problems exist within all the characteristics of ASD, particularly the sensory, motor development and social areas. We list some of these potential factors in Box 8.2 to illustrate the point.

BOX 8.2 FACTORS RELATED TO THE DEVELOPMENT OF EATING PROBLEMS

- Sensory integration dysfunction (e.g. problems with taste, smells and texture).
- Motor coordination problem (e.g. using a knife and fork).
- Social aspects of eating (e.g. eating the same foods as others).
- Need for routine (e.g. eating at the same time each day).
- Food environment (e.g. the smell of food cooking).
- Difficulty in recognising when they are hungry or full (sensory problem).
- Concurrent medical conditions (e.g. reflux, or certain medication usage that may affect appetite).

Children with ASD are known to have problems in relation to sensory and motor difficulties. There are often issues related to taste, smell, temperature or texture of food that lead to selectivity in the diets of such children. Approximately 70–90 per cent of children with ASD have sensory problems (Leekman *et al.* 2007), and we discuss sensory issues in more detail in Chapter 12. Obviously, eating involves all the senses and it can be easy to see how a child who is over-sensitive to smells, tastes or textures can associate an unpleasant sensation to a particular type of food. This aversion may have occurred so early in their lives that they are no longer able to say why they do not like the food.

Another issue which appears to have an impact is motor coordination. This may initially seem surprising, but fine motor coordination is required for many tasks (e.g. writing). In this context, motor coordination is required for the use of eating utensils, which initially involves using a spoon but progresses to using a knife and fork. These actions become increasingly socially important and can often influence eating behaviour. Parents frequently complain that their children with ASD have difficulties using a knife and fork and use their hands, which can make eating messy. This may result in meal times becoming a huge cause of anxiety for children and their families.

It should be remembered that for a lot of families meal times are a social gathering. This does create quite a complex social environment, with exposure to many of the areas that children with ASD may find difficult. Children with ASD may find the social interactions challenging and the noise volume distracting, and they may struggle to follow the normal social conventions, which can lead to additional stress. In the Western world it is usual for families to sit at a table for a meal and not to leave until the meal is finished. This is an additional problem if the child also has comorbid ADHD.

Another factor that we commonly see is children who have ASD who have a tendency to either over-eat or under-eat. In clinical practice it is not uncommon to see children, who apparently never get hungry, surviving mainly on liquids, or, conversely, they rarely feel full and seem to be constantly eating. Again, this may be a reflection of sensory difficulties in these children, with the normal feedback mechanisms around hunger often not functioning appropriately. The sensation of food in the stomach is an essential feedback on the hunger mechanism. Therefore, it can be very difficult for these children to regulate their diets. This, interestingly, can also be seen around the sensation of thirst. This may not be the entire picture or relevant to every child who under- or over-eats. We have shown already that eating is complicated and the abnormal eating patterns may be related to other aspects of the ASD, such as the rigidity of thinking or routines.

As a consequence of developing an eating problem, the child can develop quite considerable anxiety when challenged over their eating, particularly if things are changed. This anxiety can be central in preventing any meaningful change and therefore it is important that this is managed in a sensitive way. This is an area where it is easy to do too much too quickly. An example from our practice was a young child who refused to eat meat. He finally agreed to try some, but, unfortunately, was started on a piece of beef steak, which he found strong tasting, chewy and 'full of blood' (a small piece of turkey might have been more appropriate).

THINK POINT!

Children with ASD can develop eating problems for many reasons relating to their sensory difficulties, rigidity of thinking, social abilities and motor problems. This may occur so early in life that the child cannot even remember the cause of their problems.

WHAT TREATMENTS ARE AVAILABLE FOR THE CHILD WITH ASD AND EATING PROBLEMS?

So far in this chapter we have highlighted some common eating problems and some of the reasons why children with ASD develop them. It is essential, therefore, to bear these factors in mind when considering any possible treatments. A full assessment of the child, considering the different aspects of ASD, is important and it may require the involvement of different professionals. A particular professional group which is especially important to involve where possible are dieticians. These professionals are specially trained in promoting and managing different aspects of diet and nutrition. They can be useful in assessing a child's diet, particularly in those who are restricting their food, to ensure that the correct nutrients are always made available.

In our practice we often find it useful for families to keep a food diary recording the different types of food a child will eat and the behaviours around this process. It is interesting to note that in older and more able children the process of keeping the diary does sometimes facilitate their interest in trying new foods. Again, the dietician may help to facilitate this process. The main problem we often encounter in assessing and working around these problems is the child's reluctance to engage in any form of work around food, which can be a clear indication of their lack of motivation to eat more or differently. It should be mentioned at this point that of all the problems associated with children who have ASD, we have found that food issues appear to be some of the most resistant to change. However, it is not unusual for various strategies to have been tried over a number of years without success, and then at the point of resignation the child decides to eat something different by themselves. This again shows that children are constantly developing.

We have found several strategies to be useful, particularly for restrictive/refusal eaters. They aim to encourage children to experiment with food for themselves in an attempt to reduce the anxiety which is often present when trying new foods or new ways of eating. These strategies are presented in Box 8.3 and can be used as self-help strategies at home.

Social Stories™ have also been found to be an effective approach in helping with these problems. Gray (2002a) describes Social stories™ as a short story describing a concept, skill or situation in terms of relevant social cues or common responses with a goal to share social information with an individual. It is recommended that at least 50 per cent of the Social Story™ should praise the child in terms of what they do well. In the context of eating, therefore, a Social Story™ could help the individual to understand why we eat and the function of food (Gray 2002a). This technique breaks down the activity into small, digestible segments which help children with ASD understand what is going on. It can be effective at reducing the anxiety around a social situation, such as eating at the table.

BOX 8.3 STRATEGIES TO HELP THE YOUNG PERSON WITH EATING DIFFICULTIES AND THEIR FAMILY

- *Engage the child in cooking/baking* – this is to encourage their interest in food.
- *Make alternative foods visible* – for example, have fruit on a table so that it is available but non-threatening.
- *Encourage the child to try small amounts of new foods* – it is important to select foods which are initially similar in texture and taste to foods they like. Also, it is often necessary to offer the same food more than once to overcome the initial negative reaction.
- *Use behavioural interventions such as reward charts and stickers* – give rewards when the child has eaten a particular food.
- *Adopt a healthy eating approach* – educate the child about the effects of food and why healthy food is essential. This is useful particularly for more high-functioning children.
- *Use visuals* – for example, to indicate the correct meal times or to indicate what food to expect for that meal.
- *Give clear and consistent guidelines* – it is useful to establish regular routines around eating, such as the location of a meal, the amount of food to be eaten and the behaviours expected.

THINK POINT!

The management of eating problems can be quite challenging and may require significant inventiveness to overcome.

HOW DO YOU DIFFERENTIATE DISORDERED EATING FROM EATING DISORDERS?

In clinical practice, in addition to eating problems we sometimes use the term 'disordered eating' as a differential term from eating disorders. There is a wide range of eating patterns which fall under this definition, and it can often be part of another psychiatric or psychological disorder. The most common example of this is the reduced eating seen in young people with anxiety or depression, which resolves on treating this condition. It can also cover those who have some of the aspects of an eating disorder, such as anorexia nervosa or bulimia, but who do not fulfil the whole criteria for these conditions.

EXAMPLE

A teenage girl who has been feeling low in mood for the last few months and more recently has some symptoms of anxiety. She is having trouble sleeping, concentrating, feels tired and has also lost some weight. She described having had a reduced appetite and just picking at her food over the last couple of months. She just does not feel hungry. Following treatment for her mood the appetite returns of its own accord.

THINK POINT!

Disordered eating is seen fairly frequently in children with mental health problems; it is due to a multitude of factors, and needs differentiating from eating disorders.

WHAT ARE THE EATING DISORDERS?

Eating disorders are serious conditions. Unfortunately, we are seeing them more often in clinical practice and they can have significant short- and long-term health implications. Before we describe the presentation of these conditions in children with ASD, we will discuss them more broadly so that the fundamental aspects of these conditions are understood. There are three main categories of eating disorders which would be useful to understand:

1. Anorexia nervosa.

2. Bulimia.

3. Over-eating.

Anorexia nervosa is a disorder in which there is deliberate weight loss, which can lead to significant ill-health problems and, tragically, in some cases death. For the diagnosis of anorexia nervosa to be made there need to be certain characteristics present, including:

- The body weight is kept deliberately low.

- Weight loss is self-induced by either avoiding foods or using other mechanisms such as vomiting, excessive exercise or appetite suppressants/laxatives.

- There is a body image distortion and a fear of fatness.

- Hormones are affected (e.g. in women the menstrual cycle is disrupted).

- In children there can be delayed puberty.

This disorder tends to affect teenage girls and young women more than other groups, but it can affect people of all ages and there are even some cases in pre-pubescent children. In addition, approximately 6–7 per cent of cases of anorexia nervosa are male (Kjelsäs, Bjornstrom and Gunnar 2004). The exact cause of anorexia is unclear but it appears to be an interaction between biological and environmental factors, which can include family dynamics. The medical effects of anorexia nervosa are related to the persistent state of starvation and will affect virtually every organ in the body. This includes effects on the digestive system, the cardiovascular system (low blood pressure and effects on the heart), bones (reduction in bone density), and in females, effects on the menstrual cycle. Additionally, the condition appears to affect how these individuals think – they not only have distorted views about their body shape and weight and a fear of being fat, but also they are often preoccupied with thoughts of food. It is unclear whether having anorexia nervosa can make an individual more rigid in their thinking, or whether the rigidity of thought precedes the development of the condition, but this rigidity of thinking is reflected in the need to control food and eating. We recommend that you read a more specialist text on eating disorders to understand this condition more fully and we make recommendations at the end of the chapter.

Bulimia nervosa is characterised by the binge-purge cycle, with over-eating being followed by purging as a way of compensating for the fattening effects of the food. This can be seen as an attempt to control body weight. Some behavioural symptoms of such individuals include binge-eating, eating in secret, bathroom visits after meals, and the use of diet pills or laxatives. For the diagnosis to be made the following need to be present:

- A preoccupation with food and eating, and cravings for food which lead to episodes of over-eating.

- Following consumption there are attempts to counteract the over-eating by mechanisms such as vomiting, using laxatives or medications, or starving for periods of time.

- A preoccupation with body image and weight, with a fear of fatness.

Some medical consequences of bulimia are similar to those found in anorexics – individuals also exhibit tooth decay, sore throat, swollen glands and internal bleeding due to vomiting. There is some crossover between anorexia and bulimia, and both conditions can occur over time in an individual.

Although children with these conditions have an unusual attitude towards eating food, the preoccupation with food – sometimes linked to their feelings of hunger – translates into them having an interest in cooking and food in general. They can often enjoy preparing meals for other people and encouraging those around them to indulge.

THINK POINT!

Eating disorders are serious conditions which are best managed by specialist teams of professionals utilising different approaches to care for the physical and psychological aspects of the conditions.

Over-eating can be defined as eating too much in reaction to a distressing event, such as a bereavement, which has led to excessive weight gain or obesity. It is increasingly recognised that obesity itself can cause significant psychological distress, but this is an area that seems to be less well understood than the under-eating counterparts. This is a much more complex disorder to diagnose and define as having a mental health component, since eating is considered to be such a normal part of many cultures and obesity is so commonly seen in many parts of the world. Nonetheless, clinical obesity due to long-term and excessive over-eating has many negative effects on the body, causing various illnesses and health problems. Clinically obese individuals who over-eat are at risk from coronary problems, diabetes, stroke, blood pressure problems, water retention and a range of other problems which can lead to premature death.

What are the treatments for eating disorders?

The treatment for eating disorders is very specialised and is often carried out by highly skilled clinical professionals, often in specialist teams. It is our opinion that the complexity of these disorders needs a specialist input. The risk of long-term physical damage from prolonged starvation (or excessive over-eating), together with the higher rates of mortality, requires intensive support and therapy for both the child and their family. Treatment tends to involve multiple parallel formats to address different aspects of the condition. The physical aspects of treatment are important to ensure adequate nutrition, and in children it is important to ensure that they continue to grow.

Alongside this identification of underlying psychological and emotional difficulties, it is necessary to choose the correct therapeutic treatment. This treatment can take the form of individual therapy, such as Cognitive Behaviour Therapy (CBT), Interpersonal Therapy or group therapy. For children, family therapy is often a component to address any difficulties in the families. Sometimes medication, such as antidepressants, is found to be useful in reducing some of the symptoms, but this is best managed under specialist supervision. At times the situation deteriorates to a point where the child is admitted to a hospital environment for compulsory treatment. In some places there are specialist residential units which will treat these children on a very intensive basis.

What is the prognosis?

The literature on eating disorders indicates slightly variable rates of recovery and relapse. Reviews illustrate that up to 50 per cent of those in treatment will do well, 30 per cent will do relatively well but maintain some symptoms and 20 per cent will do poorly, with adolescents having a better prognosis than adults (Fisher 2003). Unfortunately, mortality rates for anorexia nervosa remain high, with some deaths resulting from suicide, while 20 per cent of cases remain chronically ill (Steinhausen 2002). It is, however, evident that different studies report slightly different figures which vary across age groups and countries, so it is difficult to be exactly sure of the percentages. Nonetheless, collectively, the research illustrates that full recovery from eating disorders is difficult, with only small numbers completely leaving their eating disorder behind them. Some of those with eating disorders will learn ways to manage their symptoms and keep the disorder under control, while others will remain chronically ill for long periods. Ultimately, the worst outcome is death from the physical effects of the disorder, or suicide.

HOW DO THE EATING DISORDERS OCCUR IN ASD?

Although eating disorders in children with ASD remain uncommon, they do occur and it can be quite a significant challenge to find an effective treatment. An overlap between anorexia nervosa and autistic traits was initially proposed on the basis of clinical and behavioural observations about 20 years ago, noting that many individuals with anorexia displayed some of the common traits associated with autism (Gillberg and Råstam 1992). There is now a growing literature on anorexia nervosa being considered in some cases to be a neuro-developmental disorder, due to some of the similarities observed in the cognitive style of both disorders. In addition to these similarities, eating disturbances (e.g. refusal of certain types of foods, sensitivity to texture or types of foods and unusual behaviours at meal times), which are common in individuals with ASD (Råstam 2008), are also found in young people with anorexia nervosa. Although none of the studies has proved the link so far, some of the recent research in this area has found similarities in the theory of mind impairment in both ASD and anorexia nervosa.

There is also other evidence which supports the link between ASD and eating disorders. There may be a genetic component with the coexistence of both conditions within families, suggesting that there may be a biological connection. Studies further show that teenage girls with a diagnosis of ASD are at greater risk of experiencing eating disorder symptoms than their typically developing peers, with 27 per cent of girls with ASD reporting symptoms of eating disorders (Kalvya 2009). Males with ASD are also at increased risk for low body weight and abnormal eating practices (Sobanski *et al.* 1999). The rigidity, need for sameness and obsessions found in the thinking style of a young person with ASD are somewhat similar to elements in the thinking style of a young person with anorexia nervosa.

Case study

Mia is an 11-year-old girl with ASD who has recently moved to a new school. She has had difficulty adapting to the change of pace at her school and finds the social scene difficult and complex. She complains to her parents that she feels isolated from her friends and does not feel able to join in their conversations. Her parents describe her as being very academic but quite controlling. Mia does like everything in its place and her life to have order. With regards to her school work, the teachers have called her a perfectionist. Until now, Mia's parents have never been particularly worried about her eating, but recently they have often found her lunch uneaten and she has become very picky about what she eats at home. Mia will not eat any foods which she describes as 'fattening', she tries to avoid breakfast and has been asking to eat alone in her bedroom. Her mother has found evidence of uneaten food under the bed. In addition, Mia's clothes appear to be less well-fitting. When her parents speak to her about this, she becomes very distressed, refusing to even talk about her eating with them.

Reflective activity

Do you feel that Mia has an eating disorder or disordered eating?
What other information would you require to make that decision?

At first glance it is difficult to tell if Mia has an eating disorder or if eating is a reflection of her mood. She may be anxious or depressed due to the difficulties she is experiencing at school and has stopped eating as a consequence of this. However, having ASD puts her at risk of developing an eating disorder and she does apparently have a need to control her environment. More concerning is her avoidance of food and her desire to eat in isolation, together with her refusal to even talk about her eating. This is probably more suggestive of an eating disorder. If possible, as professionals we would like to know Mia's height and weight, and how much weight she has lost. We would also want to know how much she is actually eating on a daily basis. In appointments we would like to explore her attitude towards food but this might be difficult due to her age and her ASD.

WHAT ARE THE TREATMENTS FOR THE CHILD WITH ASD AND COMORBID EATING DISORDERS?

Eating disorders are becoming an increasingly recognised comorbidity with ASD, but the treatment of ASD and eating disorders together can be extremely difficult. For many of the reasons we highlight in Chapter 14, engaging children with ASD in therapy can be very challenging as many of the current therapies are not adapted completely for this condition. There is often a need to control and a rigidity of thinking around the eating disorder, which can make it difficult to engage in any meaningful therapeutic relationship. The aspects of therapy, in which the therapist attempts encourage the child to see a situation from a different point of view, tends to rely on theory of mind skills, which obviously can be lacking in many of these children.

It is very interesting to note how some children develop this condition – they can develop an obsessional attitude to food following education around healthy eating. Their rigidity of thinking can reinforce the belief that all fat is bad and, in an attempt to reduce their fat intake, they will avoid any foods with fat in them. This has an issue for therapy as the child believes that healthy eating is good, a belief which is reinforced by numerous sources around them, but the therapist in their eyes, is giving conflicting advice.

The treatment pattern does tend to follow the treatment used for children without ASD who have eating disorders, and is adapted to meet their needs as best as possible. A behavioural approach can be taken to food in which the child is rewarded for eating in a particular way, with attempts made to influence their underlying thought patterns. The rigidity of thinking can sometimes result in treatment making very rapid progress – far more rapid than children without ASD – if they suddenly decide they want to eat again. This can be unpredictable and the child may relapse later in their life.

CHAPTER SUMMARY

Behaviours could range from very selective eating and food refusal to over-eating and even developing a full-blown eating disorder. It's helpful to understand that in most cases children and young people are able to maintain normal weight and nutritional status in spite of eating selectively. Only a small number are more at risk of developing complications (e.g. lack of weight gain, distress, anxiety and even aggression) and require attention. It is extremely important for the carers to be vigilant about these complications and to act early if they start to impact on the psychosocial aspects of the young person's life.

The studies done to develop an understanding of those behaviours conclude that it's not just one, but a combination of multiple factors that lead to children and young people developing food-related problems. This chapter has mainly focused on understanding those reasons and has also provided you with some useful strategies to help this particular group. These strategies are especially important if eating problems lead to more severe forms of eating disorders, such as anorexia nervosa or bulimia. This chapter has hopefully enabled you to recognise some of the early signs of those disorders and when and where to seek specialist help.

ⓘ IMPORTANT LEARNING POINTS

- Eating problems are very common in children who have ASD.
- Eating problems take many different forms and these are caused by a complex interplay of multiple factors.
- Treatment of eating problems is not straightforward and may require persistence, patience and adaptability.
- ASD and eating disorders, particularly anorexia, share some similar characteristics in terms of thinking style (with ASD being a potential risk-factor).
- The treatment of eating disorders is complex, requiring specialist intervention, particularly in children with ASD.
- A good understanding of ASD is essential when working with a comorbid eating disorder.

FURTHER READING

Bryant-Waugh, R., & Lask, B. (2004). *Eating Disorders: A Parents' Guide* (2nd Edition). Hove: Routledge.

Duker, M., and Slade, R. (2002). *Anorexia Nervosa and Bulimia: How to Help.* Buckingham: Open University Press.

Gray, C. (2002). *My Social Stories Book.* London: Jessica Kingsley Publishers.

Legge, B. (2002). *Can't Eat, Won't Eat: Dietary Difficulties and Autistic Spectrum Disorders.* London: Jessica Kingsley Publishers.

Treasure, J. (1997). *Breaking Free from Anorexia Nervosa: A Survival Guide for Families, Friends and Sufferers.* Hove: Psychology Press.

Further support and information

- *Overcoming Bulimia* – www.overcomingbulimiaonline.com
- *Overcoming Anorexia* – www.overcominganorexiaonline.com

CHAPTER 9

ASD AND OTHER LESS COMMON PSYCHIATRIC CONDITIONS

This chapter will cover:

- Introduction.
- What is psychosis?
- What are the psychotic conditions?
- How do psychotic symptoms present in a child with ASD?
- How do you treat psychosis in the child with ASD?
- What is bipolar disorder?
- Are there different types of bipolar disorder?
- How do you recognise and treat bipolar disorder in the child with ASD?
- Chapter summary.
- Further reading.

INTRODUCTION

While most children with ASD will experience the common emotional problems such as anxiety, and a significant number will have conditions such as ADHD, sometimes in clinical practice we come across children with much rarer problems. They are the sort of problems that cause considerable anxiety in those caring for the children and treatment should be sought as soon as possible. Specialist mental health settings may be familiar with conditions such as psychosis or bipolar disorder, but they may be less familiar with these conditions in the child with ASD, and this can cause difficulty in making a diagnosis. It should be highlighted that many primary care doctors will never see a case of this in their career, which means that everyone would benefit from awareness of their presentation.

In this chapter we are going to focus on conditions which influence how a child can lose touch with reality. These are the psychotic conditions, including schizophrenia, or schizo-affective disorders, and bipolar affective disorder. These occur fairly rarely in early childhood and are seen more during the teenage years. There is some controversy surrounding these conditions, particularly in terms of how commonly they occur – this is a particular issue for bipolar disorder. While this is an ongoing debate, it is important to recognise the core features so that help can be sought.

There is an extensive literature available on both schizophrenia and bipolar disorder as separate conditions and it is difficult in a book of this size to explore these issues in any great depth. However, we feel it is important that the reader understands the terms used in this area, such as 'hallucination', 'delusions' and 'mania', which tend to be used rather freely in common language, as a general appreciation of these terms will help you to distinguish these features from the typical presentation of a child with ASD. This chapter provides an overview of this complex area.

WHAT IS PSYCHOSIS?

Psychosis can be defined as an abnormality of the mind in which the individual becomes detached from reality. Determining whether somebody has lost touch with reality can be difficult in some circumstances and to a certain extent there can be a cultural element to this definition. For example, in some cultures individuals who hear voices may in certain circumstances be perceived as receiving special messages, or those who experience hallucinations may also be considered special. In many cultures throughout history the behaviours have been explained in this way. However, in the Western world the development of hallucinations, delusions, disorders of thought and the behaviours associated with this are treated as markers of serious mental illness.

In children, particularly those in pre-adolescence, the incidence of psychosis is extremely rare, but prevalence increases in older children. Although there are mental health causes of psychosis, some of the features are occasionally seen with organic (physical) causes of brain impairment, such as tumours, or transiently when the child is delirious due to high fever. Many parents have the experience of a child who is seeing things or saying strange things, particularly when unwell with a high temperature, but it is the persistent nature outside of these circumstances which defines having psychosis. Additionally, many children have very vivid imaginations with imaginary friends whom they talk to, play with and listen to, which is part of their normal development. Many of these young children will try to convince their parent that the 'friend' is real. In older children, the drive for experimentation and possible peer pressure can lead to the use of illicit substances, some of which can have unpleasant side-effects in this area – cannabis or amphetamines in particular can induce psychosis.

Case study

Susan is a 15-year-old girl who appears to be developing some strange behaviour. She complains that she is being followed and that she can hear people talking about her, even when she is alone. More recently, she describes seeing shadows at the edge of her vision. Susan describes these shadows as 'creatures'. Despite her parents' and the school's attempts to reassure her that she is not being followed, she remains adamant that somebody is watching her and recording her movements. Susan has started to take a very convoluted route when going to/coming home from school in an attempt to lose her pursuers. In response to these voices and sightings she is becoming more socially withdrawn, is reluctant to leave the house to see friends or go shopping, and is also not eating or sleeping well.

This brief case illustrates some of the behaviours which we will discuss throughout the chapter. Susan is starting to have some visual and auditory hallucinations (seeing things and hearing people talk about her) and is developing paranoid beliefs (delusions) about being followed, which have changed her behaviour.

What is a hallucination?

In understanding 'hallucination' it is essential to have some appreciation of some other terms. One of these is 'sensation'. A sensation is the way in which an external stimulus is first detected by an individual's senses (e.g. the sound detected by the ear or the smell detected by the nose). This sensation is then interpreted by the brain in a process called 'perception' (e.g. the sound is recognised as a voice or the smell is recognised as a rose). In this way the brain can interpret the world around the individual. Additionally, the brain also tends to be more aware of some perceptions and sensations than others, depending on the circumstances – basically, focusing on some and excluding others. A simple way of demonstrating this is if we were to point out that you can now feel the seat underneath you. In most cases this will now heighten your awareness of the seat; but before we mentioned it directly, most of you were not consciously aware of this sensation. When considering hallucinations, therefore, it is important to understand that they are abnormalities of perception, abnormalities in how the mind/brain sees the world.

The way the brain interprets the outside world is complicated and it is easy to see how it can be distorted. There are two types of abnormal perception which are divided into:

1. *sensory distortions*, where a real object is perceived in a distorted way

2. *false perceptions*, where a perception occurs which may or may not be in response to stimuli but in reality the object perceived does not actually exist.

In sensory distortions, the quality of the perception changes in many ways. For example, it may seem more or less intense, or different in shape and size, and sometimes this can be related to mood.

■ EXAMPLE

'Sensory distortion' is often experienced by people who are in a low mood. They may describe the world as feeling 'grey' or 'black' and their senses appear decreased. Food may taste bland and other people's voices may feel too loud or too quiet (i.e. it is the brain's interpretation of something in the real world).

False perceptions are different – a hallucination is a false perception. This is a particularly complex area of psychiatry and can therefore be quite tricky to describe. In clinical terms, it is a perception of an external stimulus in the absence of that stimulus while in a conscious state – that is, a hallucination is when the conscious person believes what they are sensing is real, when in reality it is actually absent. A hallucination has the qualities of a real sensation (perception) – for example, the qualities of a real voice or a real smell – and is said to exist in external objective space. This means that the individual experiences it as external to them and their mind and body. Importantly, hallucinations can occur in any sensory modality, such as auditory, visual, olfactory (smell), tactile or taste, and can occur singularly or in groups.

■ EXAMPLE

The classic example of a 'false perception' is the auditory hallucination. Many people describe the voice as being heard through their ears alongside other noises, rather than inside their heads. This suggests it is experienced externally to the body and mind.

The most common hallucinations described by individuals appear to be auditory hallucinations (hearing voices). This can actually take many forms:

- The individual may hear their own thoughts out loud.

- They may hear a running commentary on their actions.

- They may hear voices discussing them in the third person.

It should be appreciated that the presence of a hallucination does not necessarily always mean that someone is unwell. Interestingly, research has demonstrated that many people hear voices without being psychotic, but it is the presence of these voices together with other symptoms of psychosis which suggest an illness is present (Escher *et al.* 2002).

It is extremely common to work with children with and without ASD who say they are hearing voices; again, we should remember the younger children who often have imaginary friends. Often in our practice we are asked to see teenagers who are worried that they are hearing voices, which in many cases turns out to be an internal dialogue of their thoughts. They hear voices inside their heads debating a course of action, which feels foreign to them. Although the teenagers know that these voices are experienced internally, they tend to become worried as the voices may suggest unpleasant courses of action. Additionally, many teenagers have intrusive thoughts, which also cause significant distress. In our experience this internal dialogue tends to be perfectly normal. Nonetheless, many teenagers are worried when they first become aware of this internal dialogue, which can often occur when in a heightened emotional state but also when calm (e.g. when reading). Alternatively, others describe very realistic-sounding voices in their head, but they recognise them as being in their head and therefore part of themselves – these tend not to be thought of as hallucinations.

Reflective activity

There are other types of false perception, illusions and pseudo-hallucinations which are beyond the scope of this book. It may be useful for you to explore these further if you are interested, and we recommend you obtain a copy of the book by Casey and Kelly (2007), (see Further reading at this end of the chapter).

What is a delusion?

'A delusion is a false idea or belief which is out of keeping with a patient's educational, cultural, and social background and is held with extraordinary conviction and subjective certainty.' (Sims 1995, p.101). Basically, in this situation an individual believes something is true, despite all the evidence to the contrary. This can cause them considerable distress as it appears everyone is disagreeing with them and does not understand their point of view. Additionally, it is difficult or even impossible to convince them that it is not true, despite spending significant amounts of time and demonstrating that their view is incorrect in a number of different ways. It should be remembered that the delusion has an educational, cultural or social component and that the belief is inconsistent with this setting.

EXAMPLE 1
A teenage boy believes he has special powers similar to a comic book character and despite being unable to fly, attempts to do so.

EXAMPLE 2
A teenage girl believes she has been possessed by an evil spirit and has been instructed to punish her sister (it is important in this case to explore the religious background of the family and possibly speak to the religious leader).

There are many types of delusion, which cover all types of thinking, and we present a summary in Box 9.1 to illustrate the differences.

As explained earlier, delusions are persistent, which makes them difficult to remove through talking therapies. There has been some limited success in this area, but generally medications are needed to treat them. When treated, individuals may try to make sense of what happened to them; some gain insight into their delusional state, while others may attempt to explain their ideas in a more rational way.

Additionally, delusions should be differentiated from another concept referred to as 'over-valued ideas'. These are defined ideas which are acceptable and comprehensible, but pursued by the individual beyond the bounds of reason (Sims 1995).

BOX 9.1 TYPES OF DELUSION

- *Delusional intuition* – this is a delusion that arises suddenly with little obvious prompting.

- *Delusional percept* – the individual interprets something that they normally experience and then attaches delusional significance to it (e.g. seeing a cloud and interpreting that as the sky falling in).

- *Delusional atmosphere* – feeling that the whole world has been subtly altered.

- *Delusional memory* – remembering something that did not occur.

- *Delusions based on content* – this can be based on anything, such as:
  - delusions of persecution
  - morbid jealousy
  - delusions of love
  - delusional misidentification (e.g. someone close has been replaced by an impostor)
  - grandiose delusions (e.g. developing super powers)
  - religious delusions
  - delusions of guilt and unworthiness
  - nihilistic delusions (e.g. the feeling of having nothing)
  - hypochondriacal delusions
  - delusions of infestation
  - delusions of control (e.g. feelings of being controlled by an outside force).

(Sims 1995)

EXAMPLE

A 15-year-old boy may be intensely jealous of the time his girlfriend spends away from him. He fears she may be unfaithful and therefore he frequently follows her around. When asked about it, he realises that he has been possessive but struggles with this; and on questioning, his fears do not have a delusional intensity.

WHAT ARE THE PSYCHOTIC CONDITIONS?

Now that we have talked about some of the concepts which underpin our descriptions of psychosis, it is useful to describe them in more depth. For the purpose of this book we focus on schizophrenia and bipolar disorder as these are two of the most significant mental illnesses.

THINK POINT!

Psychosis is a state in which perception of reality is severely affected; it is associated with the presence of hallucinations and delusions.

In medical practice psychosis can occur in a number of different mental illnesses. The most commonly recognised is schizophrenia but it can also occur in other conditions such as persistent delusional disorders, drug-induced psychosis bipolar disorder or depression. We discuss schizophrenia at this point, as it is a relevant example of psychosis, but will then return to a broader discussion on psychosis.

WHAT IS SCHIZOPHRENIA?

Schizophrenia is a mental illness defined by a particular selection of symptoms. These are often divided into positive and negative symptoms to help describe the effect on an individual.

- *Positive symptoms* include hallucinations, delusions, disorganised speech and thoughts, and catatonic behaviour (see Box 9.2).

- *Negative symptoms*, which can be more debilitating, include 'affective blunting' (mood is flat), 'avolition' (lack of motivation) and alogia (lack of speech).

We summarise some of the features which affect different aspects of an individual with schizophrenia in Box 9.2 below. As you can see, there are a number of different signs and symptoms which can occur to a greater or lesser degree. It is probably unnecessary in this book to explain them in great detail but it is useful to have an awareness of them.

Schizophrenia affects approximately four people in every thousand in the general population (Bhugra 2005), but it is extremely rare before the age of ten years old. Prevalence increases throughout the teenage years and reaches its peak during early adulthood, which reinforces the need to be vigilant for it in the teenage population.

BOX 9.2 OTHER FEATURES OF SCHIZOPHRENIA

Speech/thought

- *Breaks in the train of thought* – the person also has incoherent speech.
- *Neologisms* – the person makes up new words and uses them.
- *Thinking can be vague and circumstantial* – the person fails to actually get to the point.
- *Thought insertion* – the person believes that thoughts have been put into their head.
- *Thought withdrawal* – the person believes thoughts have been taken out of their head.
- *Thought broadcasting* – the person believes that thoughts are being broadcast to everyone.
- *Thought echo* – the person hears their thoughts repeatedly.

Mood

- *Mood can be very variable* – mood can change rapidly.
- *Mood can be incongruous* – there is inconsistency between the expressed mood and the associated behaviour.

Catatonia

- *Excitement* – the person is in an exaggerated state of excitement.
- *Waxy flexibility* – the person can be put into an unusual posture in which they remain.
- *Posturing* – the person stays in one static position.
- *Mutism* – the person does not speak.
- *Stupor* – the person is in an unresponsive state.

The pathology behind schizophrenia remains unclear, but it is evident that early diagnosis and treatments are essential for a better prognosis. Although the onset of schizophrenia may be sudden, with rapid development of hallucinations and delusions, typically in teenagers the presentation of schizophrenia is more insidious. There can be a prolonged decline in social and academic functioning prior to the development of the positive symptoms. This is called 'the prodromal phase'. Unfortunately, this presentation can be non-specific, with the teenager becoming more socially withdrawn and doing less well at school/college, and this can make early recognition difficult.

Although the range of symptoms can vary between individuals, schizophrenia can be described broadly in different categories. For ease of description there are different types of schizophrenia, which we describe in Box 9.3.

BOX 9.3 TYPES OF SCHIZOPHRENIA

- *Paranoid schizophrenia* – the dominant feature is hallucinations and delusions which contribute to a paranoid state (i.e. the belief that people are watching the person).
- *Disorganised/hebephrenic schizophrenia* – in this type, thoughts and speech are very disorganised and the negative symptoms, such as avolition, are prominent.
- *Catatonic schizophrenia* – catatonic symptoms are the prominent feature.
- *Residual schizophrenia* – this is the longer-term state, which can be dominated by negative symptoms; hallucinations and delusions are less common.

Typically, schizophrenia runs a chronic long-term course, with impairment continuing to deteriorate in early adulthood. There are things which can affect the prognosis, such as the length of the first episode or the onset at a younger age (Lay *et al.* 2000), but each case is different.

At this point we would like to make a particular point. It should be remembered that schizophrenia is *not* a split personality, which is a commonly used description in everyday language. This misconception has come about due to individuals' responses to voices. In reality, a 'split personality' is probably a better description of the extremely rare 'multiple personality disorder' in which the individual appears to have more than one distinct personality. Another point that we would like to make relates to the common view that people with schizophrenia are dangerous and should be avoided or incarcerated. In reality, the vast majority of people with schizophrenia are not dangerous and in some cases should be considered quite vulnerable. Unfortunately, the media tends to focus on those few who are more dangerous (Klin and Lemish 2008) and this perpetuates the myth.

HOW DO PSYCHOTIC SYMPTOMS PRESENT IN A CHILD WITH ASD?

Unfortunately, this can be a confusing area for clinical professionals and parents. It is not unusual for children with ASD to describe unusual ideas or beliefs which can feel almost delusional. There have been descriptions of children with ASD who really believe that they can fly as they confuse fantasy with reality, or they may identify with a particular fantasy character, such as a superhero. Obviously, this can be extremely dangerous; however, this tends not to be a psychosis, but may be a function of literal thinking, difficulties with theory of mind and their obsessive way of thinking. While younger children with ASD struggle to differentiate fantasy from reality, in older children this may also occur but the child can also develop a fantasy world which can appear to have a delusional intensity. The child appears to exist in their own reality in which they can have special abilities and feel they have a special status, and it can be very difficult to shift their thinking.

Rather than being a psychosis, however, this is an expression of anxiety and can be related to many feelings including those of social exclusion. These children may be struggling with the many demands put upon them and may recognise that they are different to their peers. They may want to have friends but feel unable to socialise adequately and therefore feel rejected, which can affect their self-esteem. As a way of defending their self-esteem and coping with the stress of the world around them, they may then develop a superior and unapproachable attitude. These feelings of anxiety can result in the creation of a fantasy world, which in turn has a protective function. In their worlds they can feel safe, secure and important, which in many ways increases their resilience, despite seeming unusual to everyone else. Interestingly, when the stress is reduced, this fantasy world can quickly disappear, which is not the case for an individual with genuine psychosis. Unfortunately, it can be extremely difficult at times to differentiate between the two, and it is fairly easy for clinical professionals to feel that the child needs to start on treatments for a psychotic illness.

THINK POINT!

Although a child with ASD can have comorbid psychotic illness, care should be taken to thoroughly exclude the presentation of anxiety as the key problem.

When considering the development of psychosis in a child with ASD, the pattern can be similar to those without ASD, with the development of the positive and negative symptoms. Again, it is important to have a good understanding of ASD when assessing these children, in order to differentiate the psychotic features from the ASD. An additional difficulty for clinical professionals is to decide when the psychosis has been treated, as elements such as social withdrawal and difficulties with motivation or concentration may be inherent to both conditions. It is therefore really important that the clinical professionals assessing and diagnosing young people with ASD and psychosis are very familiar with both conditions and can tease out the different elements.

Case study

Jake is a 16-year-old boy with ASD. He attends a mainstream school but always spends a significant amount of time in a learning support environment, away from his peers. He struggles to engage with his peers, but has formed good relationships with his learning support assistant. Over a number of months Jake has become more withdrawn and difficult to talk to. He refuses to go anywhere outside of the learning support environment, saying the other children are watching him. Over the last couple of weeks his behaviour appears to have become more unusual; for example, he says that he can read the thoughts of those around him but refuses to demonstrate this. He claims that he is not of this planet and that one day he will 'ascend'. Notably, his attention to hygiene has significantly declined. This period of behaviour does coincide with some important exams and you understand that his father has recently become unemployed.

Reflective activity

What would make you feel that this young man is having a psychotic episode? What else could explain this presentation, and how could you differentiate?

With the information provided, it is actually difficult to be completely clear whether Jake is having an early episode of psychosis or whether he has developed these thoughts and behaviours in relation to the stress around him. Possibly he could even be depressed. A lot of time will be needed to properly explore Jake's way of thinking. Sometimes the picture only becomes truly clear with time.

HOW DO YOU TREAT PSYCHOSIS IN THE CHILD WITH ASD?

If the child with ASD does have a diagnosis of comorbid psychosis, it is important to recognise the condition early as delayed treatment is related to poorer prognosis. The choice of where the young person receives treatment may vary locally and internationally, but tends to depend on the risk the child poses to themself and to others. If the risk is low, it would be preferable in many instances to treat the child as an outpatient so that there is no change to their environment or routine. This means that they are still being cared for by those who understand the nuances of their ASD. Unfortunately, some children are so unwell that they require inpatient admission. This can be done on a voluntary or involuntary basis, with compulsory detention reserved for those with significant risk. This may depend on local resources, but it tends to be utilised to keep a child safe.

In ASD, as we have already alluded to, there may be significant problems with an inpatient admission as the unit may not be specifically for children with ASD and the staff may struggle with some of the specific features of the ASD. Inherently, there are going to be problems due to a change in routine, a change of people, a change of environment, changes of diet, restrictions to obsessive behaviours and sensory issues – in reality the list is endless! This can result in the child becoming more agitated, which then appears to exacerbate the psychotic presentation. Ideally, individuals with comorbid psychosis need to be cared for in a low-sensory environment which is generally calm – this is not always possible in many inpatient units.

The mainstay of treatment for comorbid psychosis remains medication – the antipsychotic group of drugs also known as 'neuroleptics' or 'major tranquillisers'. This class of treatment has been around for decades but there have been some improvements, particularly with the development of the atypical antipsychotics which have fewer side-effects than their predecessors. This is a very specialist area due to the nature of the condition and the drugs, and there can be specialist teams which work in this area.

Unfortunately, many of the medications used in psychosis have short-term and longer-term side-effects which people can find unpleasant. This can lead to young people not taking their treatments, with an increased chance of them relapsing. An additional problem often found in individuals with psychosis is that the condition can affect their insight. This is the ability for them to realise that they are unwell and need help. This can often be even worse for those children with ASD who struggle with recognising their own emotions.

It is increasingly recognised that it is important to reduce the relapse rate of a psychotic illness, such as schizophrenia, by reducing the stress an individual may experience. Obviously, this is of increased relevance in children with ASD as stress can cause such a deterioration in many of their behaviours and they are particularly sensitive to the effects of stress. It is therefore common sense to reduce the stress a child with ASD may be experiencing in order to reduce their relapse rate, which will require the involvement of a number of different services, such as school, health and social care, and a number of different professionals. In many places the recognition of the early benefit of intervention has been recognised, with the creation of specialist teams to help the children. However, these children remain complex and care needs to be individualised.

WHAT IS BIPOLAR DISORDER?

Another condition which has gained increasing publicity is 'bipolar disorder', which is also known as 'bipolar affective disorder' (it used to be called manic depression). This is an illness which is defined by disturbances in mood in which the mood can be elevated or depressed, and it is these features which define the type of bipolar disorder present. The elevated mood can be described as 'mania' or 'hypomania'. Generally, hypomania is a less severe version of mania but can still be quite debilitating. Mania is characterised by a number of features which are outlined in Box 9.4. These symptoms can occur to a greater or lesser degree and can severely affect an individual's life. These symptoms can significantly impair someone's judgement and lead them into difficult situations.

Hypomania is characterised as being a mild to moderate version of mania. Some individuals describe feeling very productive in this state, while others can be overly distracted and have poor judgement. Although hypomania may be described by some as a good experience, families and friends may feel otherwise. Both hypomania and mania can lead to excessive risk taking. Patients may get into significant debt, as they do not judge the problems inherent in spending, or they may have accidents, particularly adults involved in car accidents.

BOX 9.4 CHARACTERISTICS OF MANIA

- Elevated mood.
- Euphoria.
- Increase in energy.
- Decreased need for sleep.
- Pressured speech.
- Racing thoughts.
- Poor attention span.
- Impaired judgements (e.g. spending spree).
- Aggressive and intolerant.
- Increased sexual drive.
- Psychotic features such as grandiose delusions.

EXAMPLE

A 15-year-old boy, whom the school is worried about, appears to be extremely happy to the point of euphoria. He is talking very rapidly about anything, and it is a struggle to keep up with his train of thought. At times he becomes very aggressive and is easily irritated. He is now claiming that he wants to teach the class as if he were qualified as a teacher.

The other aspect of bipolar disorder is the depression component. This can present similarly to those who have depressive illness (as discussed in Chapter 5), with feelings of low mood, tiredness, fatigue, poor appetite, poor sleep, poor concentration and poor motivation. Individuals can also have the negative thoughts associated with this, such as guilt, hopelessness and worthlessness. Some individuals will develop suicidal ideation and, in more severe cases, they can develop psychotic features. The psychotic aspects of a bipolar disorder tend to be called 'mood congruent', which means that they tend to reflect the mood of the individual, such as delusions of poverty while in depression, or the grandiose delusions which occur in mania.

Thankfully, bipolar disorder is fairly rare in children but there is an increased risk throughout the teenage years. Approximately 4 per cent of adults and 2.5 per cent of teenagers met the criteria for bipolar disorder in their lifetime within a given year, with rates increasing with age (National Institute of Mental Health 2012b). The exact cause of bipolar disorder is unclear but, like schizophrenia, there is a strong genetic component, with children being at increased risk if a relative, such as a parent, has the condition.

ARE THERE DIFFERENT TYPES OF BIPOLAR DISORDER?

It used to be believed that bipolar disorder was a fairly circumscribed condition. However, in recent years this view has become much more blurred. Although we discuss bipolar disorder within ASD a little later in the chapter, the concept of bipolar disorder in younger children with ASD is particularly contentious. First, we will briefly describe how the condition has been divided into different types.

Classically, bipolar disorder can be classified in different ways. This can depend on whether the bipolar disorder includes manic episodes, as opposed to hypomanic episodes, or can be due to the presence of psychotic symptoms. Although many people may have the misperception that mania always has psychotic features, some episodes of mania do not and are classified by the extent of the mania. Additionally, bipolar disorders are also classified according to how often the episodes of illness occur. On average in an adult, an episode of bipolar illness will occur approximately once every two years, but some individuals appear to have the cycle far more frequently. This has been called 'rapid cycling bipolar disorder' and is defined as having four or more episodes each year, although some observers have described another condition, 'ultra-rapid cycling bipolar disorder', in which they claim the episodes occur every few days. Although the view is not universally held, some commentators claim that cycles can actually occur within a single day (Tillman and Geller 2003).

This view of bipolar disorder is fairly contentious and there are some disagreements regarding the existence of the more rapid cycling types. This is probably particularly important when considering the behaviour in children. It has been argued that the rapid change in mood in some children is the result of bipolar disorder, due to the instability of their moods and therefore their behavioural outbursts. However, it needs to be realised that much of the emotional regulation in children is a learned process and therefore putting such a strong label as bipolar disorder on a child who is emotionally immature is controversial. This difference is most apparent in the increasing rates of diagnosis within the USA data.

HOW DO YOU RECOGNISE AND TREAT BIPOLAR DISORDER IN THE CHILD WITH ASD?

It remains fairly uncommon in our clinical experience to find a case of bipolar disorder in a child with ASD. This is not to say it does not occur, but an individual clinical professional will see only a handful in their career. In most cases the condition tends to be recognised when the child develops a manic episode as this is so classical in its presentation. The child may have developed a depressive illness before this and undergone treatment, but it is the development of the mania which changes the diagnostic label.

In children with ASD this manic presentation has all the hallmarks of a classical manic episode as described earlier, with symptoms such as pressure of speech, flight of ideas and euphoria being fairly obvious. They may also develop the grandiose delusions so familiar in mania.

The difficulty comes in identifying those with less obvious swings in their mood. It is fairly common to see over-excitability in children with ASD, particularly those with comorbid ADHD, and many children with ASD can have a fairly volatile mood throughout the day. As stated earlier, children need to learn to recognise and regulate their emotions, and this process is often delayed in the child with ASD. Therefore, this fluctuating mood is a reflection of developmental immaturity.

THINK POINT!

Care should be taken when attributing significant fluctuations in mood to bipolar disorder as these could be a reflection of developmental immaturity.

The variability of mood between children with ASD can be quite challenging when making a diagnosis of comorbid bipolar disorder. While some children with ASD tend to express one mood all the time, others tend to have significant mood swings with marked problems in regulating their emotions. It would be easy for those children who have difficulty regulating their emotions to be diagnosed as having a more rapid cycling bipolar disorder, particularly by professionals who are unaware of the variability in ASD. At the present time most professionals tend not to diagnose comorbid rapid cycling bipolar disorder in these children and would only feel comfortable doing so in children in whom there has been a significant change in their typical presentation and when the changes occur for a prolonged period of time. Again, it is important to gain a clear picture of the child's particular presentation of ASD and whether there has been any significant change. In our view, bipolar disorder is felt by the majority of professionals to be an acquired condition rather than one that has been present from early childhood.

For simplicity, it is important to diagnose the bipolar disorder in children with ASD only when they have prolonged bouts of low mood or elevated mood, as a diagnosis of bipolar disorder may result in drug treatments, which have their own drawbacks.

Treatment of bipolar disorder

The issues regarding treatment for bipolar disorder in some ways mirror those of psychotic disorders. The treatment for children with ASD is similar to those without ASD, obviously with some additional considerations. In some cases admission to an inpatient environment may be the only option if the risk of the behaviours is too significant to manage as an outpatient. There may be the risk of self-harm or other risk-taking behaviours, and when children are in a manic phase, they can be extremely exhausting for their families as they may not stop to eat or sleep. Admission sometimes has to be enforced on an involuntary basis, according to the legal framework of the country. This can still occur even in young people. Obviously, for children with ASD admissions can be particularly traumatic, due to an aversion to change in routine, and so the question of whether to admit or not should probably be very carefully considered.

If managed in the community, treatment can be through outpatient or day units, but continued vigilance is required due to the risks this condition poses. It is generally recognised that in the acute phase of this illness medication is needed to improve the mood disorder. In the manic phase 'atypical antipsychotics' can be used to alleviate symptoms, particularly if they are psychotic in nature. The mainstay of treating bipolar disorder is medication, with these treatments known as 'mood stabilisers' as they tend to reduce the fluctuations in mood. These are also used in the acute episodes and to prevent relapse. The commonly recognised treatment for bipolar disorders is lithium, which was the first mood stabiliser in this area. Although it can be very effective, it tends not to be used in children due to some of the longer-term side-effects, such as effects on the thyroid and kidneys.

In children it is now more common to see medications such as sodium valproate and carbamazepine (originally anticonvulsant medications), which are used to control the mood element, particularly during the manic phases. Unfortunately, these may have some significant side-effects, and drugs such as sodium valproate should be avoided during pregnancy. In children with ASD, it is probably wise to initiate these treatments over a longer period of time as they may be more sensitive to some of the side-effects.

Although low mood is a very significant part of the disorder, it should be mentioned that antidepressants should be used with extreme care in most cases as they can precipitate a manic episode. Unfortunately, in some cases of children with ASD the antidepressants may have been used to treat an earlier episode of comorbid depressive illness or to help in the reduction of anxiety symptoms. This may pose a problem if the antidepressant was helping to reduce anxiety. Therefore it is important to look at other ways to reduce the stress on the child, using more behavioural or environmental methods.

Obviously, it is important alongside any medical treatment to include work which can reduce the stress the child may experience in order to reduce the likelihood of relapse. This includes looking at the stress at school, from family life and relationships. It is important that the individual and families can recognise the symptoms of early relapse and can therefore seek treatment early on. This may be difficult in some individuals with ASD who obviously have difficulties not only in emotional recognition but also in expressing how they are feeling.

Case study

Simon is a 15-year-old boy with ASD. Last year he was diagnosed as having a comorbid depressive illness, which responded to medication and to work which looked at his management of stress. He has been stable for some months, but his mother has called a professional with a number of concerns. She says that Simon has not slept for two nights and appears to always be 'on the go'. She is struggling to convince him to eat anything as he seems 'hyper' and he has told her about his plans for leaving school and starting his own business as a dot com millionaire. His speech is described as almost incoherent at times as he is trying to say so much, and he tends to rhyme words constantly. She wonders if there is anything the clinical professional can do to help.

Reflective activity

It is fairly obvious from this description that Simon is suffering from a manic episode. What would you recommend Simon's mother to do? What support do you think she needs to get Simon and herself through this episode?

This is a potentially difficult situation as Simon will need urgent treatment to help with his mania. As mentioned earlier, in some cases antidepressants can exacerbate this problem and therefore should be stopped. The main issue that is important in this situation is for the specialist mental health service to make an assessment of the risk-factors for Simon. It is important to look at how his illness can be treated without causing him too much distress. It does sound like Simon needs an inpatient admission to keep him safe, monitor him closely and initiate treatments. His mother will obviously need some support as this will be a traumatic time for the family.

CHAPTER SUMMARY

Psychosis and bipolar disorder are rarely seen in children with ASD. However, if they do occur, the young person needs assessing carefully. It is important to recognise the features of ASD, particularly those related to anxiety or emotional dysregulation, which can present as either of the conditions and would need very different care.

Psychosis has a very particular group of symptoms (e.g. hallucinations and delusions), which need to be understood so as not to mislabel similar features in those with ASD. It is, however, very important to recognise when they do occur, as early recognition and treatment of the psychotic illness is associated with a better outcome.

Classical bipolar disorder can also present in a very distinctive way with significant mania and depression. The difficulty lies with the more recent interpretations of bipolar disorder and whether they occur in the more rapid cycling forms, which are more controversially diagnosed in children with ASD. This is an expanding area in the literature and continues to present challenges for clinical professionals and parents. Early recognition of bipolar disorder is, however, beneficial for those affected.

ⓘ IMPORTANT LEARNING POINTS

- Psychosis is an abnormality of the mind in which the individual becomes detached from reality. It can occur in both schizophrenia and bipolar disorder.

- Schizophrenia affects approximately 1 per cent of the population and is characterised by psychotic features such as hallucinations and delusions.

- Psychotic illnesses can occur in children with ASD, but care should be taken not to confuse this presentation with that of extreme anxiety.

- Bipolar disorder is characterised by a disturbance in mood – both low mood and elevated mood.

- Recognising bipolar disorder in children with ASD requires an understanding of the child's typical presentation, but there is controversy around some of the subtypes of the condition.

FURTHER READING

Casey, P., and Kelly, B. (2007). *Fish's Clinical Psychopathology: Signs and Symptoms in Psychiatry*. London: The Royal College of Psychiatrists.

CHAPTER 10

REDUCING STRESS, AND STRATEGIES THAT HELP

This chapter will cover:

- Introduction.
- Is there a way to understand stress in children with ASD?
- How do we identify the stressors?
- What are the practical self-help strategies that can work to reduce stress?
- When should specialist help be sought to reduce stress, and what does it add?
- Why are families so important?
- Chapter summary.
- Further reading.

INTRODUCTION

While the first part of this book concentrated on helping to understand and recognise mental health conditions in children with ASD, we now want to focus to a greater degree on what can be done to help these children and their families. From a personal perspective we recognise that having a child with ASD in the family can feel a bit like a roller-coaster experience, and this sentiment is often supported by what families tell us in clinic. Although the whole experience is physically and mentally demanding and often frustrating, it can at times be rewarding and is nearly always interesting.

One of the problems that is evident for many people is their lack of access to specialist help for the additional mental health problems. Furthermore, the life-long nature of ASD can mean that help needs to be accessed intermittently throughout the lifetime, and may be difficult to find. In earlier chapters we have referred to stress as an underlying feature in the development of mental health problems. In this chapter we will use the word 'stress' to describe the effect of risk-factors on the mental health of children with ASD.

▮ EXAMPLE

Many children with ASD describe feeling 'stressed' when they hear loud noises, which is a reflection of their sensory problems. This makes them less likely to cope with additional pressures.

Also in this chapter we propose a broad framework to look at the build-up of different stressors and how they may affect the child's mental health, and thus the development of any comorbid problems; we also look at the different ways of identifying and managing them. There are obviously some factors which affect mental health which cannot be eliminated (e.g. the genetic risk), but we are firm believers that the risks can be ameliorated by reducing stress, and treatment also follows this model.

IS THERE A WAY TO UNDERSTAND STRESS IN CHILDREN WITH ASD?

Children with ASD are stressed by many things and have to live in an environment which poses considerable challenges for them on a daily basis. When working or living with these children, some stresses can be quite easy to see while others are much less obvious. In an ideal world we could provide a model of care which would cover all eventualities and enable everyone to identify all the stresses, but this is probably overly optimistic. What we will provide here are some ideas to help work with these children. Unfortunately, ASD can be a bit unpredictable and sometimes it appears impossible to know the full extent of the stresses on the child. While we offer you an overall picture, it is necessary for you to adapt and translate this guidance to suit the individual child.

Although some children seem very sensitive to a particular stress (e.g. a change in routine, which at the time may seem insignificant to the outside observer), many children with ASD develop their problems as a consequence of a build-up of different stressors throughout the day. We are often asked to see challenging children who are being physically aggressive and we can be told there seems no reason for this behaviour. In our experience, in the vast majority of cases there *is* a cause for the behaviour but it is not immediately apparent. It is in these cases that there has been a build-up of stress throughout the day, with something minor actually triggering the outburst. Many parents have described to us the difficulties they have with their child when they return home from school, due to the stressors that have built up over the course of the day, as well as how long it can take for the child to unwind.

> **THINK POINT!**
>
> Challenging behaviour or meltdowns may be a consequence of a build-up of a number of different smaller stresses.

A useful way to consider the build-up of stress is to consider each stress as a layer of a cake – a 'stress cake' – with candles igniting at the top representing the child's outburst. By way of illustration, see Figure 10.1 below.

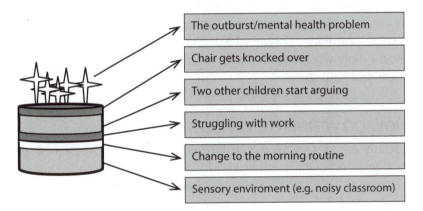

The outburst/mental health problem

Chair gets knocked over

Two other children start arguing

Struggling with work

Change to the morning routine

Sensory enviroment (e.g. noisy classroom)

Figure 10.1: The 'stress cake'

What this example illustrates is that the child is experiencing a number of stresses which are built up in the classroom environment. The first of these could be sensory issues in an overly noisy school classroom. This causes some stress, which is then exacerbated by a minor change to the morning routine. Additionally, the child struggles with the tasks set during the morning, and the situation is made worse by listening to their peers in dispute. Therefore, when a minor incident such as the chair getting knocked over occurs, the child explodes. Although this model is useful to explain the outbursts or meltdowns of children with ASD, a similar model can be applied to the development of some mental health problems.

When considering mental health, there may be a number of layers to this cake which are present on a persistent and chronic basis. Although these stresses do not lead to any apparent outbursts, the continued experience of multiple stresses does appear to have an effect on the child's mental health. It is not difficult to see how this chronic stress level could lead to mental health problems, such as anxiety or depression, and also how constant feelings of stress/anxiety affect the presentation of other mental health problems. Again, it is useful to consider many children with ASD being chronically stressed by interacting with the world around them and finding it very difficult to manage. Thinking about ASD in this way lends itself to thinking about what can be done to help the child, and, although this may not be the most scientific way of assessing the situation, in practical terms it is very useful. For example, it is often useful to think of the child's routines being a way in which they manage their stress by keeping everything controlled and the same. These routines develop as a consequence of finding the world a confusing place and therefore anxiety-provoking. This may be described for children with ASD, but most people would say that they, too, have some routines which help them deal with stress.

HOW DO WE IDENTIFY THE STRESSORS?

Identifying the stressors can be difficult, particularly for those who are new to working with children with ASD. We have developed a short acronym to help you remember the main issues so that the problems can be identified. The acronym we use is SCOPER but please feel free to come up with any other acronym that you feel is useful. We have kept this one as short as possible, with each letter covering more than one issue.

Structure.

Communication.

Others.

Physical.

Environmental.

Rigidity.

Structure/support

Structure/support covers all those mechanisms which have been put in place to help the child and is also a way of looking at routines. It is important to identify the structures which are currently being used to support the child, and to see if problems have occurred if any supports have been recently changed. There may be missing ones which need to be reinstated or new ones may need to be introduced. Structures are useful as they provide a consistent framework for the child and are therefore predictable. Home and school life are often easier if things are structured in a more ordered fashion. There can be instances, however, when the child has responded so well to this consistency that if the particular structure (e.g. a visual timetable) is removed, the child becomes increasingly stressed. When looking at structures and support, it is essential to recognise all those supports for the child (formal and informal) that are being used. Schools and families are often surprised at how much they have naturally put in place to help a child with ASD, without even realising it.

■ EXAMPLE

A teenage boy with ASD, who has recently started at secondary school, is expected to go into the dining hall at lunchtime. In his previous school he always had lunch in a separate room as he found the dining hall overwhelming. His stress level is now rising due to the lack of support or structure around this meal time.

Under this area it is also useful to consider routines, as they are often the structures the child is using to manage their anxiety and stress. Obvious stressors for children with ASD are the changes which can occur in their routines, often on a fairly daily basis. Unfortunately, life is far from predictable, and although major routines may remain the same, the smaller ones can often be affected. It is surprising how small changes can affect children with ASD, and so it may be useful to look at what changes are happening in their lives and what routines are evident day to day. Many children with ASD can find unstructured times (e.g. play-time/recess), difficult, as the rules around this time are less clear. These routines may not be immediately evident to those looking after the children and it may be a surprise when they become aware of all the routines that exist.

Communication (and social communication)

Communication is obviously essential to address wants and needs. There are many aspects of these children which are affected by communication difficulties – both verbal and non-verbal. When looking at communication, it is essential that it is examined fairly closely and no assumptions are made. Even children who appear to have very good verbal abilities may have difficulties in understanding what is said to them. In this situation it may be easier for the child to acquiesce rather than disagree with a family member or teacher. It therefore needs to be made clear that everyone working with the child must really understand their true level of communication abilities and the best way of communicating with them. Even with children who have good spoken language, other mechanisms for communication such as email or text may be more useful. For those children who are non-verbal, other communication aids, such as pictures, can help with this problem.

It is important that these children are able to express themselves as clearly as possible as it can be frustrating for them not to be able to do so. This frustration can then soon turn to additional stress, which can present with anxiety or aggression. Most children with ASD struggle to express their emotions in a verbal form and therefore tend to express themselves behaviourally or not at all.

An assessment should be made of the child's understanding in the particular areas which are causing them stress. Many children have poor auditory processing (this translates to a poor ability to listen), or/and slower information processing (the speed in which new information is understood). They obviously struggle with aspects of speech such as metaphors, irony and sarcasm, and all these difficulties place additional stress on the child.

▮ EXAMPLE

A child is being quite disruptive in a classroom environment as they are having trouble understanding the work, despite appearing to have the ability.

Others

'Others' in this context covers outside influences and other people. This is a category used to cover a broad range of potential stressors. There are many outside influences which can cause stress to the child with ASD. We provide some examples of these in Box 10.1.

BOX 10.1 POTENTIAL EXTERNAL STRESSORS

- Interpersonal interaction.
- Bullying/rejection.
- Family relations.
- Life events.

Obviously, for many children with ASD, interactions with the world around them, particularly interpersonal interactions (engaging with people or groups in person), are a source of considerable stress and anxiety. This is often something that children avoid or struggle to do well. It is important to recognise if the child is feeling that they are being coerced into interactions they find uncomfortable or if there are unrealistic expectations of their social abilities. There may be expectations that they will take part in activities which they find uncomfortable, as participation is expected for their age, or they might be encouraged by adults to become more independent when they are not emotionally ready.

Bullying and social rejection, often by the peer group, is a fairly common experience for children with ASD. Although some appear unaware of the bullying, others are much more affected by it. An additional problem is that the child may be finding the experience unpleasant, but due to their difficulties in communication and social awareness they have difficulty sharing this with other people, particularly those who can help. Unfortunately, the stress and anxiety may be expressed in a different environment to the one causing the problem, so bullying at school results in a change in behaviour at home.

Despite having ASD, the child does not live in a vacuum. There are a number of events which can occur in any child's life that are unlinked to ASD. The most common of these events can be bereavements or parental separation, which can obviously have an effect on the child. What is interesting is that the child with ASD may be less affected by these events than would be expected and it may be the ASD-related issues, such as the change in routine at home, which they find distressing. People may then believe that the child is unhappy because their parents live separately, when in reality it is because their routine has been disturbed. It can be difficult to get to the bottom of these problems as the child may be reluctant to talk about them.

EXAMPLE

A boy with ASD, following the bereavement of his father, displayed aggressive behaviour at home and was referred to specialist services. Upon consultation with the child and family it became clear that the behaviour was linked to ongoing bullying at school, not the bereavement, but the boy had felt unable to tell his mother about it.

Physical

While consideration of a child's mental health is important, they are obviously affected significantly by the normal physical needs such as sleep, hunger and thirst. Although the problems of hunger and thirst may only be a transient in this model, they may constitute one or more of the layers of the 'stress cake' we referred to earlier. In isolation they may not be much of a problem, but quickly escalate when added to other stresses. Often these sorts of stresses are present when the child first returns home from school, and this is a time when behaviour can be quite volatile. It may be necessary to think of ways to address this, such as giving the child some space on their own and having a snack and drink available without them having to request it. Another biological issue to consider is that of pain. This becomes a particular problem if the child is unable to express verbally what is happening. Chronic pain is very stressful and it is helpful to recognise this as a stressor in order to be able to treat it effectively. There have also been cases of girls with ASD for whom things are worsened by pre-menstrual symptoms. Unfortunately, it is the difficulty many children with ASD have in recognising social norms which results in their lessened control over these physical factors.

EXAMPLE 1

Anecdotally, a number of children with ASD appear to suffer from persistent headaches. It is often unclear whether this is a reaction to feeling stressed or whether it is an additional cause of further stress. In some cases it can be both.

EXAMPLE 2

A child is noticed to become irritable before lunchtime each day in school, but this has been helped by giving them a mid-morning snack.

Environmental

'Environmental' in this context is used to describe the immediate environmental influences on the child, particularly the sensory environment, and for schools the learning environment. The sensory world for many children with ASD can be confusing or overwhelming. This is covered in more detail in Chapter 12, but it is a necessary consideration in SCOPER. It is important to look at all the sensory modalities which are affecting the child as this is the only way that environmental considerations can be addressed. This can sometimes be difficult – for example, the noisy school dining environment can be hard to change – but alternative options may need to be explored. All the senses (auditory, visual, olfactory, touch, taste, vestibular, proprioception – see Box 10.2) can be involved. However, unfortunately, there may be no local access to a formal sensory assessment.

BOX 10.2 THE SENSES
- *Auditory* – hearing.
- *Visual* – sight.
- *Olfactory* – smell.
- *Touch* – touching.
- *Taste* – tasting.
- *Vestibular* – sense of balance.
- *Proprioception* – sense of body position.

Children can feel over-stimulated or overwhelmed by the sheer volume of sensations that their body and brain are having to process, and this can often raise the stress level quite considerably. Unfortunately, many of these children will only reveal how much difficulty they are having in this area on being asked directly, so it can be a factor which is easily missed.

Most children with ASD attend school and therefore the learning environment within the school becomes an essential aspect of any assessment for stress. Looking at the influences on the child's ability to learn is helpful as it will enable them to access the curriculum. This can involve looking at the immediate learning environment of the classroom or the school as a whole. In the classroom, in addition to looking at the sensory environment, it is useful to consider the child's academic abilities and in particular whether the work is differentiated to accommodate the learning style of a child with ASD. This may involve more visual aids to learning, and making the work less abstract. A child who is struggling to follow the curriculum will obviously be developing layers on their stress cake. Interestingly, some children appear not to have any academic difficulties at first glance, but they have to put in so much effort to stay on top of the work that this continued level of work causes them stress. In addition, it is useful to look at the support provided during unstructured times, such as breaks (recess) and lunchtime, as some children find this time stressful. Many schools can help by providing an area where children may be able to relax during the day.

Rigidity

The world generally requires some adaptability and flexibility of thinking to cope with the often 'grey' areas of daily living. The rigid thinking style of many children with ASD thus causes quite significant stress to them as they struggle to adapt to any changes. It may be necessary to look at the effect of their thinking style on their interactions with others. Some children can become quite distressed due to their need to control situations, thus making them predictable, and the failure to do so can raise their anxiety quite significantly. These difficulties often require the adaptation of those around them, with the child remaining very much the same. This means that the adults will often need to change their way of interacting with the child, rather than expecting the child to change their way of thinking.

Although we have discussed each of these factors separately, there is obviously a significant interaction between them. We provide an example of the interplay between these stressors below in the case study.

Case study

Abby has ASD and has just transferred to her new secondary school. After a few days she is becoming very distressed and aggressive in the classroom. She has taken to running to the toilets and locking herself in a cubicle for a few hours. She will only come out when all the other children have gone home. It is difficult to get Abby to express her feelings, but it becomes apparent that she has obviously found the move to a new school difficult as this has changed her routine both at home and at school. Abby feels she is struggling to understand the lessons and describes the school as noisy, smelly and too crowded. It appears that she has also been affected by her 'best friend' now going to a different school.

Reflective activity

Using SCOPER, what are the influences which are affecting Abby?

SCOPER provides a way of conceptualising the different stresses that may be affecting Abby. First, it is helpful to look at the structures and supports provided to Abby in the school environment which have been used in her transition to her new school. It may be useful to look at what was provided in her previous school and note whether this has been replicated or not in the new one. It is obvious that there has been a significant change in Abby's home and school routine and this has unsettled her. Although we have found out that Abby has found the change difficult, there were some communication problems in getting her to express her feelings and obviously time needs to be taken over this. The 'Others' aspects of SCOPER that needs to be considered as an additional stress, are the loss of her best friend, who was probably providing a significant amount of support for Abby, and her negative reaction to the school environment as it is noisy and smelly. Abby is also struggling to understand her lessons, which could be environmental or as a consequence of her rigidity of thinking.

SCOPER covers the basics but there are obviously other things that affect the presentation of these children, which are covered in other chapters in this book. Once stresses have been identified and there have been some attempts to address them, there may still be some problems. This situation is particularly prevalent in certain mental health disorders. A child with ASD and comorbid ADHD may still need treatments for attention and hyperactivity, or a child with comorbid bipolar disorder may still need help in addition to the stress reduction.

THINK POINT!

Think SCOPER!

WHAT ARE THE PRACTICAL SELF-HELP STRATEGIES THAT CAN WORK TO REDUCE STRESS?

The practical strategies that are useful in reducing stress will vary according to what has been identified as causing the child's stress or anxiety. In reality, working with these children depends upon understanding the effect of ASD on the particular child. With every child having some similarities but also differences, what needs to be put in place will differ. However, there are certain techniques which do tend to work. What we are aiming at is reducing the anxieties which affect these children's ability to function well. Strategies which can be used include the following:

1. Try to be pro-active in your care of these children. It is much better to plan what is going to happen in an ASD-friendly way, rather than react to a 'meltdown'. There is an active need to pre-empt any possible change and educate the child on what is going to happen.

2. Make sure that there is enough structure and routine within their daily timetable to enable them to be clear on what will happen and when. The difficulty with the rigid style of thinking in ASD is that too many routines can lead to further anxiety if they are not strictly adhered to, thereby creating more anxiety. Unfortunately, there is actually a fine-line between enough structure and too much.

3. Ensure that the child understands as much about a new situation as possible in advance. This may help to prevent their negative reaction to the unexpected. This can range from understanding an academic task in the classroom, to why they have to stand in a queue at a theme park. Careful explanation is often required, but the communication issues are often evident when explaining something new so it may be useful to use techniques such as Social Stories™ (Gray 2002a) or other visual aids. Verbal instructions should be kept fairly short and simple, and it is probably best to avoid metaphors, jargon or complicated terms. It is important to remember that the processing of information may be slower and time should be given for a child to listen to instructions and construct an appropriate response. Again, this is true even for those children who are verbally able.

4. Ensure that the sensory environment is modified to reduce its impact on the child. This may not always be possible but if it can be reduced, this may still help. The use of ear defenders for sound, or a 'move and sit cushion' for proprioception may be helpful. It may be necessary to get a sensory assessment from a professional to assist with this.

5. Attention to the child's physical needs, particularly sleep, is essential.

WHEN SHOULD SPECIALIST HELP BE SOUGHT TO REDUCE STRESS, AND WHAT CAN IT ADD?

Towards the end of most of the chapters in this book we have suggested when specialist help might be sought for each problem discussed. Seeking specialist help is actually a personal decision, depending on the situation and the child's needs. It is sometimes difficult to know what to do, and the outside perspective of somebody else can be very useful. When talking about specialists, there are a wide range of professionals who can help with the management of difficulties in children with ASD, and they come from a range of different backgrounds (we discuss these in the final chapter in more detail). If we think about mental health in its broadest sense, then many of these people can help with many of the problems seen. However, at some point it may be necessary to see a more specialised mental health professional.

As discussed in this chapter, there are many ways to reduce the stress and anxiety levels in children with ASD and these may be enough help. It is probably best to see a specialist in mental health when the functioning of the child is being impaired to such a degree that it is significantly affecting their life and that of the family. There is some variation in the specialist knowledge of mental health problems specific to ASD, even in professional groups, so getting the right help may require some persistence.

When is therapy useful?

We discuss this in greater detail in Chapter 14, but in general therapy depends on certain factors. The main factors to determine whether any particular therapy will be effective are the *child's insight* into their problems (i.e. whether they think they have a problem) and their *motivation to change* (i.e. whether they are prepared to do anything about it). These things are obviously important for any verbal therapies but actually they are also fairly essential for non-verbal therapies such as music, art or play therapy.

Family therapy may be useful in helping the family as a whole to cope with the stress/pressure of having a child with ASD. This can be carried out with or without the child with ASD present and may potentially help the family adapt to the effects on their life.

What can be achieved through therapy obviously depends on what is affecting the child. For example, Cognitive Behavioural Therapy

(CBT) can be used in a modified form with these children and can be particularly useful for anxiety problems.

Why use medication?

In some cases of mental health problems, the best option tends to be a pharmacological approach. Many professionals still feel uncomfortable with giving psychiatric medication to children and it remains controversial at times. The problem can also be that a child may require more than one medication or that they may be more sensitive to certain side-effects. It is important that good advice is sought from expert professionals in this area and that they are able to give a clear picture of the risks and benefits of any particular treatment. Many children with ASD struggle with aspects of the psychological therapies and therefore medication may be the only option to treat their comorbid mental health problem.

■ EXAMPLE

The child who experiences comorbid depression may struggle with the therapy associated with this but improves when given antidepressants. This may actually enable them to then access therapy to a greater degree.

It should be recognised that none of these treatments should be provided in isolation. Children tend to benefit from problems being approached from multiple angles – for example, by reducing the stress and using a combination of therapy and medication.

Integrated care

The following case example is useful to show the approach to a mental health problem which requires a reduction in stress levels and integrating this with other therapeutic options. In many cases of mental illness, the integration between specialist therapy and working with the child on a daily basis is essential in improving their mental health, which demonstrates the need for joint working between agencies/ professionals and a partnership approach with parents.

Case study

Darren is a 14-year-old boy with ASD. He has developed an increasing phobia of contamination and germs and is washing his hands over 60 times in a day. This is getting worse and he has developed sores on his hands and gets distressed when he cannot leave lessons to wash. You know that a family member has recently recovered from a serious illness and this has thrown out Darren's routine at home. He is also struggling to understand much of the work he has been given at school, despite being intellectually able.

Reflective activity

What do you do for Darren?

It is evident that Darren has developed comorbid OCD (see Chapter 7 for Obsessive Compulsive Disorder). This may be in response to the anxiety he has experienced about the changes at home or may be due to his distress at not understanding the academic curriculum. Interestingly, it may be both or neither. In such a case, considering SCOPER we would look at the stresses which might be impacting upon Darren to see if some of his worries could be assuaged. Although this might help to some extent, many cases of OCD need referral to a specialist service to assist with the comorbid disorder. A professional would then assess whether Darren was suitable for a therapy which could then try to help with his symptoms. In addition, he might be started on medication to facilitate the therapy or in place of the therapy if it proved to be unsuccessful.

WHY ARE FAMILIES SO IMPORTANT?

This question may feel blindingly obvious, but the effect on the family of having a child with ASD can be considerable. ASD has been described as the disability which causes the most stress on the family (Bromley *et al.* 2004). The persistent nature of ASD, together with the difficulties in interpersonal relationships, can cause significant strain but for many this is often worsened by a lack of resources and services available. In addition to parents, the effect on siblings can be quite profound. The reality of managing or preventing mental health problems is keeping families mentally and physically healthy to deal with the day-to-day challenges. This reinforces the advice in the next chapter (on sleep) as it is hard to work with a tired parent. While therapy can help with some major problems, it is the families that have to reduce the daily stress on the child with ASD.

CHAPTER SUMMARY

In this chapter we have attempted to provide a framework for thinking about problems faced in caring for a child with ASD. We have used the term 'stress' as a way of describing the pressures which affect these children, how this may affect their mental health and the need to reduce this. The concept of the 'stress cake' demonstrates how stress may be cumulative and that different interventions can be used for the different layers of the cake. SCOPER is a useful acronym for remembering most of the factors which can impact on a child's stress levels and also helps to identify possible solutions. Sometimes it is necessary to use therapy, either psychological or pharmacological, but these do need to be incorporated with the other ongoing interventions.

ⓘ IMPORTANT LEARNING POINTS

- Children with ASD are often affected by multiple stressors which can contribute to the development of a comorbid mental health problem or worsen an existing one.
- These stresses can occur in any aspect of a child's life but may not be immediately obvious.
- SCOPER (Structure, Communication, Others, Physical, Environmental, Rigidity) is a useful way of identifying the stresses which affect these children.
- Practical strategies which address many of the key domains should be developed to reduce these stresses.
- Sometimes mental health requires specialist therapy and/or medication to help with these problems, and there might be a need to access specialist services.

FURTHER READING

Baron, M., Groden, J., Groden, G., and Lipsitt, L. (Eds) (2006). *Stress and Coping in Autism.* Oxford: Oxford University Press.

Plummer, D. (2010). *Helping Children to Cope with Change, Stress and Anxiety: A Photocopiable Activities Book.* London: Jessica Kingsley Publishers.

CHAPTER 11

ASD AND SLEEP PROBLEMS

This chapter will cover:

- Why are sleep problems included in this book?
- What is sleep and why is it important?
- What are the sleep problems commonly seen in children with ASD?
- What are the treatments for sleep problems in the child with ASD?
- Chapter summary.
- Further reading.

WHY ARE SLEEP PROBLEMS INCLUDED IN THIS BOOK?

It may seem unusual or out of place to have a chapter on sleep problems in a book on the mental health aspects of children with ASD. However, most parents of these children do describe sleep difficulties with their children, either some or most of the time. Sleep potentially has significant effects on the behaviour and learning of the children and sometimes more significantly the energy and functioning levels of the parents/carers. Chronic tiredness can be truly awful and can make looking after these children much more stressful. The thing that parents have often appreciated most from clinical appointments is the treatment of sleep problems in their children and therefore an improvement in their own sleep.

Managing the challenges of a child with ASD can require extensive patience and fortitude, and the exhaustion that comes from sleep deprivation does not help. Sleep has become an increasingly recognised factor for physical and psychological well-being, and as part of our practice it has a valuable place in the assessment process. In more than one case, the behavioural problems and some mental health problems have improved as tiredness is reduced in both the child and their parents. It is amazingly important for parents to get a break from their children in the evenings.

In this chapter we will discuss the 'science of sleep', as it is important to understand the sleep cycle and what happens during sleep so that any treatments make sense. We will make the links between sleep difficulties and mental health and discuss the sleep problems commonly seen in children with ASD. In this chapter, unfortunately, we are unable to cover all aspects of sleep problems but we will concentrate on the most common. Some guidance and solutions, with suggested further reading, are provided towards the end of the chapter.

WHAT IS SLEEP AND WHY IS IT IMPORTANT?

Sleep is one of the essential functions of life, and severe sleep deprivation is actually very harmful. Sleep is a universal need in all mammals, with different species requiring different amounts. Although sleep is ubiquitous, it is not clear why we need it and, although there are a number of theories, there is no universal agreement. The theories that do exist include the use of sleep for physical recuperation, processing the information from the day or as an energy-saving exercise.

In humans the amount of sleep needed can vary, but generally we sleep during the night and are awake during the day. This cycle is based on something called the 'circadian rhythm'. This is a physiological process in which the body regulates, and adjusts for its needs, over a 24-hour cycle. The level of hormones, for example, are increased and decreased throughout the day and night in relation to what the body expects will be happening. A good example is those hormones associated with eating and sleeping which are more active at different times. It is interesting to note that although we work to a 24-hour cycle, humans actually work to a 25-hour cycle, with daylight correcting this on a daily basis.

When understanding sleep, the most important thing to recognise is that sleep has different stages: there appear to be six parts of the sleep cycle. Sleep is also differentiated by eye movement, divided into 'rapid eye movement' (REM) sleep and 'non-REM' sleep. Non-REM sleep is further divided into four aspects, labelled simply as one, two, three and four. An extra aspect of the sleep cycle is waking episodes, which occur normally during sleep. Most people are unaware that they do this, but anyone who has looked after a child with ASD who has a sleep problem, realises that this happens frequently. Once the sleep cycle is understood, the waking is explainable. This sometimes enables us to find ways of helping with this waking, but it can continue to be challenging. The phases of sleep can be illustrated using a diagram called a 'hypnogram' (see Figure 11.1), which demonstrates a common pattern of sleep in an adult (without ASD).

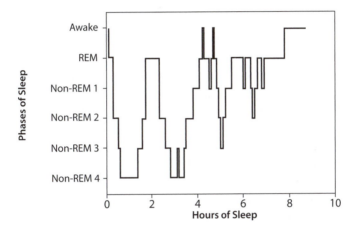

Figure 11.1: Phases of sleep

In normal sleep there is a transition from being awake to deep sleep in the first cycle (non-REM 4), and then there is a move back through the phases to REM sleep before going back into deep sleep. This phase lasts approximately 90 minutes, which is why some children with ASD wake up an hour and a half after being put to bed. Throughout the night the sleep cycles tend not to become so deep, with more REM sleep and episodes of wakefulness.

THINK POINT!

There are different phases of sleep, which include short episodes of wakefulness which can be problematic in children with ASD.

REM sleep is the cycle of sleep which is typically associated with dreams. In an adult this accounts for approximately one quarter of sleeping time and is felt to be an important phase of the cycle. Although the idea is contentious, it is thought that REM sleep is important for learning and memory (for an overview, see Siegel 2001) and that it facilitates the development of longer-term memories. Research has shown its importance as having been deprived of sleep, the brain will spend a greater proportion of time in REM sleep when allowed to sleep again (Beersma *et al.* 1990).

Although it is recognised that REM sleep is associated with dreaming and dreams are probably present in all mammals, it is unclear why we have dreams. Dreams can have a strong emotional content and be extremely vivid and 'weird and wonderful', yet it is unclear what the content represents. There remains significant interest in interpreting dreams, which was popularised by Sigmund Freud, but the world of science remains sceptical. It is obvious that dreams do serve some function, at least biologically, given that REM sleep is essential to well-being, but the issue remains unresolved.

In managing sleep problems, it can be seen from these phases that sleep is not just a single continuous entity but has cycles to it, which can explain some of the difficulties seen in children. Notably, in children the hypnogram would be slightly different, and again this would be different in a child with sleep problems. In babies the sleep cycles are shorter, starting at around 30–50 minutes, and these increase throughout childhood. Like adults, children do have the waking phases of sleep but most learn to self-settle after these episodes. REM sleep accounts for approximately half of all the sleep of a newborn baby, again decreasing as the child gets older. It reaches adult levels during the teenage years. This may explain why children wake more often than the 90-minute cycles typical in adulthood.

Understanding brain rhythms in sleep

For a proper grounding in the basics of sleep, it is important to understand the electrical activity in the brain, as this varies with the different stages of sleep. This is classically measured using an Electroencephalogram (EEG). During an EEG, electrodes are placed on different areas of the scalp to measure the electrical activity under the electrode. See Figure 11.2.

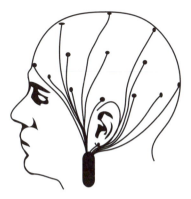

Figure 11.2: Image of an EEG

The different types of brain waves seen are shown in Box 11.1.

BOX 11.1 BRAIN WAVES

- *Alpha* – these are associated with brain states when the person is awake.
- *Beta* – these are associated with alertness and occur during thinking.
- *Gamma* – these are implicated in information processes in the brain.
- *Delta* – these are characteristic of deep, slow-wave sleep.
- *Theta* – these are associated with inhibition in the brain, when trying to suppress something.

During the different phases of sleep there are certain brain waves which are dominant. Delta-wave sleep (also known as 'slow-wave' sleep) is characteristically seen in non-REM stages three and four (the deep sleep phase). It is during this phase of sleep that the individual is in the deepest stage of sleep and when it is most difficult to wake the person.

As part of the circadian rhythm, including sleep, there is the release and inhibition of certain body processes, and the release of brain chemicals and hormones. For clinical purposes the most significant is 'melatonin'. Melatonin is a hormone produced in the pineal gland, which is located in the centre of the brain and is important in the regulation of the sleep/wake cycle. It is released at different times over 24 hours and promotes sleep by helping to cause drowsiness and a lowering of the body temperature – in some ways it acts like a natural sedative. It is released typically when it is dark, and the production of melatonin is inhibited by light hitting the retina (in the eye). This indicates the need to promote darkness when the child is trying to get to sleep and to keep the room as dark as possible for the duration of the night.

Sleep deprivation

Most adults put in a darkened room soon fall asleep. Sleep deprivation is a very common phenomenon, particularly in adults. Put simply, sleep deprivation is not having enough sleep and can either be acute or chronic. Certain jobs are associated with poor sleep (e.g. shift work). People who have had babies who sleep badly will know the feeling of exhaustion and it is also very common to find this in parents of children with ASD. Sleep deprivation has significant physiological and psychological effects and is associated with longer-term health problems (Colten and Altevogt 2006). Some of the more relevant effects are listed in Box 11.2.

As can be seen from Box 11.2, sleep deprivation may affect many aspects of a child's behaviours. It can make children irritable and aggressive, and exacerbate anxiety; or in conditions such as ADHD, it can make the hyperactivity or attention problems worse. It is perhaps unsurprising that sleep deprivation is used as a form of torture.

BOX 11.2 EFFECTS OF SLEEP DEPRIVATION
Physiological
- Aching muscles.
- Tremors.
- Headaches.
- Malaise.
- Feeling cold.
- Bags under eyes.
- Yawning.

Physical (long term)
- Risk of diabetes.
- Increased blood pressure.

- Risk of obesity.
- Effect on growth.

Psychological
- Irritability/increased stress.
- Decreased cognitive functioning (memory and attention).
- Impaired concentration.
- Risk of low mood/depression.
- Risk of elevated mood (mania).
- Hallucinations/risk of psychosis.
- ADHD-like symptoms.

What is the relationship between sleep problems and mental health problems?

There is a fairly strong relationship between sleep problems and mental health problems. Sleep problems are often found as part of mental health problems but also the lack of sleep/sleep deprivation can itself lead to some mental health problems. Box 11.3 shows how sleep is affected by these conditions.

BOX 11.3 MENTAL HEALTH PROBLEMS AND SLEEP
- *Depression* – early morning wakening, difficulty getting to sleep, reduced/increased levels of sleep.
- *Bipolar disorder* – depends on the phase (mania leads to reduced sleep, depressive as above).
- *Anxiety disorder* – initial insomnia, early morning wakening, reduced/increased sleep.
- *Psychosis* – disrupted /disordered sleep.
- *ADHD* – difficulty getting to sleep, repeated wakening in the night and reduced length of sleep.

There is some evidence that sleep deprivation can lead to mental health problems as the lack of sleep induces fatigue and reduces resilience to daily stress. This tends to be seen more in adults than in children, although, as we have noted, there can be significant effects on sleep-deprived children.

WHAT ARE THE SLEEP PROBLEMS COMMONLY SEEN IN CHILDREN WITH ASD?

Sleep problems have been increasingly recognised in children with ASD. Approximately 25 per cent of all children (including those without ASD) will experience a sleep problem during their childhood, with increasing numbers in those with learning disabilities (Sheldon, Ferber and Kryger 2005). Approximately two-thirds of children and young people with ASD have a sleep problem at some point during their childhood, which is significantly higher than other groups of children, and also the sleep problems are more persistent (Wiggs and Stores 2004). This prevalence of sleep problems has been verified by a number of studies using parent–report measures and also sleep measurement studies.

THINK POINT!

Sleep problems are extremely common in children with ASD and can affect any part of the sleep cycle.

It appears that those children with lower levels of functioning are more likely to have significant and severe sleep difficulties. However, for those with higher-functioning ASD there is still a significant number who experience sleep problems. The sleep problems can affect any aspect of the night in a child with ASD. It basically divides into:

- settling problems (difficulties in getting children to go to bed or stay there)
- initial insomnia (insomnia at the start of the night)
- recurrent waking
- reduced duration of sleep
- early morning wakening
- anxiety about going to sleep.

While other things, such as nightmares, night terrors and sleepwalking, may occur, it is unclear if these are more common in those with ASD.

Settling problems

Settling problems are difficulties getting settled into bed and occur in approximately two-thirds of children. This may be related to a lack of tiredness at bedtime, but may be compounded further by the child's perception that the social rules and boundaries of bedtime do not apply to them. Children with ASD may have developed a routine of sleeping downstairs or sleeping on the sofa, rather than in their bed, or they may become unsettled by any attempt at subtle changes in routine. Children with comorbid ADHD in particular have a problem settling, as often their prescribed medication may wear off in the early evening.

Initial insomnia

Initial insomnia is a problem that is very commonly raised, with parents describing that their children sometimes take hours to get to sleep at night. It is not unusual for a parent or child to describe the inability to get to sleep until the early hours of the morning. We also have experience of children who do not sleep at all some nights. In this situation the child can become distressed but more often will repeatedly get up or call out, thus disturbing the rest of the family. It is only when overwhelming tiredness takes over that they are able to sleep. This is often the problem parents struggle with the most as it encroaches on any free time they may have in the evening; indeed, parents have described feeling quite resentful towards the child. Families will try anything to overcome this, including sitting in the child's bedroom, trying to sleep with the child, or using 'blackout' blinds/curtains. It is advisable to stop the child playing on the computer or watching television too close to bedtime as the bright lights can increase initial insomnia. However, preventing a child from playing with their toys or video-games can potentially make the problem worse as, unfortunately, this may lead to arguments with the child, which obviously is not conducive to good sleep!

Waking in the night

As illustrated by Figure 11.1 earlier in the chapter, there are brief periods of wakefulness in a normal sleep cycle. Unfortunately, in children with ASD this can translate into night wakening, which may disturb the rest of the family. There are a number of aspects of ASD which can make this worse. Although the child may recognise that they need to go to bed earlier, once they are awake they feel that the night is finished. This is complicated by longer summer days, when it can become light in the early hours and therefore reinforces the idea that it is daytime. The child may actually not feel tired any longer, and therefore convincing them that they need sleep can be problematic. The ensuing argument can wake them up even more. This problem of getting back to sleep can result in a child being up for many hours or even staying awake for the rest of the night. Even if the child is left to their own devices, their lack of social awareness can result in them engaging in noisy activities, preventing others in the household from sleeping. Many parents who have been woken from their own deep sleep can find this very debilitating.

Reduced duration of sleep

Many families report that their child with ASD appears to need a lot less sleep than the average child. Some children with ASD appear to need extremely short periods of sleep, sometimes only two to three hours all night. This is extremely fatiguing for the parents and they are often desperate for help. Parents try to cope with this by putting the child to bed later so at least they sleep during some of the same period as the parents. Alternatively, some parents end up taking turns to be awake with the child, while the other sleeps. Again, this can be worsened by the longer summer days, with children being sensitive to early morning light.

Early morning wakening

Many parents of children with ASD complain about their children waking very early in the morning, sometimes at two or three o'clock, and then not going back to sleep. Many parents express their dread of the summer months, when the days are longer, as their children wake so early. As can be seen in the previous hypnogram (Figure 11.1), there are periods of waking associated with the natural sleep cycles, but, unfortunately, some children with ASD are fully awake once the earlier cycles are complete. This problem is also associated with those children who have coexisting ADHD.

Anxiety and sleep

Many children with ASD have anxiety symptoms. Anxiety is also associated with sleep difficulties, particularly in the initial phase.

Some children with ASD who become anxious will present with difficulties settling and it is evident that they are worrying, even if they are unable to express themselves. This worrying can have an obsessive quality to it, with the worry constantly present, which can prevent the child sleeping for some time. In addition, as many children with ASD do develop some imagination, the normal fears which affect children, such as fear of the dark or fear of monsters, become an issue. Parents have reported that their children are only able to get to sleep if they lie down with the child, as this calms the child's anxiety. Unfortunately, this is often not a viable long-term solution, particularly as it may become part of the child's routine.

Case study

Adam is a six-year-old boy with ASD. His parents describe themselves as totally exhausted. He can take hours to get to sleep and will repeatedly try to get up for a glass of water or to play with his toys. Once asleep, he wakes about two or three times each night, and his parents have taken to sleeping with him to get him back to sleep. In addition, they describe how he flails around during sleep and how they have bruises from his kicks. Despite not getting to sleep until late, he can be up at a very early hour and this disturbs the whole household. The parents have resorted to sleeping with him in 'shifts' so at least they get some undisturbed sleep. They are now seeking help as things are not getting better and their relationship is under strain.

Reflective activity

What type of sleep problems do you think Adam is displaying? Keep this example in mind when reading through the next section on treatments to see what advice you would give Adam's parents.

Adam is demonstrating the overlap between the different sleep problems and the fact that they commonly coexist. He has problems with initial insomnia, night waking and early morning waking, and his parents are now sleeping with him due to the desperate nature of the situation. This is a scenario which we frequently see in clinical practice, and although we have not mentioned it earlier, like Adam, these children are often restless in their beds (e.g. flailing around). Treating Adam's sleep problems is challenging, but we make some suggestions on what to do in the remainder of the chapter.

WHAT ARE THE TREATMENTS FOR SLEEP PROBLEMS IN THE CHILD WITH ASD?

Before considering the approaches to treating a child with ASD, it is important to make a thorough assessment of their sleep problems. This will involve looking at all aspects of the child's sleep during the night, the behaviours around sleep and any factors which influence the ability to sleep. The basics of the assessment will be looking at 'sleep hygiene', which refers to the routine activities performed to promote good sleep. For example, going to sleep at a regular time and not playing computer games in bed. We outline some of the features of assessment in Box 11.4.

BOX 11.4 ASSESSMENT OF SLEEP PROBLEMS

1. *History taking* – this involves the clinical professional asking the parents about the child's sleep problems.

   a) Establish how long there has been a problem with sleep – Is it a new problem or longstanding? How did they sleep as a baby/toddler/young child? Have they ever established any sleep routine?

   b) Establish what the routine is before going to sleep – For example, is there a calm period for the child before bedtime? Is there a similar routine each night at bedtime such as bath time? Does the child know when bedtime is? Are they playing computer games (or other stimulant activities) very close to bedtime?

   c) Bedtime – Is this the same each night? Is there a developed routine at this time to help keep the child calm? Is the bedroom suitable for sleep – for example, is it dark, quiet and comfortable?

   d) During the night – How long is it taking the child to get to sleep? When does the child tend to wake? What do they do when they wake? What do the parents do when the child wakes? What time does the child get up in the morning?

2. *Tried techniques* – What techniques/treatments have the parents implemented previously?

3. *Information gathering* – This can be achieved using a diary of the sleep cycles of the child. Information can be collected from the school related to tiredness and sleep during school hours.

4. *Observation* – If resources are available, direct observation can be achieved in the child's home or via video-recording. Alternatively, the child can be brought to a specialist sleep clinic.

Behavioural management

Before thinking about the use of medication to help a child sleep, it is essential to look at how sleep can be promoted by changing the behaviour of the child and the household. This behavioural management can often solve or at least improve some of the problems. In managing sleep problems, it is essential to identify the difficulties which are occurring in the different parts of sleep (see Box 11.4 above) as this will obviously dictate what the treatment needs to be. It is always essential to remember that these children have ASD and it is necessary to work with their thinking styles and capabilities. In many instances it is useful to work with their need for routines and structure as this can aid the development of good 'sleep hygiene'. We provide a framework of behavioural management in Box 11.5, but the suggestions made in this book are not exhaustive.

BOX 11.5 HOW TO PROMOTE SLEEP IN A CHILD WITH ASD
Putting the child to bed

- Develop a regular evening routine.
- Keep the routine calm towards bedtime.
- Avoid (if possible) consoles/computer games (including all forms of bright screen) at least one hour before bedtime.
- Establish roughly the same time for bedtime each night.
- Establish a routine at bedtime itself – for example, brushing teeth, listening to stories, reading in bed and so forth.
- Get the child to sleep in their own bed/bedroom (if possible).
- Keep the environment low stimulus – for example, a darkened, quiet room.
- Encourage the child to stay in bed and try to go to sleep – use rewards where appropriate.
- Avoid watching television or the use of mobile/cell phones in bed.

On waking

- Encourage the child to stay in bed (this may help them learn to return to sleep after natural waking cycles).
- Maintain a low-stimulus environment when they wake – for example, avoid putting the lights on, avoid getting upset, distressed or shouting at the child, avoid putting on the television.
- If possible, avoid getting into bed with the child as this may soon become a routine.

> **Early morning wakening**
> - Put up 'blackout' curtains or blinds on the window to prevent sunlight filtering through.
> - If the child wakes, try to encourage them to occupy themself quietly without disturbing the household.

As the more vigilant among you may have noticed, we are not fans of computers, consoles or bright screens (including smart phones) around bedtime. Children with ASD appear particularly sensitive to the stimulant effect of the bright lights but also to the intensity of many computer games. This does appear to put many of these children in an overly-stimulated state, and it can then take considerable time to settle them. This instruction can obviously cause some conflict, particularly with teenagers who may be extremely reluctant to come off their screens. However, it is something that is worth insisting upon as this can make a big difference. Although we do understand that many children with ASD do need the escape of the computer/consoles and that it is embedded in many contemporary cultures, the reality is that sleep is very important.

THINK POINT!

Behavioural strategies should be the first line of management in helping with any sleep problem.

Medication

Sometimes when the behavioural techniques are insufficient at enhancing sleep, there is a need for a pharmacological treatment. This is somewhat contentious (as with many other medications for children) but can improve sleep considerably. Most of the sleep medications available (called 'hypnotics') are designed to treat a change in sleep (i.e. sleep was previously normal but has changed in some way). The difference in children with ASD is that the sleep problem tends to be a persistent, long-term developmental issue which started at a very young age. Therefore, typically, the hypnotics are used for short-term improvements in sleep and are not really for longer-term problems. Most of them are also not recommended for use in children and can have unwanted side-effects. Some of the older hypnotics can be addictive.

The options which are used in children typically include the melatonin and sedative antihistamines. Melatonin, as we noted earlier in the chapter, is a hormone which is released when it is dark and is a natural sedative in the brain. The sensitivity of the melatonin system to light may be the mechanism which causes the problems of early wakening in the summer months, together with normal wakening in the natural sleep cycle. As we mentioned earlier, this indicates a need to promote darkness in the room where the child is trying to get to sleep and to keep the room as dark as possible for the duration of sleep hours. In some children with ASD the mechanism which causes melatonin to induce sleep appears 'faulty', but it is presently unclear what the exact mechanism is for this problem. The 'shut down' cycle simply appears not to work and therefore the use of medication can promote sleep in the child.

It is becoming increasingly common to treat the sleep problems in children with ASD with additional melatonin supplements. These can come as short-acting or long-acting preparations, and may be useful to treat the different elements of the sleep problems. Short-acting treatments may be better for initial sleep problems with longer-acting preparations helping with waking, although these can also be effective in initial insomnia. There is little data on the long-term use of melatonin and what dosage to provide in children and therefore some caution should be exercised in its usage. However, it can be very effective when used in conjunction with good sleep hygiene. It is important to recognise that although melatonin can make some children drowsy before going to bed, it tends to work by promoting sleep when the child is actually trying to go to sleep. In that way it is not a hypnotic like some of the sleep-inducing medications for adults. There are few side-effects reported with this treatment (the main one is daytime sleepiness), but care should be taken when giving children any type of medication.

In some cases of sleep problems which are not amenable to behavioural management or melatonin, the use of sedative antihistamines may be useful. These are pharmacological preparations which can also be used as antihistamines but have the side-effect of being quite sedating. They tend to be used in the short-term, but some families find that they need these medications for a longer period of time and that the benefits of sleep outweigh other considerations. Again there is little data on the long-term usage of these treatments.

THINK POINT!

The use of medication such as melatonin can be useful but is best used in conjunction with good sleep hygiene.

Does sleep treatment help ASD children's mental health?

As can be seen, children with ASD often have sleep problems which can impact on themselves and on the family. Other chapters in this book talk about the comorbid mental health problems which can develop in children with ASD. As part of a treatment package we feel it is important to look at the sleep characteristics in these children in addition to considerations of other treatment options. Tired children and tired parents struggle with any other behavioural changes or therapy and therefore it puts them in a better frame of mind if they have had more sleep.

There are thus potential benefits for many aspects of the mental health of children with ASD when their sleep is improved. Anecdotally, children with comorbid ADHD can have improved attention and concentration from just helping their sleep, while other children with anxiety or low mood also may report feeling better. We would argue, therefore, that sleep remains an under-recognised problem in this area and that more needs to be done to better understand these issues and to help families cope.

Case study

Rachael is a ten-year-old girl with ASD who has become very withdrawn. She appears to be worrying about school all the time and this is most evident when going to bed. Although she has always had difficulty getting to sleep, this has become worse and she is not getting to sleep until the early hours of the morning. She has a tendency to sit in her bed playing with her mobile phone because she cannot get to sleep. During the day she looks tired and her parents have noticed that as her sleep has deteriorated, her anxiety has worsened. Rachael is now sometimes falling asleep during the day and this is leading to less sleep at night. Her parents are becoming exhausted themselves and seek some advice.

Reflective activity

What could be done to help Rachael and her family?

It should be recognised that Rachael already had some sleep difficulties before this episode and that her anxiety has made them worse. Obviously, a fuller assessment of her sleep is necessary and also an assessment of her anxiety as this may be the underlying problem. In this situation there is a need to manage her anxiety and to reinstate a better sleep routine. The daytime sleeping has to be reduced and the use of the mobile phone also requires some attention. These are both reducing her ability to sleep. Ideally, this situation could be managed by these simple behavioural strategies, but the history of longer-term problems may be an indication that she may require some sleep medication.

CHAPTER SUMMARY

In this chapter we have considered the relevance of sleep in relation to the comorbid mental health problems that some children with ASD encounter. As most children with ASD have sleep difficulties, this has the potential to impact heavily on the family and cause disruption and distress. This chapter has provided a concise overview of how normal sleep patterns operate and has differentiated adult and child cycles to provide some context for the sleep routines of children with ASD. It then moved on to descriptions of the more common sleep problems experienced by children with ASD, with discussions around early morning wakening, anxiety, initial insomnia and settling problems. We concluded the chapter by discussing some of the main treatment options available to families and considering their usefulness.

ⓘ IMPORTANT LEARNING POINTS

- Sleep is an essential function for children and adults and is required for healthy living.
- There are different phases of sleep, which cycle throughout the night, intermixed with short periods of waking.
- Sleep deprivation has both psychological and physical effects and can be very debilitating.
- Sleep problems are common in children with ASD, affecting all aspects of the sleep cycle.
- The treatments for sleep problems in children with ASD are predominantly behavioural, although some medications may be used.

FURTHER READING

Aitken, K. (2012). *Sleep Difficulties and Autistic Spectrum Disorders: A Guide for Parents and Professionals.* London: Jessica Kingsley Publishers.

Colten, H. and Altevogt, B. (2006). *Sleep Disorders and Sleep Deprivation: An Unmet Public Health Problem.* Washington, DC: The National Academic Press.

CHAPTER 12

SENSORY PROCESSING PROBLEMS AND EXECUTIVE FUNCTIONING DIFFICULTIES

This chapter will cover:

- Introduction.
- What are the sensory processing issues in ASD?
- Why does this matter to mental health?
- How are sensory problems treated?
- Why does this chapter include executive functioning?
- Chapter summary.
- Further reading.

INTRODUCTION

As with the chapter on sleep, it may seem strange to a have a chapter on sensory problems in children with ASD in a book primarily focused on comorbid mental health problems. We have included this chapter because we want to describe briefly how sensory problems affect the mental health of children, and also to look at some of the other issues, such as difficulties in organisation skills, which appear to become relevant to children's mental health at different points during childhood. There are some fairly well-known comprehensive texts (we list two of these at the end of the chapter) on sensory problems, which provide a more complete understanding of these difficulties, and we encourage those interested in this area to read these books. What we provide in this chapter is a simplified overview in relation to mental health.

Sensory processing problems are increasingly recognised as being significant factors for many children with ASD, and commonly in clinical practice children describe the stress they feel under from managing the sensory information in the world around them. Sensory problems have the potential to affect any child on the spectrum, whether high- or low-functioning. While other aspects of ASD obviously cause children significant distress, sensory problems are the one area that children themselves, often identify as problematic. We see children who describe their classroom as 'too noisy', and say they have to cover their ears. These problems can be seen at all ages but typically the younger children appear more susceptible to the sensory environment, with older children having problems in other areas.

Our earlier model of the increasing layers of stress (the 'stress' cake – see Figure 10.1) is useful in considering how sensory problems impact on the child and while we may have mentioned these difficulties in earlier chapters, it is now useful to go into them in a little more depth. In this chapter, in addition to sensory problems, other difficulties which impact on a child's mental health will be discussed. This includes problems such as motor difficulties and executive functioning. We aim to describe these problems but also to provide suggestions for strategies to help.

WHAT ARE THE SENSORY PROCESSING ISSUES IN ASD?

We live in a sensory environment and are constantly bombarded by multiple sensations: sights, sounds, smells, tastes and touch. All the sensations are listed in Box 10.2 in Chapter 10, and you may want to refer to this now to remind yourself of them. The brain has to constantly process these sensations into a coherent form and also to filter the significant from the insignificant. The brain has to interpret these senses and does so using previous experience as a point of reference. (For example, the smell of a flower is recognised as a rose because of prior experiences of that particular smell.) This process develops throughout life but obviously exists in an accelerated form in childhood as the child is exposed to new experiences. Difficulty in processing sensory information is commonly seen in children with ASD, but is also reported in other neuro-developmental and neurological conditions; it is even seen in people who are very tired. For example, when you are tired, the noise of children seems louder and more intrusive and the ability to block out this noise is reduced. This ongoing development in the ability to interpret the sensory environment and the changes throughout childhood may explain why younger children with ASD have more profound problems with sensory processing, which tend to improve as the child gets older.

The ability to receive and modify these sensory problems is not a consistent feature in all individuals with ASD – clinically, it appears to occur more frequently in those children with comorbid conditions such as ADHD. In addition to this, the presentation of sensory problems differs significantly from child to child, with children being over-sensitive (hyper-sensitive) and under-sensitive (hypo-sensitive) to different sensations. Adding to the complexity is that children can be over- or under-sensitive to different things within the same sensation.

EXAMPLE 1
A child refuses to work with a teacher at school because of the smell of her perfume, and the hyper-sensitivity to this smell leads to aggression.

EXAMPLE 2
A child who goes out in the snow in just their T-shirt and jeans, claiming that they are not cold, may be hypo-sensitive to the sensation of temperature.

EXAMPLE 3
A child plays their own music very loudly at home but becomes agitated in shops when loud music is being played – are they hyper- or hypo-sensitive?

The boundary between senses being considered hyper- or hypo-sensitive can sometimes feel a bit artificial. Everybody experiences the sensory environment in a slightly different way, depending on previous experiences, personalities and state of mind (i.e. mood). It is difficult to describe to others exactly how we perceive a particular sensation. (Is my red the same as your red?) Regarding children with ASD, who may be experiencing the world in a very different way, it becomes clinically important if sensitivity to their environment is causing them distress, discomfort or affecting their ability to function (e.g. noise sensitivity which prevents the child from attending school).

How does the brain process information?

With the huge amount of sensory information it receives every second, the brain adopts the strategy of filtering out any information not considered relevant at that point in time. It is important to recognise that this is a subconscious process which is done effortlessly by most people. Evidence from cognitive psychology and related disciplines demonstrates that people selectively attend to things in their surrounding environment which they find interesting or relevant to them. The classic example of this is that in a busy environment, such as a crowded restaurant, you tend to hear your own name if it is spoken across the room, even if it is spoken at the same level as the background noise. Additionally, to cope with the sensory environment, the brain will tend to make interpretations by filling in details based upon past experience. This is the basis for many optical illusions. Consider Figure 12.1

Figure 12.1: What do you see?

Most of you will look at Figure 12.1 and see a face, when in reality it is simply a constellation of shapes, this is a phenomenon known as pareidolia. This is because your brain is filling in the lines around it to close the gaps. You are drawing upon your familiarity with faces to understand that there are two eyes, a nose and a mouth. A good way to understand this is how we see shapes in clouds and actively try to find forms that we recognise in them.

THINK POINT!

We live in a highly stimulating sensory environment, which can be difficult for children with ASD to cope with.

What are the sensory processing problems for the child with ASD?

Children with ASD may struggle to filter out all this background information. Conversely, they may be under-sensitive to all the information reaching them. It is the former group which tend to be recognised, as this overload of sensory information can have significant effects on behaviour or be responsible for emotional difficulties such as anxiety. This overload may be recognised by those around the child or may go unrecognised due to the different presentations. Some children will have sudden outbursts of aggression or tantrums, while others will become progressively more withdrawn or say they are tired.

Those who are under-sensitive to sensory information can be more difficult to identify and tend to be less commonly recognised. The problem tends to be under-sensitivity to certain sensory inputs, which we will discuss later in this chapter. These children can be difficult to motivate or to involve in activities such as school lessons. There is no easy way to test for these sensitivities, and it is often identified through the reported history of the family or child, or by direct observations. We provide some examples in Box 12.1 to illustrate this.

BOX 12.1 EXAMPLES OF SENSITIVITY

- *Children who are very over- or under-sensitive to smell.* Some children find the smell of certain foods revolting and this may be implicated in why some children are such picky eaters. Other children are under-sensitive and therefore seek out smells (e.g. they sniff people on meeting them).
- *Children who are very over- or under-sensitive to taste.* Those children with hyper-sensitivity find certain tastes unpleasant or strong and may gag when given some foods. This sensitivity problem may result in a limited diet. Those who are under-sensitive to taste may attempt to lick or taste *anything*, including other people, or may tend to seek out strong-tasting foods, including spicy or salty food.
- *Children who are very over- or under-sensitive to sound.* Those with hyper-sensitivity to sounds tend to be frightened by sudden noises such as fireworks, telephones and fire/smoke alarms. These children can also be bothered by less obvious noises such as a ticking clock, which goes unnoticed by most people. They will often cover their ears to block out the noise. Children who are under-sensitive may seek out noise or create the sounds themselves.
- *Children who are very over- or under-sensitive to touch.* Classically, those with over-sensitivity do not like to be touched (e.g. they may not like having their hair cut or wearing certain fabrics). Those who are under-sensitive may actually enjoy the sensation of tight clothes and being hugged. There appears to be some difference between light touch and the feeling of deep pressure, such as hugs, with the same child avoiding light touch but being relaxed by tight hugs. The appreciation of temperature is often distorted in these children, so they choose inappropriate clothing for the weather, but the hypo-sensitive children may appear to be unaware of wounds or burns.
- *Children who are very over- or under-sensitive to visual stimuli.* Some children may be hypo- or hyper-sensitive to light levels or may be

affected by too many things within their visual field. Classically, those with over-sensitivity will struggle with brightly coloured, visually stimulating classrooms, especially ones with hanging decorations. Also, they appear to be aware of the flicker in fluorescent tube lighting.

- *Children who have vestibular difficulties (balance).* Children with hyper-sensitivity in this area may have difficulties with spinning, jumping or coping with unstable surfaces. In our experience they also tend to have motion sickness (e.g. car journeys). Those who are hypo-sensitive, on the other hand, enjoy the sensations of spinning or swinging and seek out these movements through equipment and rides in parks and theme parks. This may be a reason why some children spend time rocking or spinning in circles.

- *Children who have proprioception difficulties (knowing where parts of the body are without the use of the other senses).* The most commonly recognised form is hypo-sensitivity, where children are unaware of the position of their limbs/body. This can present in the child needing to move constantly to 'remind' themself where their body is, often using touch to confirm. This may be interpreted as fidgeting and misdiagnosed as a component of ADHD. Children may also bump into objects or lean on furniture to stimulate a tactile sensation. In addition, those who are hypo- or hyper-sensitive to proprioception may have difficulty regulating the sensation of hunger, resulting in over- or under-eating.

From these examples it can be seen that a child's behaviour is affected by their sensitivities. Behaviours can be divided into sensory-seeking or sensory-avoiding. Sensory-seeking behaviours are often seen in children who have hypo-sensitivity to a particular sense and are seeking out the sensations to regulate themselves. An example of this is the child who uses a spinning chair to compensate for vestibular (balance) hypo-sensitivity. Sensory-avoiding children avoid sensations which they find unpleasant or uncomfortable, and their behaviours will reflect this. Many children with ASD dislike ticking clocks in clinic rooms.

THINK POINT!

When looking at sensory problems in children with ASD, consider all the senses.

WHY DOES THIS MATTER TO MENTAL HEALTH?

As is apparent from discussions in earlier chapters, positive mental health is dependent upon a number of factors which affect a child at any one time. The sensory environment in which the child exists is obviously a very significant factor on a daily basis and can be a constant challenge. This may form one of the layers of the 'stress cake' or may be the factor that ignites the candles (see Figure 10.1). Coping with the continued difficulty in regulating the senses can cause children significant anxiety, which may be a factor that leads to other mental health problems. We are often involved with children who are very anxious within the school setting but much calmer at home. Although being in the school does challenge the child with ASD in many different ways, such as social expectations or academic pressures, the impact of the sensory environment can often be a significant stressor. The sensations at school can be very strong, particularly in the areas of sound, smell and vision. You may like to reflect on your own school days, particularly going into the school cafeteria/dining hall. It is not unusual for children to seek quiet, low-stimuli environments to 'calm down', which can be interpreted as sensory avoidance – they need to down-regulate the sensory overload they may be experiencing.

Unfortunately, the evidence supporting the view that sensory problems impact on mental health is fairly limited and tends to be anecdotal. However, it does seem self-evident that sensory problems are so significant to many children with ASD that it must impact upon their mental health. Unfortunately, with so many aspects of ASD affecting how a child presents, it is difficult in clinical research to isolate a single factor, such as sensory problems, as causing a comorbid mental health problem. It is equally difficult to 'prove' that any work to reduce the sensory problems, such as providing a 'sensory diet' (Wilbarger 1995), is responsible for an improvement in the mental health condition. (A sensory diet is a programme providing children with activities to regulate the over- or under-sensitivity, such as spinning activities for children with vestibular problems). This is a problem which besets those who are looking at the use of sensory integration therapy as a treatment for children with ASD.

HOW ARE SENSORY PROBLEMS TREATED?

The availability of assessments for sensory problems is quite variable. Much of the work in this area has been developed by occupational therapists, who still remain instrumental in assessing children for these problems and developing interventions. However, many other professionals have received training in sensory problems so may be able to provide guidance. The key to any difficulty is an assessment of the problem, which tends to consist of a combination of history taking, direct observation and engaging children in sensory-stimulating activities. Unfortunately, there is no definitive test currently available for the problems.

Intervention tends to be based on the individual's needs and on the available resources. Much of the work consists of consultations with families and organisations, such as schools and colleges, on how to modify the sensory environment to meet the child's needs. It may also involve training professionals, such as teachers or learning support assistants, in techniques to regulate the child's sensory needs – either to down-regulate heightened senses or to up-regulate those which are under-active.

Case study

Tim is a nine-year-old boy with ASD and is in mainstream education. It is becoming increasingly difficult to get him to go to school and when he is there it is difficult to get him to do any work as he says he is tired. It is also obvious that at any opportunity Tim is keen to be out of the classroom. When his parents ask for help with Tim, it becomes obvious that the classroom is very 'busy' (i.e. very visually stimulating). There are lots of bright pictures on the walls and decorations hanging from the ceiling. From talking to the teacher it transpires that this reluctance to go to school has coincided with preparations for the Christmas season in which the children wanted to decorate the classroom in a festive way.

Reflective activity

Is there a relationship between the decorations and Tim's behaviour?
What do you think you would do to help Tim in the classroom?

Tim is obviously having difficulty coping with the Christmas season and this could be for a number of reasons. Although he may be stressed by the changes in routine, it appears that he does not want to be in a classroom which has become very visually stimulating. As a consequence, he is avoiding the classroom. The tiredness may be a reflection of him feeling overwhelmed and his need to withdraw from the environment. This is a difficult situation. Ideally, we would suggest that the school remove as many 'dangly' things as possible, but this might upset the other children. Tim might be able to cope if he had a low-stimulus area in the classroom or if he had set periods out of the classroom each day.

What techniques could be tried for sensory problems?

We are aware that not everyone can get a formal sensory assessment, but many families and professionals are aware of the common sensory difficulties. It is often evident in clinical practice that families have adapted their home-life to accommodate many of these problems. For example, children who have sensitivities to smells or tastes are not given the foods which upset them (unfortunately, the family tends not to be able to have them either). A problem can arise if two children in the family have opposite sensory problems (i.e. one likes spicy, strong-smelling food while the other prefers food to be as bland as possible). The mere presence of the strong-smelling food can cause distress to the other child, while the sensory-seeking child may refuse to eat bland food.

There are some techniques which can help children with their sensory problems and we provide suggestions in Box 12.2.

BOX 12.2 SUGGESTED TECHNIQUES TO HELP CHILDREN WITH SENSORY PROBLEMS

- First, it is important to identify which sensory issue the child is experiencing.
- Modifications to the environment to reduce or increase the stimuli might help with the behaviours.
- Suggested modifications could include the following techniques:
  - Making a learning space for the child which is less visually stimulating (e.g. creating a pale-coloured, uncluttered environment).
  - Removing irritating stimuli such as fluorescent lighting or ticking clocks for children who have auditory over-sensitivity.
  - Allowing the child to wear headphones/earplugs to reduce noise.
  - Pre-warning children of any known sudden noises (such as testing the fire alarm, or school bells).

> ○ Being aware of the effect of certain smells, such as perfumes, disinfectants or the smell of school dining halls. The child may need to eat elsewhere and certain smells should be avoided where possible.
>
> ○ Awareness of temperature regulation in the child to avoid over-heating or becoming cold. A child may need to be told, using a thermometer for visual representation, that they need to put warmer clothes on or take them off.
>
> • The list is endless and you may need to use your imagination. The adaptation needs to be applied to the individual child as children are all so different. Although earplugs can be suggested to help with noise, children may find the sensation of wearing them uncomfortable.

WHY DOES THIS CHAPTER INCLUDE EXECUTIVE FUNCTIONING?

We briefly described 'executive functioning' in Chapter 1. Executive functioning is a term used to describe the way in which certain psychological functions affect the pattern of thinking. An example of executive functioning is the ability to plan or make decisions. This is obviously an important process in all aspects of life, but, due to the increasing independence of the child, it becomes more important as the child grows older and matures. It may seem strange to include this section in a book on mental health, but in clinical practice these abilities do appear to become more of an issue as the child gets older, and we will often see issues relating to these abilities causing problems for the child and their families. Most commonly, this comes to light with homework, which requires such abilities as self-organisation, motivation, planning and reasoning. The child may suffer some distress and stress as they struggle with these tasks, and they often take out their frustrations on family members. These factors do tend to be more of an issue in those children who are higher functioning as there is an expectation that they will work or live more independently. However, these factors impact on any child with ASD.

Exasperated parents often complain that, although they understand the basics of ASD, it is the inability of their child to become independent which is the most frustrating aspect of the condition. Parents have described situations where their child struggles so badly to motivate themself and organise their time that they will follow their parents around the house and even into the toilet. It is also one of the possible reasons why these children tend to spend so much time in front of various screens such as televisions, computers and consoles. These machines and games inherently provide structure and motivation for the child. Games in particular have certain qualities which seem to maintain attention, such as colour, instructions and feedback on progressively more complex play. It is notoriously easy to allow a child to spend inordinate amounts of time with this technology, particularly when many of their peers are also spending time this way; finding the alternatives can often be challenging for family life. Unfortunately, there is some concern that children who spend so much time on these activities may not have the opportunities for social learning within the family setting, which they so obviously need. Some expert advise that it is better to limit children's time with technological screens to about two hours per day. This can be exceptionally challenging for some households, who will struggle to find alternative activities that the child will engage in. (It is not unusual for families to describe a child being on the computer from the time they get in from school up to bedtime.)

What are the executive functions?

There are several executive functions, which are introduced in Box 12.3.

BOX 12.3 THE EXECUTIVE FUNCTIONS AND THEIR IMPORTANCE

- *Planning* – the ability to coordinate a plan of action.
- *Working memory* – holds information for a limited period of time for immediate processing.
- *Attention* – the cognitive process of selectively attending to particular aspects of the environment while ignoring other things.
- *Problem solving* – the use of particular methods to find particular solutions to problems.
- *Verbal reasoning* – understanding and reasoning using words.
- *Inhibition* – restraining a behavioural desire or impulse.
- *Mental flexibility* – the ability to handle different situations in different ways.
- *Multi-tasking* – this is the ability of an individual to engage in more than one task at a time.
- *Initiation* – starting tasks.
- *Monitoring of actions* – this is the skill to monitor one's own behaviours and modify to suit expectations or environmental factors.

How does executive functioning affect mental health?

While we have already referred previously to the issues with homework, for higher-functioning children with ASD this can be a particular area of stress and potential conflict. Although there are international variations, and there are new specifications for UK GCSE and A-Levels, there is typically a requirement for school-aged children to undertake some homework. Homework potentially requires a multitude of skills, to complete these tasks. Projects may require the ability to plan, multi-task, problem solve, initiate ideas and keep attention, among other things. This is hard enough for most children, but for those who have difficulties in these areas it can be overwhelming. Some schools manage the situation by giving children with ASD minimal homework, but this may result in their eventual academic attainment not matching their intellectual abilities. In addition to the issues around homework, executive functioning is required on a daily basis, from dressing oneself, to washing, to successfully preparing a meal. It is fairly common to work with a very intellectually able child who cannot successfully use the microwave or know how to turn down the temperature on the shower.

It is therefore easy to see how the child with ASD, who is trying to cope with the complex social environment and then has to increasingly manage parts of their lives, becomes stressed by these demands. As they get older the demands can get greater, which they find more difficult, and when combined with the changes associated with adolescence (e.g. the hormonal and bodily changes), this can lead to considerable impact on their mental health.

THINK POINT!

When looking at the factors which affect a child with ASD, do not forget executive functions.

There have been no consistent research studies which illustrate the effects of executive functioning skills on mental health, but in practice, when seeing families over many years, these issues appear to become more and more prevalent. It is sometimes difficult to know if the child is struggling more in this area or if the family has become less tolerant of their difficulties, with the expectation that they will be able to become more independent. It may be that some of these children develop these skills later in life – in their twenties and thirties – thus enhancing their ability to live alone. Conversely, and this is a good example of how ASD can present in so many ways, some of these children have extremely good executive functions. They can be very organised and good at problem solving, and are able to work through a number of tasks. However, there do still appear to be difficulties with mental flexibility as would be expected.

Case study

Alex is a 15-year-old boy who comes to clinic due to increasing anxiety. Things have been fairly settled at school over the last few years and academically he is in the top stream. Unfortunately, he became stressed at school while doing a project in history in which he had to work with others and each individual was given specific tasks to complete. Alex struggled to coordinate his activities with other members of the group and fell behind. He then felt that the group blamed him for a low grade, which made him distressed. He admitted to having difficulties planning his part of the project and anticipating what would be required at different stages. While he tends not to have any difficulties with attention and basic problem solving, he struggled when the group tried to take the project in a different direction.

Reflective activity

It is obvious that Alex has some difficulties in organisation. What can you do to help Alex?

To answer this question we provide you with some possible strategies below, while acknowledging that this area is not straightforward.

How do we help with executive functioning problems?

This requires some inventiveness on the part of those helping the child, and there has to be an individualised approach. We would emphasise that this area may require a lot of patience as it can be frustrating, and for some parents, very difficult to understand. Parents will sometimes accept the child's social and communication difficulties more easily than their executive functioning problems. There are, however, some strategies that may be beneficial:

- The use of technology can be helpful. Most teenagers have a mobile phone with a number of functions, including a diary and a 'to-do list'. This will remind them of some of the tasks they need to complete and will often give deadlines.

This interactive modality is one that is familiar to many teenagers and has various functions, such as alarms, that assist.

- Other visual aids may be useful to break any activity down into manageable and meaningful chunks. This may utilise the strength some children with ASD have with visual processing.

- Dividing any task into smaller, more manageable components may make the overall task feel less overwhelming. Children with these problems struggle to multi-task and therefore single, small tasks can be focused on more easily.

- Timetabling the activity may take advantage of the child's need for routine and predictability.

Obtaining support in any setting to help facilitate the above tasks is obviously essential in achieving a better outcome.

CHAPTER SUMMARY

The difficulties in social and communication skills for children with ASD are significant, but there are other areas which impact upon them, including sensory processing difficulties and executive functioning problems. We live in a sensory environment and children with ASD can struggle with modifying how they process these sensations. This can affect any of their senses and can cause quite considerable stress and distress. This has the potential to affect their mental health and needs to be considered when working with them. Although there is no set treatment in managing these problems, sensible measures can be adopted to reduce the impact. Many children with ASD, particularly those who are high functioning, are affected to a considerable degree by limitations in their executive functioning. These skills are required to live and work independently and can become more clinically significant during the teenage years. This is yet another factor increasing the stress in these children which needs to be addressed when looking at mental health. Again, there are no clear treatments for this and some imagination will be required.

① IMPORTANT LEARNING POINTS

- Children with ASD live in a highly stimulating sensory environment.
- Sensory processing difficulties are a common feature in children with ASD.

- Sensory processing problems can occur in all the different senses, and children can be over- or under-sensitive to these sensations.
- Sensory processing difficulties can be an additional stress, potentially affecting mental health.
- Sensory processing problems have to be managed by simple practical measures.
- Executive functioning difficulties are commonly seen in children with ASD. Executive functioning skills are essential for independent living.
- Problems in this area can lead to increased stress.

FURTHER READING

Bogdashina, O. (2003). *Sensory Perceptual Issues in Autism and Asperger Syndrome: Different Sensory Experiences – Different Perceptual Worlds.* London: Jessica Kingsley Publishers.

Kranowitz, C. (2005). *The Out-of-Sync-Child: Recognizing and Coping with Sensory Processing Disorder.* New York: Skylight Press.

CHAPTER 13

ASD AND SELF-HARM

This chapter will cover:

- Introduction.
- What do we mean by 'self-harm' and what is the language used to describe it?
- How common is self-harm and why do children harm themselves?
- What factors influence self-harm?
- How common is self-harm in children with ASD?
- How does self-harm present in children with ASD?
- How do we assess and treat self-harm/suicide ideation in the child with ASD?
- When should you seek help?
- Chapter summary.
- Further reading.

INTRODUCTION

Self-harm is a rather emotive subject but unfortunately it is fairly common in young people. In child and adolescent mental health services self-harm can make up a significant proportion of the referrals. It is an area which can cause considerable distress and worry to individuals, families and organisations such as schools. One of the problems that we find in clinical practice is that the term 'self-harm' is often used very freely and can mean different things to different people. This can range from children who are harming themselves on purpose with the intention of killing themselves, to those children who are hitting themselves as a sign of distress. Both these scenarios can be seen in children with ASD but tend to affect a different cross-section of children.

In this chapter we explore the different terms used for self-harm as well as some of the issues which arise from working with young people who do this. The main point we want to make throughout this chapter is that although self-harm can be the visible aspect of a young person's behaviour, the essential aim of assessment is to look for the underlying reasons for it. Before we discuss self-harm in ASD we will look at the subject of self-harm more broadly, including the terminology.

WHAT DO WE MEAN BY 'SELF-HARM' AND WHAT IS THE LANGUAGE USED TO DESCRIBE IT?

There are many terms used to describe self-harm. Obviously, at one end of the scale is suicide, which is a final and devastating action, while at the other end of the scale a child may be engaging in risky or self-injurious behaviours (discussed later in the chapter). There is no universally agreed way to define self-harm, but, basically (for discussion purposes), it is the deliberate action of harming oneself. As a consequence, this term can be used very broadly and covers a wide range of different behaviours. Other terms which are commonly used in everyday language include:

- 'parasuicide'
- 'deliberate self-harm'
- 'self-injury'
- 'self-destructive behaviour'.

These terms are often used interchangeably, but more often the term 'deliberate self-harm' is used in clinical practice. Nonetheless, it is useful to have some appreciation of what these different terms mean.

The term 'parasuicide' was originally coined by Kreitman *et al.* (1969) as a way of describing overdoses or self-cutting behaviour of low medical lethality. It is not often used now in contemporary practice, probably because the word 'suicide' is so emotive. At other times behaviours are labelled 'self-destructive behaviours', which can include excessive uses of substances and alcohol or engaging in risky behaviour. In these situations it is sometimes difficult to determine if a young person's behaviours are self-destructive or part of youthful experimentation. The important thing is that professionals/carers explore the reasons behind the behaviour, and again we reiterate here that this factor is important in all types of self-harming. It is the reasons behind the behaviour, rather than the behaviour itself, which are vital to understand.

■ EXAMPLE

A young person continually drives recklessly following consumption of alcohol with the intention of having an accident to harm themself. It is this intention to harm themself that differentiates the behaviour from a young person who is driving under the influence of alcohol as part of youthful rebellion.

The difficulty when assessing young people for self-harm is deciding if the episode of harming was a true attempt at suicide or had another meaning such as 'a cry for help'. A cry for help is seen by services as behaviour used by the young person to let people know how miserable they are feeling. Assessing the intention behind behaviour in reality can be very tricky, but again it is the intention of the behaviour which truly determines the risk. This does sound a bit strange as some episodes of self-harm can appear quite dramatic and can result in emergency hospital admissions, but in practice even some of those who needed intensive care did not really want to kill themselves.

■ EXAMPLE

One young person may take five paracetamol, thinking that it will cause significant harm, while another may take a whole packet, thinking that it will be harmless as you can purchase it over the counter.

From our experience in actual practice, sometimes gauging a teenager's intent can be extremely difficult and they may be fairly reticent in giving the true picture of what is going on in their lives. It can take some time and patience to get a clear sense of their true intentions and therefore it helps to have experienced and skilled professionals doing these assessments.

THINK POINT!

The intention of the self-harming behaviour is the most important factor to assess in children.

HOW COMMON IS SELF-HARM AND WHY DO CHILDREN HARM THEMSELVES?

Approximately one in every ten young people in the UK will self-harm at some point (Royal College of Psychiatrists 2012), with similar figures reported in Ireland (Morey *et al.* 2008). In Morey *et al.*'s study of 15–17-year-olds, 9.1 per cent self-harmed, with approximately two-thirds cutting and approximately one-third overdosing. A study of prevalence across the globe reports figures as high as 16.1 per cent (Muehlenkamp *et al.* 2012).

Unfortunately, the definitions of self-harm do vary between countries and research studies, which makes comparisons internationally quite difficult. Due to the broad nature of self-harm, it can be difficult to include all behaviours which may be of a harming nature, and there are also significant variations in the health services in different countries which detect and treat these problems. This makes measuring the exact prevalence very challenging. In addition, it needs to be recognised that most children and young people who self-harm never present to medical services, so in reality the prevalence is probably much higher than statistics suggest. Therefore, there are a considerable number of children who are self-harming without anyone knowing about it.

Thankfully, the figures for suicide in teenagers are relatively low, at approximately 7.4 in 100,000 (Wasserman, Cheng and Jiang 2005). The act of suicide remains very rare in young children, but, unfortunately, the rates increase steadily throughout the teenage years and reach their peak in young adulthood.

Both the acts of deliberate self-harm and suicide need to be differentiated from self-harm intent or having ideas of self-harm, which have been found to be much more common. Studies have found that suicidal ideation is very common in the teenage years – it has been estimated at 25 per cent in females and 14 per cent in males over a 12-month period, when teenagers were asked the question 'Have you seriously considered suicide in the last 12 months?' (Centers for Disease Control and Prevention 2000). This obviously seems a very high figure and does appear quite worrying, but it must be remembered that adolescence is characterised by change and turmoil (particularly emotional), and in most young people this can be seen almost as part of their development. It is important, however, that we do recognise those young people who are really struggling and who have a much more serious intent to harm themselves. This can be very difficult and at present remains a challenge.

Methods of self-harming

There are a number of different methods of self-harm. The most common form is self-cutting, but this tends not to be seen as a means of suicide. The most commonly seen method for self-harm with suicidal intention is the ingestion of tablets or substances (e.g. bleach). We present the main methods below in Box 13.1.

BOX 13.1 METHODS OF SELF-HARM
- Ingestion of tablets (most commonly over-the-counter medications).
- Cutting or burning oneself.
- Head banging.
- Scratching.
- Biting.
- Neglect of self-care (emotionally and physically).
- Alcohol and substance abuse.
- Risky behaviour.
- More violent methods (e.g. hanging, firearms).

The method chosen for self-harm can obviously be very variable and may relate to what is available. This is reflected in the common use of over-the-counter medicines and why in some countries the use of firearms is more common than in others. In general, self-harm among adolescents is approximately twice more common in females than in males. However, the number of teenage girls who present to services is disproportionately greater as the methods they tend to favour often require medical attention. This is because girls are more likely to ingest tablets, thus highlighting their needs to services. Although ingestion of tablets is still very common in males, there is also a tendency towards greater use of violent suicidal methods, such as hanging and firearms.

Self-cutting is usually seen on the arms, but can be on any part of the body. Although from our clinical experience it appears that self-cutting among teenagers is a common occurrence, in most cases it does not continue, but is a passing phase of their adolescent development.

However, in some individuals the cutting can become a recurrent behaviour, potentially with the cutting becoming deeper and more widespread and resulting in scarring. As with all methods of self-harm, it is the intention behind the cutting behaviour that is important. In the majority of cases, cutting does not have a suicidal intention but is a way of inflicting pain in response to distress. In some individuals it is the pain or visible blood which is sought, but in others, who use cutting as a way of coping with anxiety, it becomes a stress-relieving action. In these individuals the cutting is used to relieve feelings of stress and this becomes a habit. Then again, others will use cutting as a way of punishing themselves. Obviously, the treatment for these problems relies on understanding the underlying reasons for the behaviour.

■ EXAMPLE

A teenage girl starts cutting her arms after a relationship breakdown as a way of 'coping'. She feels that the pain helps, but, unfortunately, she tends to rely on this method more frequently when she is feeling stressed. Therefore, this cutting becomes a 'maladaptive way of coping'.

THINK POINT!

The method of self-harm can be extremely variable, but it is the perceived lethality of that method which is the important factor.

WHAT FACTORS INFLUENCE SELF-HARM?

Assessing self-harm can be a complex process and one in which all the factors which influenced the action need to be considered. There can be a significant number of factors which lead to a young person self-harming. These can occur individually or it can be a build-up of issues which leads to the ongoing problem. The most striking example of this is the teenage girl who takes an overdose after the breakdown of a relationship, which in our experience is the most common presentation in teenagers. It is often useful to think about these factors in three ways, known as 'predisposing', 'precipitating' and 'perpetuating' factors. These are listed in Box 13.2 below.

> ### BOX 13.2 THE THREE 'P'S
> - *Predisposing* – these are the factors which make the young person at risk from self-harm and are often those which increase stress in the child.
> - *Precipitating* – this is the event which causes the child to self-harm.
> - *Perpetuating* – these are the factors which may lead the child to continue to self-harm.

The risk-factors

Obviously, the risk-factors for self-harming can come from any aspect of a young person's life which is causing them stress and distress. They may occur as a single, overwhelming factor or as a number of different problems which may lead them to self-harm – the so-called 'predisposing factors'.

When thinking about these risk-factors, the most important one to consider is whether the child has an underlying mental illness as this is strongly associated with the risk of self-harm and suicidal behaviours (Thompson *et al.* 2005). The most significant mental illness which raises the risk is a depressive illness, particularly if associated with feelings of hopelessness or worthlessness. Anxiety disorders and eating disorders are also associated with suicidal ideation, due to the stress experienced by the young person, but all mental illnesses can have an effect. It should be remembered that previous history of self-harm is a very significant predictor of future self-harm and even suicide, so this should be taken seriously. It is therefore essential that any assessment process is able to draw out the existence of a mental health problem so that the individual can be treated appropriately. We list the risk-factors to self-harm in Box 13.3 and the protective factors in Box 13.4. While it is important to look at the factors which increase the risk of self-harm, it is also useful to consider those which are protective (i.e. reduce the risk).

BOX 13.3 RISK-FACTORS IN SELF-HARM

- *Individual risk-factors* – the existence of mental health problems, poor coping strategies, personality factors, impulsivity, poor problem-solving skills, sexuality.
- *Family factors* – interpersonal conflict (e.g. arguments, divorce, domestic violence), family history of self-harm/suicide, poor parenting.
- *Peer factors* – peer rejection, peer conflict, bullying, isolation.
- *Social factors* – alcohol and substance abuse, homelessness, poverty, economic stress, children in care, young offenders.
- *School factors* – being out of education, bullying, academic failure, academic stress/pressure (e.g. exams), not fitting in.

BOX 13.4 PROTECTIVE FACTORS IN SELF-HARM

- *Individual factors* – good social skills, good problem-solving abilities, 'internal locus of control' (the feeling that you control your own destiny).
- *Family factors* – family cohesiveness, support from family, good family communication.
- *Peer factors* – good peer relationships, development of friendships.
- *School factors* – academic success, enjoyment and involvement with school, feelings of inclusion.

HOW COMMON IS SELF-HARM IN CHILDREN WITH ASD?

We have spent the first part of this chapter looking at self-harming as it occurs in the general teenage population since this can form a basis for further exploration of the relevance to children with ASD. In clinical practice we do see children with ASD who self-harm, and while there are similarities to the general population, there are also some differences. It is unclear how common it is for children with ASD to self-harm. There are very few studies that explore the prevalence of this problem in children with ASD and most evidence appears anecdotal. One study conducted in 1979 suggested that self-harm occurred in 43 per cent of children with autism aged 6–14 years old (Ando and Yoshimura 1979). Of course, this figure needs to be treated with caution as our terminology and definitions of ASD have changed considerably since the 1970s, but it is a reflection of the lack of information in this area.

In determining self-harm in children with ASD, it is important to differentiate what function the self-harm has for the child. We recognise that children with ASD may self-harm in a similar way to children without ASD. However, there is also a considerable body of children who are harming themselves for different reasons. For this discussion we would like to differentiate self-harm from self-injury. Self-harm can be seen as the desire to harm oneself in relation to a more complex and often longer-term emotional stress, whereas self-injury is inflicted by those who injure themselves as a way of communicating distress. This is often seen in younger children or those who have difficulty expressing themselves verbally. This is obviously an arbitrary division, which does become blurred, but it is nonetheless important when dealing with a child who has ASD. Again, it is important to elicit the intent and reasons behind this self-harming behaviour.

When we consider self-harm and suicide, rather than self-injurious behaviour, it is thought that the rates of self-harm are raised in children with ASD, particularly during adolescence. The most common reason is probably the link between self-harm and depression and the increased rates of comorbid mental health problems in this group. It is easy to see that self-harm may be a response to the stress the young person is experiencing and is a marker for them needing help.

Anecdotally, although we have seen children with ASD who are depressed and talk about self-harming, very often there is no apparent intent to go through with it. They appear to deal rationally with the idea, often saying 'I thought about it but I don't want to do it', citing the reasons why it would be unnecessary. The problem is that with children with ASD (who are struggling to express their emotions), it is difficult to know if this is the true picture. It is especially difficult to guess the future behaviour of those who have additional impulsivity traits, or what will happen if they consume alcohol.

THINK POINT!

When looking at why a child with ASD has self-harmed, consider all the different factors which may be affecting that child.

HOW DOES SELF-HARM PRESENT IN CHILDREN WITH ASD?

Self-harm in children with ASD can present in a very similar way to how it presents in children without ASD. However, the problem is that the child with ASD may not report their behaviour or self-harm until a later time as they may not see the relevance of involving anyone else. Unfortunately, the presentation of these children can be very variable. In practice there are instances when the child will harm themselves in front of family members as an attempt to show their distress, anger or anxiety; or they may harm themselves in an isolated environment and not feel that they need to discuss it with anyone. In addition to this, there are younger children or those with learning difficulties who may use a self-harming type of behaviour – self-injury – as a way of expressing how they are feeling.

What is self-injurious behaviour?

'Self-injury' is often used interchangeably with the term 'self-harm', but classically in the field of mental health the term 'self-injury' is reserved for younger children or those with a learning disability – often those who are hurting themselves as a way of expressing their emotions when they find it difficult to express things verbally.

■ EXAMPLE 1

The three-year-old child who bangs their head repeatedly against a wall as part of their temper tantrum after being disciplined.

■ EXAMPLE 2

The teenager with ASD and a learning disability who bites themselves in response to a change in routine which they find distressing.

■ EXAMPLE 3

A ten-year-old with ASD and a learning disability who is constantly punching themselves in the face in response to toothache, when they are unable to express how they feel in any other way.

There is no specific definition of self-injury, but it tends to include actions such as self-biting, gouging, scratching, head banging, self-punching or kicking – basically any way in which the child can harm themselves. What differentiates this behaviour from self-harm, as described earlier, is the function of the harming behaviour. While this differentiation can seem a little artificial, its importance becomes evident when considering the appropriate treatment options. It is important to understand the cause of the behaviour in order to select the correct action. Consider the case study below.

Case study

Stephen is a nine-year-old boy with ASD. He is fairly verbal but has regular tantrums when he is unable to get what he wants, and more recently he has started head banging quite vigorously during these episodes. Stephen's parents are obviously very worried about this behaviour and are concerned he will give himself a head injury. They have therefore taken to giving in to his demands in order to stop the behaviour. Unfortunately, the head banging is getting worse. Stephen says he is doing this because he wants to die.

Reflective activity

Do you think that Stephen is displaying self-harming behaviour or self-injurious behaviour? Why do you think this?

From this information it appears that Stephen is engaging in self-injurious behaviour for some obvious gain (i.e. to get what he wants). He head bangs to express his distress at not having his demands met, and, unfortunately, as a result of his parents giving in to these demands, the head banging has worsened as he has found that this is a strategy that works. Due to his young age, he does not realise that this behaviour may cause a head injury, and he is just doing it for short-term gratification.

Although Stephen is saying that he wants to die, the understanding of death in this age group is very variable and he is probably using this term as it has evoked a significant reaction from his parents in the past and it worked. While children with ASD do struggle to read the emotions of others, the reactions of parents can often be so great as to be evident even to these children. This behaviour does not have the hallmarks of classical self-harm as the intent is not the harming in itself, but to meet some other need. For Stephen the self-injurious behaviour could be replaced with alternative behaviour such as screaming to achieve the same result, which is not true in the vast majority of self-harm cases.

Young people who cannot express their emotions, possibly due to their poor verbal skills or intellectual disability, have to express their feelings in some way. They may be upset with a change in their routine or be feeling anxious or stressed about something else in their environment. Very commonly, children with ASD in this group who are experiencing pain can have a significant change in their behaviour. They may become aggressive, agitated, or they may self-injure as they are distressed by the pain. The obvious example is toothache, which may not be obvious to their carers but can be extremely uncomfortable. The self-injurious behaviour may reflect where the pain is being experienced. However, this is not a 100 per cent guarantee.

THINK POINT!

Self-injury behaviours do have a meaning to the child and they are often used as a way of expressing their needs or feelings.

HOW DO WE ASSESS AND TREAT SELF-HARM/ SUICIDE IDEATION IN THE CHILD WITH ASD?

It is important to remember that self-harm has an underlying meaning for the child with ASD. Self-harming, although very distressing, is typically a sign of a problem and therefore the assessment needs to look at, and explore *why* it is occurring. A central feature of the assessment process is the ability to assess the risk of further self-harm. This looks at a number of factors which indicate whether the risk is raised or reduced. In anyone, including those with ASD, the risk is assessed on factors as diverse as whether the individual planned the self-harm (which would raise the risk) and their appreciation of how dangerous the self-harm is (e.g. their perceived lethality of an overdose).

An impulsive overdose tends not to be considered high risk in clinical practice as the lack of pre-planning indicates a lower intent of killing oneself. The assessment of risk is also mediated by other factors, such as seeking help, the event, and also the child's feelings about the self-harm during the assessment process. The majority of young people who self-harm regret their actions when interviewed a few hours later and tend to feel embarrassed. In children with ASD the assessment of risk has to be done carefully, and from our experience it can either be more difficult or, conversely, it can be more straightforward than with children without ASD. Some children with ASD can be very literal and open in their communicating of the event, and therefore the risk can be assessed completely. However, others struggle to convey their feelings, which may lead to a degree of uncertainty regarding risk and therefore problems in predicting whether the child will repeat the harming behaviour.

Other aspects of the assessment include looking for the presence of a comorbid mental health problem, which in many ways can be considered the most important part of the assessment. Again, this may be difficult in the young person with ASD and it may be essential to obtain objective information from carers/parents. As we will discuss in subsequent chapters, it may take some skill to assess these problems and the assessment should not be rushed. As can be seen from this discussion, the assessment of risk is an inexact science and the probability of a child harming themselves again can be challenging to estimate. It may be difficult to know what support will be required to minimise the risk in future.

What is the concept of death for children with ASD?

When talking about suicide ideation and assessing suicide risk in children with ASD, it is important to think briefly about their understanding of death as a final outcome. Even for adults and professionals it is sometimes difficult to conceptualise fully the meaning of death. A central component of understanding death is the notion of irreversibility, but medical science has made the notion fairly ambiguous (Cole 1992). For example, the advent of advanced resuscitation can mean that the heart can be restarted, whereas previously the person would have been considered to be dead. In fact, the medical world has argued for years about what constitutes death, focusing on whether brain death or heart death defines the person as deceased. Medical science now tends to argue that a person is deemed dead when brain activity ceases (Hossain 2008). Part of the difficulty in defining death relates to the contrast with life, given that death is considered to signal the end of life. Notably, in some cultures death is viewed more as a process than a single event as the person makes a transition from life into death (Metcalf and Huntington 1991); and in some ways religious beliefs complicate the matter further.

Although these arguments are important for our understanding of death, it is more important clinically to assess the child's understanding of death. Research indicates that young children (5–7-year-olds without ASD) do have some understanding of what death means, in terms of it being irreversible, that the body stops functioning and that death is universal (Speece and Brent 1984), and this may be linked to their increasing understanding of how the body functions (Slaughter 2005). However, there appears to be little research evidence about how children with ASD conceptualise death or what this means for their self-harming or suicidal ideation. It could be postulated that their emotional immaturity reflects a delayed understanding of death, but that this can be mediated by a number of other factors, such as their personal experience of bereavement, death, or their level of intelligence. Those with intellectual disabilities are less likely to understand the concept of death in the way other children do. However, research with adults with intellectual disabilities indicates that individuals do have some understanding of death and that they experience some levels of grief when bereaved (MacHale, McEvoy and Tierney 2009). In children with ASD this delay in understanding of death or an unusual understanding of death may pose some hazards. See, for example, the case study below.

Case study

Luke is a nine-year-old boy with ASD who is causing some alarm to his parents and school. He has a tendency to climb the trees at school because he like heights but he also likes to jump from progressively higher points. He says that is does not matter if he dies as he would like to see what death feels like. Problematically, Luke fails to appreciate that he will not see his parents again after this point and thus does not understand the irreversibility of death. This could easily be mistaken for suicide ideation, when it is not.

WHEN SHOULD YOU SEEK HELP?

Ideally, help should be available for any child who self-harms. However, in the real world this is often not possible. The decision to seek help can depend on the circumstances. Obviously, those who present to medical services such as Accident and Emergency (Emergency Room) will be assessed for the risk and referred for a specialist assessment as necessary. However, in other children with ASD, help will need to be sought depending on the judgements of those around them or the child themself. This contrasts with children with ASD and learning disabilities who are displaying challenging self-injurious behaviours since they may require assessment and help from a behavioural specialist to reduce the intrusion of the behaviour.

Another example of deciding when a child needs help could be children who are scratching themselves superficially (leaving marks on the skin). They may not need a referral to anyone at that time, but it is important to look for the underlying causes. Any possibility of mental health problems or worsening of this problem suggests that help should be sought. This is one area where, if in doubt, it is best to ask for professional advice.

CHAPTER SUMMARY

It is fairly common for young people to have suicidal thoughts at some point during their teenage years. Some of these young people may go on to self-harm, which can be dependent on the different risk-factors which are affecting their lives. The self-harm can include different methods, such as cutting arms, overdosing or risky behaviours, but it is important to recognise that self-harm is just a symptom of an underlying feeling of distress. In children with ASD the situation is unclear, with a limited evidence base. The higher incidences of mental health problems may go some way to explaining the probable increased rates in this group, so it is important to screen for problems such as depression when self-harm is seen. In parallel to self-harm and suicide, some children with ASD self-injure, as a way of expressing their feelings, but in this group it is also important to discern the underlying meaning so that appropriate help can be sought.

(!) IMPORTANT LEARNING POINTS

- Self-harm and suicide ideation are common in young people.
- There are a broad range of methods of self-harm, but it is their intent which is important.
- It is important to assess for the individual's underlying motivation for self-harm, particularly evidence of a mental health problem.
- When assessing risk, look at a range of factors which increase the likelihood of self-harm, or which may be protective.
- Self-harm may be increased in young people with ASD and is probably related to higher levels of mental health problems.
- Assessment of young people with ASD needs to take account of their difficulties with emotional expression or their ability to give the correct information.

FURTHER READING

Hawton, K., and Rodham, K. (2006). *By Their Own Young Hand: Deliberate Self-Harm and Suicidal Ideas in Adolescents.* London: Jessica Kingsley Publishers.

CHAPTER **14**

THE USE OF THERAPIES

This chapter will cover:

- Introduction.

- Therapies and ASD.

- What is Cognitive Behavioural Therapy (CBT)?

- What is family therapy?

- What is psychodynamic psychotherapy?

- What are the non-verbal therapies and when are they used with ASD?

- What is the role of the alternative therapies?

- Chapter summary.

- Further reading.

INTRODUCTION

Most people, when they think about mental health problems, consider 'talking' therapy/counselling as a solution. Talking therapies are often seen as the best way to tackle the problems that arise in relation to the stresses and strains of modern living. Over the last few years there has been increasing interest in specific therapies for the treatment of problems in child mental health, particularly therapies such as Cognitive Behaviour Therapy (CBT). The history of therapies dates back throughout the centuries but it is often seen as developing since the pioneering work of Sigmund Freud. Freud, an Austrian neurologist, was instrumental in the development of psychoanalytical psychotherapy, and this was the pre-eminent therapeutic framework in the first half of the 20th century. While this work made a significant contribution to progressing in the field of mental health, in some fields it was misunderstood. Unfortunately, the poor understanding of ASD during this time and the dominance of psychoanalytical thinking led to the belief that the relationship of carers, particularly mothers, was responsible for the development of ASD, and the term 'refrigerator mother' was coined (Bettelheim 1967; Kanner 1943). Obviously, the field of ASD practice and research has moved on considerably since then, together with the developments and interventions.

Over time there have been ongoing developments in all therapies and the creation of new ones. While new therapies have arisen in child mental health, family therapy, CBT and psychodynamic therapy are the most commonly used modalities. During this chapter we will discuss the issues around the 'talking therapies' for children with ASD, but also other strategies, such as the non-verbal therapies including music and art therapy. As you may appreciate, there is a vast area of literature on these and therefore we only briefly describe the principal uses and limitations for children who have ASD and comorbid mental health problems; supplying an understanding of the framework of these therapies is our main objective.

THERAPIES AND ASD

In routine clinical practice parents naturally ask what treatments are available to help with the mental health problems experienced by their children. This is only to be expected and reinforces our belief that professionals in this line of work should have a good understanding of all the therapeutic options available, particularly when working with children who have ASD. For children who do not have ASD, the therapeutic choices can often be clearer than for those children with ASD. This is for a number of reasons, which we will go on to explain as the chapter progresses. An example of this is the treatment for a phobia. The typical choice of treatment for children is CBT and we will explain this therapy in more detail later. However, for children with ASD and a comorbid phobia, other things need to be taken into account before deciding the best course of action. For the sake of simplicity, these can be encapsulated as insight, motivation, personal factors and supports, which we will refer to using the acronym IMPS below:

Insight.

Motivation.

Personal factors.

Supports.

Insight

Seeking help for a mental health problem implies that it is difficult to deal with these problems solely within the family or with the current help available. The first issue for any therapy is whether the child recognises that there is a problem at all – we call this their 'insight'. This can be a challenge with a lot of child mental health work as it can be the child's family or school who believe a problem exists rather than the child themself. In clinical practice with children who have ASD this can be especially difficult. These children often lack the ability to reflect on their thoughts and actions from another's perspective (a theory of mind problem) and instead see it only from their own perspective. This has the consequence of many of these children becoming distressed or angry, even when the problems are described to the professional, as they vehemently disagree with that viewpoint. Insight is not only the recognition that a problem exists, but also that the problem requires treatment. We have come across children who do agree that there is a problem, but do not feel that they need any treatment for it.

Motivation

The second issue for any therapy is intimately linked to insight. Once an individual recognises that they have a problem and that they need treatment, they then need to be 'motivated' to do something about it. Therapy can be hard work – the child may find it emotionally uncomfortable and difficult to continue with. This has implications for any child, but particularly those with ASD who may not be entirely convinced they need any treatment. *All* treatments can be hard work in terms of time, resources and emotional effort, and can take significant periods of time.

■ EXAMPLE

A good example when considering the difference between insight and motivation is the treatment of phobias. Many people recognise that they have a fear of heights (insight) but the fear has to reach a point where they want to get treatment for it (motivation). This may be difficult as it involves going up to high places and invokes anxiety, but to be treated properly they need to complete the course of therapy. The same can be said for any phobia (spiders, snakes, aeroplanes, etc.).

Motivation, therefore, may depend on many personal factors and the extent to which the issue is interfering with daily living. Both insight and motivation should be considered carefully when working with children with ASD, remembering that motivation and insight may change over time. Care should be taken when suggesting a course of treatment, as there may be implications in coercing a child into therapy when they are not ready. They may start treatment but quickly drop out. It would therefore be better to wait to see whether they want to engage with the process in the future.

THINK POINT!

Insight and motivation are essential in engaging children with ASD in any talking therapy.

Personal factors

Finding the right therapy for any child or family is affected by a number of factors which are 'personal' to that particular situation. In the right context this will make the treatment more appropriate and, it is to be hoped, increase the chances of success. This can depend on whether the therapy is for the child themself (e.g. CBT) or looks at the wider context (e.g. family therapy), and also what the goal of the overall therapeutic process is. Some therapies will look at changing the thinking styles or behaviour that a child is expressing and therefore focus on helping the child to take responsibility for making changes. Other therapies will look at the supports (i.e. family around the child) and how changes in this area can improve the mental health of the child and facilitate a more supportive environment. There are a number of personal factors which can affect the process of therapy and we show these in Box 14.1.

When considering all children, including those with ASD, it is important to look at the attributes of the child and the wider social arena. Obviously, when considering any therapy it may be necessary to consider the age of the child. This is essential when considering the child's cognitive development (i.e. the way in which they understand the world and themself). They need to have some understanding of the thought processes around their mental health problem and, if these are affected (as is the case, for example, in depressive illnesses), they will need to recognise and be able to rationally evaluate them in order to change them. This can be a particular challenge in those children who have a coexisting learning disability with their ASD as they struggle to understand the therapeutic process.

> **BOX 14.1 THE PERSONAL FACTORS AFFECTING THE PROCESS OF THERAPY**
> - *Age* – some therapies are more effective in older children.
> - *Cognitive ability* – this is central to understanding the therapeutic thinking required.
> - *Emotional maturity* – affects the emotional understanding of the therapeutic process.
> - *Language ability* – some therapies require significant verbal skills.
> - *Interpersonal skills* – some therapies require an understanding of relationships.
> - *Thinking styles* – certain mind-sets struggle with certain therapies.

Linked with the child's cognitive ability is the emotional maturity of the young person. Particularly in the area of ASD there can be a discrepancy between a child's cognitive ability and their emotional development, with the emotional development lagging behind to some degree. Recognising how emotions affect behaviour can be important for many therapies, and the therapeutic process will often need this link to exist so that any work on the emotions or thoughts behind them can have a positive effect on the behaviour. Children need to be able to recognise their own emotions and the emotions of others to facilitate normal interactions, but this is obviously difficult for many individuals with ASD. Many children with ASD, particularly those with comorbid ADHD, struggle to regulate their emotions and this can affect how they manage therapy.

Obviously, when considering a talking therapy, language plays a central role. Many children with ASD are non-verbal and others, by definition, have communication problems. The ability to listen and understand the therapy needs to be considered carefully. Any given therapy may require some adaptation to suit the needs of a child with ASD. In addition, a 'talking therapy' is a two-way interaction, with the expectation that the child will join in with the interaction. This may be problematic for some children and may actually increase their anxiety within a therapeutic session. This, potentially, can make therapy counter-productive. Although this can happen in all children, a one-to-one interaction could be particularly difficult for some children with ASD. Some therapies require group settings and the complex interactions can be a particular challenge.

We briefly described the thinking styles of children with ASD earlier in the book. When applying this to therapy, it becomes apparent that the thinking styles of the child can impact on the progress and outcomes of any intervention. Theory of mind relies on an individual seeing a situation from the perspective of another person, which is a process commonly used in therapy. Many therapies involve asking children about hypothetical situations, but those with ASD who struggle with social imagination may find this impossible. The abstract nature of some talking therapies can thus make progress challenging.

Supports

Therapy needs to be built upon a firm foundation (i.e. a platform which enables the child with ASD to engage and get the maximum benefit from any therapy). The most obvious 'supports' around the child are the family and the educational setting. When thinking about any therapy, it is useful to consider how these can be modified to enable the therapy to be successful.

It is fairly clear that families need to have a good understanding of the need for a particular therapy and what the realistic goal of any therapeutic modality would be. Essentially, it needs to be clear what could be achieved, but also what the limitations are. Families need to be motivated to support the child as they may need to undertake work on a regular basis at home and outside of any clinic. Some therapies require frequent attendance, which may pose a strain on other work and family commitments. Due to these factors, it is our experience that often only one parent is able to attend most of the appointments and this does limit the potential engagement of the whole family. However, most professionals recognise this as a reality of modern life and therefore are sympathetic.

Children spend a vast amount of time in school; hence school can become instrumental in helping the overall treatment process. On a practical level, the child may need to be absent from school on a regular basis to attend appointments, which can affect their academic progress and their attendance record. The schools may need to take this into account. In addition, the school may be involved in the overall monitoring of the child, giving feedback on the child's progress. Some schools are also involved with therapy. In some instances, for therapy to be effective, other stresses which may be affecting the child will need to be reduced. For example, it may be necessary for a child with ASD who is having therapy for low mood to reduce the number of subjects studied at school, thus reducing their overall burden. This can only be facilitated by a supportive educational setting. In our experience, schools are often very helpful, despite the demands and pressures put upon them, and a good working relationship between the therapist and the school does appear to help the eventual outcome.

Finally (often unacknowledged), there is the role of the therapist. We have emphasised throughout this book the importance of professionals having a particular understanding of the mental health problems which can occur in children with ASD and the need for them to understand the nuances of this condition. Any therapist needs to understand this when working therapeutically with these children, as they will need to adapt the therapy according to a child's particular needs. Although children with ASD have a general pattern of problems, individually they can be very different, which can present a challenge to the therapist's skills. In addition to having a good therapist, the therapeutic environment needs to be conducive to the overall care, with changes made which will make the child feel comfortable (e.g. the removal of the sound of a ticking clock or the hum of a computer, which some children with ASD find very distracting, thus interfering with the process of therapy).

THINK POINT!

There are a number of factors, both individual and environmental, which are essential to consider when finding the right therapy.

Case study

Charlotte is a 14-year-old girl with ASD who is supported fairly successfully at a mainstream school but is described as very shy. Despite being academically bright, over the last few months she has become increasingly anxious about going to school and her parents struggle to get her there each morning. Charlotte denies that there is a problem except that she reports that she 'does not like school anymore'. Her parents have noticed that she is also increasingly anxious when going to new places and they have sought help from child mental health services. Charlotte attends the clinic appointment very reluctantly and refuses to talk during the session. From the history, the clinician identifies Charlotte as having a comorbid anxiety disorder, but fails in the attempt to engage with her, except for her to say, 'Nothing's wrong'.

After the session Charlotte tells her parents she did not like 'that man or that place' and felt that the family were forcing her to go. Her parents struggle to know what to do next as Charlotte will not go back.

Reflective activity

Considering IMPS as a framework, what factors do you think could be affecting Charlotte's engagement with treatment?

This is a fairly clear case where a young person does not want to engage in the therapeutic process. If we use IMPS as a way of considering the possibility of using therapy with Charlotte, we can identify a number of problems. Charlotte does not feel she has a mental health problem such as anxiety, therefore she does not feel she needs any treatment. With no significant insight, her motivation to attend any clinical setting is very low and she feels forced to attend. There may be some indications of her struggling with interpersonal interactions; however, if she were engaged in the process, her cognitive ability would be a positive for any therapeutic process. Her parents sound very supportive of her, which is a benefit as they will have to support her throughout this problem. There may come a point when Charlotte does have improved insight and motivation, at which point she may be more suitable for therapy.

There has been an explosion in the numbers and types of therapy becoming available over the last few years, with many new therapies emerging. There are very few therapies in common use for children with ASD, and the evidence of their effectiveness for reducing comorbid mental health problems is variable. Even the most commonly used therapies have limited evidence when utilised with ASD. CBT, for example, still has a fairly slender evidence base with this group. We will now discuss the most commonly recognised therapies used with children with ASD, considering both the uses and limits for this particular group of children.

WHAT IS COGNITIVE BEHAVIOURAL THERAPY (CBT)?

CBT is a well-researched method of therapy which has an extensive evidence base for treating typically developing children for a range of mental health problems, particularly disorders such as anxiety and phobias. It is used extensively in the treatment of Obsessive Compulsive Disorder (OCD) and also has applications for the treatment of depression. It has even been used for individuals with psychosis. Before we discuss the use of CBT with children who have ASD, it is essential to understand the underlying model. The goals of CBT are to identify and treat certain thoughts ('cognitions') which are considered to be unhelpful for the individual and to identify and treat the behaviours which are linked to these thoughts (Beck 1991). An example of this is an individual's avoidance ('behaviour') of crowds due to the fear and thoughts that something 'catastrophic' will happen to them. In CBT these cognitions are often distinguished as having three different levels. The commonly used divisions are:

- 'core beliefs'
- 'dysfunctional assumptions'
- 'negative automatic thoughts'.

(Westbrook, Kennerley and Kirk 2011)

The core beliefs are the individual's fundamental beliefs about themselves (e.g. they may believe that nobody likes them). This eventually leads through the process of dysfunctional assumptions to negative automatic thoughts. These are the appraisals or interpretations of ourselves or the world around us which have a negative feel to them as they relate to the negative core beliefs. These thoughts are central to any CBT approach as they need to be identified and challenged. They are called 'automatic' as they occur without any particular active thought or effort. Some examples of negative automatic thoughts include:

- *All-or-nothing thinking* – looking at things in an absolute 'black-or-white' way.
- *Over-generalisation* – where an individual takes an individual event and generalises it to other aspects of their life in a negative way.
- *Personalisation and blame* – the individual blaming themself for something they were not responsible for.
- *Jumping to conclusions* – predicting things will turn out badly or be a disaster.
- *Discounting the positives* – failing to recognise anything positive.
- *Mental filter* – noticing all the negatives and ignoring the positives.

Considering there can be difficulties with both thinking and behaviour, the therapy has to manage both components. Generally, the model of treatment emphasises four components (Chorpita 2007):

1. Assessment.

2. Psycho-education.

3. Cognitive restructuring.

4. Exposure.

It is fairly self-explanatory that the assessment component is required to fully assess the extent and nature of the problem and to devise the appropriate treatment. Essential to CBT is psycho-education, in which the therapist helps the child identify their thoughts and the behaviours which are causing them problems. Surprisingly, often it is the psycho-education which can be therapeutically powerful, and many children can make significant improvements once they understand their condition (Kendall 1993). This is commonly seen in those who have panic attacks and feel relieved to have an explanation for their attacks, now realising that they are not going to die. Once this has been achieved, the therapist uses cognitive restructuring to challenge the negative/dysfunctional thoughts and help the child develop alternative thoughts or interpretations through using different techniques, such as questioning or homework exercises. The final component of treatment is that of exposure. In most CBT this is considered central to success and involves the child being exposed to key situations to challenge the thoughts and remove the avoidance behaviour (Davis and Ollendick 2005).

▮ EXAMPLE 1

A child who fears dogs during the early stages of the therapy will be gradually exposed to dogs. This may begin with a picture of a dog (in vitro) and move gradually to being asked to hold a toy dog. Eventually, the child goes to the park to watch dogs from a distance before finally touching a real dog (in vivo).

▮ EXAMPLE 2

A child who has OCD may have the thought that they need to wash repeatedly to eliminate germs. The child may be asked to reduce hand-washing, therefore exposing them to the thoughts of contamination, which will need to be managed by therapy. Gradually the child will be asked to touch something associated with germs, such as a their shoes, and refrain from hand-washing for a short period.

The role of exposure is to elicit the unhelpful thoughts in situations where the child is exposed to the anxiety-provoking object or situation (Davis and Ollendick 2005), such as asking about a child's thoughts when they are looking at a picture of a spider. This can be done in person (*in vivo*) or in their imagination (*in vitro*). If possible, the *in vivo* exposure is better. This teaches the child to face their anxiety and manage their thoughts and behaviours in a more positive manner. This means that the child needs a sustained period of gradual exposure to the anxiety-provoking object to develop new ways of thinking about it. In understanding this part of therapy, it is important to recognise the natural history of an anxiety episode. See Figure 14.1.

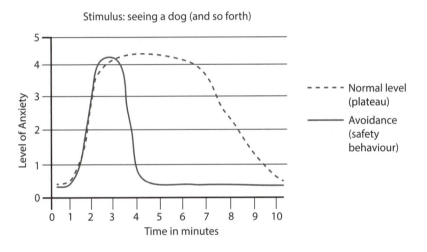

Figure 14.1: Natural history of an episode of anxiety

When exposed to any anxiety-provoking situation or object (stimulus), anxiety quickly rises. Given enough time, the feeling of anxiety will actually plateau at a particular level and then over time it will naturally gradually reduce to its original level, the level prior to the anxiety provocation. Unfortunately, people who struggle with anxiety may never get to the plateau point or to the point where the anxiety is reducing, and classically they have the fear that the anxiety will keep increasing out of their control. As a consequence they develop some behaviour to manage this feeling. Typically, people use avoidance behaviour (i.e. leaving the situation), which causes the anxiety to rapidly reduce. The problem with this solution is that it can worsen the situation. The mind remembers the fear and the solution to it which was previously used (i.e. avoidance); therefore it tends to suggest the same course of action in this situation again, which sustains the anxiety. Behaviours such as avoidance or even the compulsions in OCD (which are ways in which the person reduces their anxiety) can be called 'safety behaviours' (i.e. they make the person feel safer). The role of CBT is to challenge the safety behaviours (as they are making the situation worse) and the thoughts behind them and to encourage the individual to experiment with an alternative option. With children, the involvement of the parents is often very important to motivate the child and continue the exposure outside of the therapy environment.

■ EXAMPLE

A child has developed a fear of crowds. This started during a music concert when he became very anxious. The situation only improved from his perspective when he left the auditorium. Unfortunately, this fear has spread to other situations with crowds, and the child is now avoiding any situation where there are large numbers of people, obviously making school attendance difficult. CBT would find a way of exposing the child to this anxiety-provoking situation in a safe way and exploring the thoughts which lead to the avoidant behaviour.

What factors are important when using CBT with children with ASD?

While CBT has been shown to be a very effective therapy in the general population, there is less evidence to show its effectiveness in children with ASD (White *et al.* 2009). Most of the research studies exploring CBT for children with ASD have demonstrated some improvements when using the therapy; however, this needs to be seen in context. Most of these studies compared the use of CBT against children on waiting lists (no treatment), which does limit the ability to interpret the success of this treatment. However, in our routine clinical practice there does appear to be a place for CBT, albeit with certain modifications made to the treatment and the need to understand its limitations when used with children who have ASD.

To determine which aspects of CBT are applicable to the child, it is important to consider an individual child's level of functioning – the huge range of ability of children with ASD makes a 'one size fits all' approach extremely difficult. In reality, factors such as cognitive ability, speech and rigidity of thinking determine whether the cognitive part is easily applicable. A number of children do benefit from a more behavioural approach to modify their behaviours but may still be left with some problematic core beliefs. There have been a number of different suggestions regarding how treatment might be best modified for children with ASD, which include changes such as:

- considering the child's developmental age when shaping the therapy tasks (Beebe and Risi 2003)

- extending the number of therapy sessions and involving parents in the process (Beebe and Risi 2003)

- using role-plays and visual cues to aid understanding (Attwood 1999)

- the use of more direct, in-person strategies to help the generalisation of skills (Anderson and Morris 2006).

Many of the limitations of using talking therapies, discussed earlier in the chapter, apply to CBT, and can be thought of in terms of IMPS. In other words, CBT can be limited by the child's insight and motivation, and there are personal and support/structural factors which shape its success with children who have ASD.

WHAT IS FAMILY THERAPY?

Family therapy is a form of therapy which sets out to examine the interactions which occur between family members and to change these in order to help improve the mental health of individuals and/ or improve family functioning. Family therapy views the family as a dynamic entity where the interactions between individuals can affect the unit as a whole. Where there are problems in these interactions, the family therapy addresses them. Obviously, the definition of what constitutes a family is open to debate, but in this context the therapist will work with those individuals who have a significant and lasting effect on the family as a whole.

There are a number of different theories which underpin the practice of family therapy, which have developed over the course of its history. Different forms have developed since its inception in the mid-20th century; but despite the differences, the focus remains on helping families. For those interested in understanding the nuances of the different approaches, there is further information on-line, or in family therapy books (e.g. Barker and Chang 2013).

Family therapy relies upon seeing the family for a number of therapeutic sessions. The number of therapy sessions for each family can be quite variable, depending on their needs. Family members can be seen together or individually, depending on the situation, with the child normally included. However, engaging children can sometimes be challenging (O'Reilly and Parker 2013), as parents may talk about the child in rather negative ways (Parker and O'Reilly 2013). The therapist will explore the relationships between individuals and how these influence others in the family. The therapist is looking for the unhelpful ways in which families view situations or if individuals feel blamed, and will help the family to reframe their views of each other. Notably, family therapy makes use of a reflecting team in which other therapists will view the session with the family, often behind a one-way mirror and then discuss their perspectives on the family at points during the session (Andersen 1987). This requires particular skills to implement effectively (Parker and O'Reilly 2013).

When is family therapy used with ASD?

Despite family therapy having been around for a long time and extensive research on the outcomes made possible by this therapy (Stratton 2010), there is surprisingly little literature available on family therapy for families with a child diagnosed with ASD. This may support the view that it is not widely used in this context. Although there is little available evidence it is a therapy which may be useful in certain situations for families.

There is little to suggest that family therapy will make a significant change to the behaviour or emotional expressions of a child with ASD when used in isolation. However, it does have a role in looking at the dynamics in the family of those who are living with the child. Caring for a child with ASD has been described as more stressful than caring for those with other types of disabilities (Bromley et al. 2004), and places considerable strain on families, emotionally and economically (Sharpe and Baker 2007).

Parents may have feelings of guilt or blame and may feel isolated from each other or their wider family. They may feel lonely in dealing with the problems they face in living with their child. In addition, having a child with ASD can impact on the relationship with siblings, which may result in conflict or 'attention-seeking' behaviours. Young siblings may also model their behaviour on their older autistic sibling.

The therapist can examine all these dynamics and suggest practical ways in which they can be addressed. This has the potential to reduce the stress within the family, which may in turn impact positively on the emotions of the child with ASD.

WHAT IS PSYCHODYNAMIC PSYCHOTHERAPY?

Psychodynamic psychotherapy is a form of therapy which explores how the unconscious processes of thinking affect the behaviour and interactions of an individual. According to this perspective, the individual struggles to function or interact with the world around them to a certain degree due to the unconscious mechanisms that work in their mind. This way of thinking generally develops early in life and then colours the ongoing life story. Due to the unconscious nature of these thoughts, the therapist needs to explore the problematic behaviour and then help the individual to explore how events and memories have shaped this behaviour in order to help them seek alternatives. This is primarily done through the process of talking and reflecting with the therapist on the processes which have resulted in the maladaptive functioning.

Although there is some relationship between psychodynamic psychotherapy and psychoanalytical therapy, psychodynamic therapy tends to rely more on the interpersonal relationship between the therapist and the individual. The therapy can be quite variable in its intensity, generally ranging from weekly therapy to even daily therapy.

When is psychodynamic psychotherapy used with ASD?

There is limited research evidence on the use of psychodynamic psychotherapy in children with ASD. To a certain degree there is reluctance to use this therapy with these children, as children with ASD tend to struggle to recognise their conscious processes and emotions, and therefore recognising unconscious ones is especially complex. This therapy does also tend to rely on the child talking, which can be especially problematic for those with ASD. There are some international differences in the approach of psychodynamic therapy to ASD, with some health-providers being keener to employ this therapy than others. Although some clinicians have their doubts about the use of this therapy for children with ASD, the different approach to the children and their families can sometimes be useful as it gives a different perspective.

WHAT ARE THE NON-VERBAL THERAPIES AND WHEN ARE THEY USED WITH ASD?

It should be fairly obvious that in children who struggle verbally, therapy should look at all forms of communication, both verbal and non-verbal. Despite this, there is often limited availability of these therapies for children with comorbid mental health problems, which may be a consequence of factors such as financial limitations, the lack of trained specialists, the dominance of the verbal therapies and the limited evidence base which exists. Three of the non-verbal therapies most commonly used for children with ASD are music therapy, play therapy and art therapy.

Music therapy

Music therapy uses music to help individuals explore and improve their health both physically and emotionally. Music therapy uses musical experiences and the relationships developed through the exploration of these experiences as a mechanism for change (Bruscia 1982). In the area of mental health music is used to explore the child's mental state. Different techniques are employed to achieve this, which include free and structured improvisation of music, songs (singing and writing) and listening to music. Therapists need to be multi-skilled, applying music to a wide range of current psychological theory and practice. Music therapy with children can be done either individually or in a group setting using a wide variety of different musical instruments.

Unfortunately, there is very limited evidence about the use of music therapy applied to children who have ASD and comorbid mental health problems. Studies tend to have focused on music therapy improving communication with children who just have ASD, with one trial demonstrating that music therapy was slightly better than verbal therapies in reducing behavioural problems (Gold, Wigram and Elefant 2010). (Due to the nature of music therapy, it would be complex to design a research study to measure outcomes for treating mental health difficulties alongside all the other influences which affect these children.) Despite the lack of evidence, music therapy may be a useful way to engage children with ASD in a non-threatening manner and enable them to express their emotions in a safe way. The therapist can then use this information to help the child.

Although not all children with ASD have access to music therapy the use of music is fully supported by the authors as a way of helping to relax many children with ASD. In our experience children with ASD tend to like music, which may be a consequence of the repetitive nature of some lyrics. Unfortunately this can become irritating for parents, who may hear the same song hundreds of times. The use of earphones can be a blessing!

Play therapy

Play is considered to be a normal part of a child's development. Play therapy is a modality of therapy which is generally used with younger children and is a way for them to express their emotions through play. Play therapy can be used not only as a diagnostic tool (e.g. by observing the child playing with certain toys and thus identifying the cause of their distress), but also as a way of helping them resolve this distress (Cattanach 2003). In addition to looking at the objects and patterns of play, the interaction with the therapist forms part of the therapeutic method. There are two types of play therapy: 'directed', where there is significant structure and guidance by the therapist; and 'non-directed', in which the child is encouraged to play freely and is therefore able to resolve their own problems (LeBlanc and Ritchie 2001).

There is, as with many other therapies, limited research evidence on the efficacy of this treatment, particularly in working with comorbid mental health problems with ASD. Like music therapy, play therapy may be useful in enabling a child with ASD to express their emotions in a non-threatening environment. For example, the child can express their aggression through play.

Art therapy

Art therapy is similar to music therapy in that it uses art techniques to engage the child and to help explore their emotions and distress. It does this through the process of making art but also by exploring the relationship between the art therapist and the child. The creation of art is utilised to explore the emotional and mental health aspects of an individual, with a therapist who integrates the creative process with knowledge of psychotherapy (American Art Therapy Association 2012). Like the other non-verbal therapies, it provides an opportunity for individuals with ASD to express themselves, which in turn functions as a conduit for their emotional states. Again this enables the explanation of worries in a non-threatening way.

WHAT IS THE ROLE OF THE ALTERNATIVE THERAPIES?

Despite the growth in 'mainstream' therapies, there has been significant growth over the last few years in the field of complementary and alternative medicine/therapy. The problem with using treatments with children who have ASD (as should be fairly obvious from reading this book) is that there is a limited availability of therapies with a strong evidence base. Additionally, because of the nature of ASD, it is challenging to find a treatment that makes a significant difference. The lack of any mainstream viable and realistic ways of reducing the core symptoms of ASD may result in families seeking alternatives away from classic healthcare services and this is only to be expected. There are a multitude of alternative therapies and medicines which claim to help alleviate difficult symptoms or behaviours in these children, but care needs to be exercised in choosing such an approach.

Some treatments are fairly benign and are well recognised. Many parents have tried fish oils, probiotics and vitamins to see if there is any benefit. While these are inexpensive, other treatments can be expensive and invasive. The evidence for the effectiveness of complementary and alternative medicines in children with ASD is often controversial, with many treatments lacking any systematic appraisal (Golnik and Ireland 2009). Professionals are often divided in their attitudes to this area (O'Reilly *et al.* 2012), which can make it difficult for parents to get a clear view. We would advise parents to seek advice and guidance from reputable sources, including the professionals in health, social and education services, before embarking on a course of alternative treatments.

CHAPTER SUMMARY

The use of therapies for comorbid problems in children with ASD is an expanding field and remains under development. There are a number of different therapies available which can be used to treat different aspects of mental health problems in these children, and it is important to understand their particular applications and limitations. There are a number of factors which affect a child's engagement with therapy, which we conceptualise with the term 'IMPS' (Insight, Motivation, Personal factors and Support). Insight and motivation are essential to the therapeutic process and these appear to be the major factors which limit the success of any particular treatment. Particular treatments, both verbal and non-verbal, are summarised in this chapter, but it appears that the therapist's clinical understanding of ASD may be one of the most important factors.

ⓘ IMPORTANT LEARNING POINTS

- Talking therapies are a common treatment for mental health problems for children and adolescents.
- When using these therapies with children who have ASD, insight, motivation, personal factors and supports (IMPS) need to be considered.
- Adaptations need to be made to therapies to make them appropriate for children with ASD.
- Different therapies may be useful for different situations and different problems.
- Non-verbal therapies may be more suitable for some children.
- There is little evidence available at present on many of the therapies in the context of ASD.

FURTHER READING

Barker, P., and Chang, J. (2013). *Basic Family Therapy* (6th Edition). Oxford: Wiley-Blackwell.

Westbrook, D., Kennerley, H., and Kirk, J. (2011). *An Introduction to Cognitive Behaviour Therapy: Skills and Applications* (2nd Edition). London: Sage.

CHAPTER **15**

THE ROLE OF DIFFERENT PROFESSIONALS

What this chapter will cover:

- Introduction.
- Where are professionals based?
- Why do professionals see the same problem from different angles?
- The child and adolescent psychiatrist.
- The paediatrician.
- The clinical psychologist.
- The mental health nurse.
- The primary care physician/General Practitioner.
- The speech and language therapist/pathologist.
- The occupational therapist.
- The specialist teacher/specialist educator.
- The educational/school psychologist.
- The social worker.
- Specialist therapists.
- The role of the voluntary/charity/community sector.
- Chapter summary.
- Further reading.

INTRODUCTION

Sometimes it can be quite daunting looking after or working with a child who has ASD. The issues can be very complex and emotionally and physically tiring. There is considerable variation internationally and also within countries on the provision for children with ASD, and this can even be seen at the time of diagnosis (Karim, Cook and O'Reilly 2012). For example, in the UK, provision tends to be driven by the National Health Service (NHS), while in countries such as the USA, there is a greater private provision and involvement of health insurance organisations. This may shape what is locally or nationally available. In reality, the access to care can be patchy and the diagnostic process can be prolonged and emotionally draining. The complexity of ASD can result in a number of different professionals being involved at this early stage, and post-diagnosis there may be several more, particularly if the child is identified as having additional mental health problems.

With ASD being a long-term condition, it is inevitable that new problems will arise, and this has been the focus of much of this book. As a consequence, parents and those working with children with ASD will need to come into contact with a variety of professional groups. It can be confusing for anybody to understand the particular roles of different professionals and how they relate to each other. In our experience, parents often describe being unaware of why they are seeing a particular professional, what their background is and how they might be able to help the child and family. This is obviously not very useful. In this chapter, therefore, we feel it is important to describe briefly some of the professionals who may be involved with children with ASD, concentrating on those who would probably work with the comorbid mental health problems. Unfortunately, no list can be all-inclusive, and we should take time to acknowledge all the valuable work which is undertaken by everyone working in this field, even those not mentioned directly.

WHERE ARE PROFESSIONALS BASED?

Usually, when considering the role of any particular professional, it is important to recognise the underlying agency that they represent. This tends to separate into health services, education services, social/welfare services and the voluntary/charity/community sector. Obviously, there can be some overlap with professionals working across different agencies, but it is sometimes useful to consider professionals as being from these groups as it helps to understand their various responsibilities. While we can describe how a professional in a particular role (e.g. a child psychiatrist) may generally work with a child, there are obviously considerable differences in the actual application of that role, from country to country.

In general, children with ASD come into contact with professionals from all these groups, with each group playing a part in looking at the comorbid mental health problems. It is now fairly common for agencies to work together to help a child, and this is generally viewed positively by children and their families (O'Reilly *et al.* 2012). However, they do play different roles in the care of the child, and it is helpful to understand this. In general, professionals from health play a role in diagnosing and treating these comorbid mental health problems, but there is a significant role in maintaining the emotional and mental health from the other groups. Children spend a considerable amount of time within educational settings such as schools, so to underestimate the impact of this environment would be foolish. Indeed, research tells us that health professionals believe that knowledge of education is helpful to their practice (Vostanis *et al.* 2012). The role of social/welfare services in supporting these children and their families is essential in maintaining the well-being of the children, although we acknowledge that there are considerable differences in this provision. It should be appreciated that the delivery of services can depend on the economic and financial circumstances of the family, with resources being variable between countries; delivery can also depend on the availability of state or private provision. This can result in services being provided in some countries by the state and in others by private companies, or there may be a combination of the two. Even if services are available from state sources, some families will seek out private care to augment what they are already receiving. With the advent of evidence-based practice, it has become essential to justify a particular therapeutic approach using research, and this can affect what is provided to children, particularly in the area of ASD, where evidence may be limited.

WHY DO PROFESSIONALS SEE THE SAME PROBLEM FROM DIFFERENT ANGLES?

The one thing that parents sometimes complain about is that they see different professionals (or even professionals from the same background) who tell them to do different things to help their child. This obviously causes some confusion and frustration and can result in parents doubting the competence of the individual or service. This confusion may lead to the problem not being addressed, due to these conflicting solutions. This may be a consequence of professionals not explaining themselves fully or it may be that the problem is seen in different ways by different people. In considering this issue it is important to make some points which we hope will help:

1. Professionals may have received different types of training.

2. They may see the problem as being caused by different things.

3. There are sometimes multiple ways of dealing with any particular problem.

It is necessary to realise that different professions from different groups may have had quite considerably different training and education which influences their understanding of ASD and the comorbid mental health problems associated with it. Even within mental health services, professionals are trained differently and the ongoing training they receive within the service can be variable (see Edwards *et al.* 2008). There are different ways of thinking about ASD, which often reflect the underlying values and principles which underpin training. The understanding that mental health problems can have a biological, psychological or social causation (or a combination of all three), will lead particular professionals to concentrate on a particular area. However, different perspectives can often be helpful in identifying and treating any problem to a satisfactory level. Although this book has tried to provide a framework to consider when working with children with comorbid mental health problems, it is appreciated that there are often multiple ways of addressing a particular problem. The variation between children and the presentation of their ASD means that an open mind is needed to find the best way to help each individual child.

As a consequence of this and the general lack of research evidence for the treatment of children with ASD, most professionals work on the premise that although all children are different and that treatments will need to be tailored accordingly, the treatments that they have tried previously which have been successful will work with the child in front of them. Unfortunately, in this field there is still significant scope for 'educated guesses'. It is to be hoped that this guess is well informed, but different people will favour different solutions, hence the confusion. Nonetheless, by working together, professionals can offer useful and insightful strategies which can promote the child's well-being. Again, this reinforces our contention that professionals working with children who have ASD must have a comprehensive working knowledge of this condition as we feel this will lead to better outcomes. A good example of the need for professionals to work together is shown below.

▉ EXAMPLE

In the case of a child who is anxious at school, professionals from education will be essential in reducing the anxiety through modifications of the curriculum and by differentiating the learning; an occupational therapist may be involved in advising on the sensory environment; and a psychiatrist may be assessing for an anxiety disorder.

When looking for somebody to help with the child it is important to understand the services which are available in your community. We cannot consider here the specifics of how services are commissioned in each individual country but we can give an outline of the professionals who may be available. We present these groups in no particular order in respect to their role in mental health.

THE CHILD AND ADOLESCENT PSYCHIATRIST

The child and adolescent psychiatrist is a doctor by background and will have undertaken a medical degree. They will have additional postgraduate training in terms of diagnosing and treating a range of mental health disorders and problems which affect children and young people. They tend to have expertise in the use of a range of therapies, which include medication and talking therapies. They specifically have expertise in the prescribing of psychiatric medications such as antidepressants, antipsychotics and treatments for anxiety. Child and adolescent psychiatrists have the expertise to treat the more severe mental illnesses which can significantly impair a child. In extreme cases, psychiatrists are allowed to detain individuals for their own safety. Some child and adolescent psychiatrists actively specialise in ASD.

THE PAEDIATRICIAN

The paediatrician is a doctor who holds a medical degree. Postgraduate training involves specialisation in understanding the physical and developmental problems which exist in children. Some paediatricians will specialise specifically in children with developmental problems (such as ASD) and they are often essential to the diagnostic process, particularly in younger children. They have specific expertise in managing the comorbid physical aspects of ASD, such as epilepsy or bowel disorders. There is a growing group of paediatricians who are interested in child mental health problems and who may see a range of behavioural and emotional problems. Paediatricians can prescribe medication and, depending on their training, will use medications indicated for mental health problems.

THE CLINICAL PSYCHOLOGIST

Clinical psychologists tend to have a degree in psychology and postgraduate training in clinical psychology, often at doctorate level. They have specific training in diagnosing and recognising mental health problems and are often trained to provide a wide range of psychological therapies. They can specialise in a particular area, such as Cognitive Behavioural Therapy (CBT), family therapy or psychodynamic therapy. In addition, they are trained in the application and interpretation of psychometric testing (including personality and intelligence tests). They can be involved in all stages, from diagnosis to treatment.

THE MENTAL HEALTH NURSE

Mental health/psychiatric nurses have a nursing background and qualification. They tend to choose the option to specialise in mental health nursing early in their training and can specialise in child and adolescent mental health. The role of the mental health nurse can be extremely variable and they may work in outpatient or inpatient settings. There has been a considerable increase in the role provided by this group over the last few years, with specific training in therapeutic modalities such as CBT or nurse prescribing becoming more common. Mental health nurses tend to provide a holistic approach to supporting families and working with children. They tend to work closely with the child/adolescent psychiatrist and clinical psychologist in providing the appropriate care.

THE PRIMARY CARE PHYSICIAN/ GENERAL PRACTITIONER (GP)

This is a medically trained individual who, following their medical degree, has undertaken additional training in the area of primary care. They are usually the first point of contact in health services when individuals have a health-related problem (either physical or mental/ emotional). Their training gives them a wide knowledge of all the branches of medicine and can then help guide individuals in seeking specialist help. Some of these professionals have additional training in particular areas of medicine, such as mental health. In some countries the GP may have a role in helping to coordinate the care provided, but in others it may be a much more peripheral role. Primary care physicians/GPs may have minimal training in ASD, but this may vary from person to person.

THE SPEECH AND LANGUAGE THERAPIST/PATHOLOGIST

Speech and language therapists/pathologists (the term depends on geographical location) is an individual who has received specialist training and education, usually at degree level. They work with different elements of speech, communication and language to improve these areas through therapy. They manage a wide variety of communication problems in both children and adults and are often involved in the assessment process in children with ASD. Communication difficulties are a core component of ASD and can contribute significantly to the mental health of these children. Therefore, the speech and language therapist/pathologist plays a key role in reducing the stress created by the communication problems.

THE OCCUPATIONAL THERAPIST

The occupational therapist is an individual who has studied occupational therapy, typically at degree level. The occupational therapist is trained to help people of all ages improve their daily living skills through the use of activities or interventions to improve function. Some occupational therapists specialise specifically in mental health, and in this role they work by helping an individual cope with the demands placed on them. This can include assessment of basic motor functions (such as coordination) and, more specifically to children with ASD, they can assess the child's sensory processing. They can be involved in the ongoing therapy for children with comorbid mental health problems, identifying particular stressors and how to manage them.

THE SPECIALIST TEACHER/SPECIALIST EDUCATOR

The specialist teacher/specialist educator is an individual who, following their teacher training, has become trained in a specific area of education. There can be specialist teachers/educators for those children who are visually impaired, hard of hearing or with learning difficulties. In many areas there are specialist teachers/educators for children with ASD and they will either work directly with the children in a specialist teaching environment or will advise schools on the best provision for an individual child. They can provide guidance on differentiating the curriculum and modifications to the teaching environment. As the child will spend so much time in school, they may be one of the first points of contact if a child is having problems. Many specialist teachers will understand mental health problems in children with ASD.

THE EDUCATIONAL/SCHOOL PSYCHOLOGIST

The educational/school psychologist undertakes specialist training in educational psychology after a psychology degree or qualifications in teaching. They apply the theories and principles from psychology and education to the diagnosis and management of problems found within the educational environment. These problems can range from learning difficulties to behavioural problems which impact on the child's academic performance. They are often involved in the diagnosis of children with ASD and will be involved in supporting teachers and other educational professionals in helping the child. They are trained in psychological assessments and sometimes provide counselling for children. If a child with ASD develops a mental health problem, the educational psychologist may be an early point of contact for the school. Their role can vary between countries and they can be a central point of contact in the overall care of the child.

THE SOCIAL WORKER

The social worker tends to be educated in the principles of social care up to degree level. The role does vary significantly internationally and covers a wide range of social needs. There can be specialist social workers for different age groups and abilities. Where children are involved, social workers have a particular role in child protection, but also in helping to improve the welfare of vulnerable children. The input from social care for children with ASD can be important as social workers may be able to identify the necessary support structures and mobilise services, thus helping families. The role can be very challenging and it may depend on your local area how much social workers are involved with your child.

SPECIALIST THERAPISTS

There are a wide range of specialist therapists. As discussed in the previous chapter, children with ASD can have access to therapies such as family, music, play and art therapy, and the therapists in these areas will have different training backgrounds. In choosing a specific therapist it may be useful to research the underpinning principles of a particular therapy to understand their role in ASD. We discussed many of these in the previous chapter, so please refer back for more information.

THE ROLE OF THE VOLUNTARY/ CHARITY/COMMUNITY SECTOR

Despite ASD being more commonly recognised and an increasing number of children being diagnosed with the condition and having comorbid difficulties, it is clear that provision of services is limited. The role of the voluntary sector cannot be underestimated in the support and ongoing work they do with children and families. This sector can make up a significant element of the care provided for children with ASD and includes a range of organisations from charities to support groups which may all have different roles. In any locality it is important to research what support is available for families or if there are more extensive services available.

CHAPTER SUMMARY

ASD is a long-term condition which can involve a number of different professional groups throughout childhood. As new problems arise, different professionals can be involved, and, generally, situations can be helped when professionals work together. However, depending on the background of the professional consulted, families can be given different solutions to the same problems. With the lack of a clear treatment in ASD, professionals often resort to educated guesses which may depend on their own knowledge and experiences. The different professionals come from a variety of sectors including health, education, social care and charity/voluntary services, and often a multidisciplinary approach to care is the most effective.

ⓘ IMPORTANT LEARNING POINTS

- Different professionals from different agencies tend to be involved in a child's care.
- Professionals can see the same problem from different angles and this may depend on their training and background.
- The multidisciplinary approach, where professionals work together, tends to have better outcomes.

FURTHER READING

Dogra, N., Parkin, A., Gale, F., and Frake, C. (2009). *A Multidisciplinary Handbook of Child and Adolescent Mental Health for Front-line Professionals* (2nd Edition). London: Jessica Kingsley Publishers.

GLOSSARY OF TERMS

Aetiology	Refers to the cause of something, it means the cause of an illness or a disorder.
Agoraphobia	A fear of open spaces and being outside.
Antihistamine	A type of medication to help control or prevent allergic reactions.
Anxiety	A feeling of being nervous or worried, accompanied by physical sensations in the body such as raised heart rate, sweating and nausea.
Bipolar disorder	Also known as bipolar affective disorder, it is a mental illness characterised by periods of elevated and depressed mood. It can be associated with psychotic features.
Central nervous system	Part of the nervous system, consisting of the brain and spinal cord.
Chronic	Something that happens over a long time, and that is persistent or reoccurring.
Circadian rhythm	The circadian rhythm is a physiological and behavioural cycle associated with changes in bodily functions, such as hormone levels, over a 24 hour period.
Cognition	The mental process of thinking and understanding.
Comorbid	A coexisting or additional issue or problem.
Coprolalia	The involuntary utterance of obscene words or derogatory remarks.
Copropraxia	The involuntary usage of obscene or offensive gestures.
Delusion	A false idea or belief that is held with complete conviction that is out of keeping with the person's educational, cultural and social background which is resistant to evidence demonstrating the contrary.
Depression	Also referred to as depressive illness, is characterised by a low mood, fatigue, limited enjoyment, and the biological symptoms such as poor sleep, poor appetite, decreased concentration and motivation. It is also associated with negative thoughts and feelings.
Deprivation	The state of having necessary things withheld, such as food or water.
Dyscalculia	A difficulty with numeracy and numbers.
Dyslexia	This is a general term referring to individuals who have difficulties with literacy.
Echolalia	The automatic repetition of the spoken words of others.
Efficacious	A successful result is produced, which is desired.

Ego dystonic	Found in Obsessive Compulsive Disorder, referring to the behaviours and thoughts which are in conflict with a person's actual feelings and causing them distress as they realise the behaviours and thoughts are irrational.
Electroencephalogram	A measure of the electrical activity in the brain.
Empathy	The ability to understand how someone else feels.
Emotion	A mental state representing the feelings of an individual.
Executive functioning	In psychology this is seen as the cognitive system which controls the cognitive processes. This includes working memory, attention, verbal reasoning, inhibition, multi-tasking and mental flexibility.
Hallucination	A false perception which occurs alongside normal perceptions and is often perceived by the individual as being real. They can occur in any sensory modality.
Hyperactivity	Overactivity in the child – typically behaviours such as fidgeting, over-exercising, playing with the hands and so forth.
Hyperventilation	Rapid breathing which may cause dizziness.
Hypnogram	A graph depicting the rhythms of sleep.
Hypomania	This is a mild form of mania marked by hyperactivity and elevated mood.
Ideation	Relates to the formation of ideas and concepts. It refers to the process of creating new ideas.
Impulse/impulsivity	An 'impulse' is a strong or inexplicable urge to do something without planning. 'Impulsivity' is the inability to control one's impulses and the need to act on how one feels at any given moment.
Interpersonal	Relationships with others, such as peers.
learning/intellectual disability	Refers to problems in intellectual functioning. These may be global problems or in specific areas. It is also known as intellectual disability, and can be graded from mild to profound.
Mania	A mental state marked by elevated mood, often euphoria, overactivity and possible psychotic features.
Medical model	A psychology term coined by Robert Laing in 1971 which claims that abnormal behaviour is a result of physical problems and thus should be treated medically. This has been challenged, and alternative models such as the social model have been developed.
Melatonin	A hormone that plays a significant role in sleep.
Mental health	A level of psychological well-being or absence of mental disorder.
Mental illness	This is not clearly defined but tends to reflect impairments in the individual's cognitive, emotional and behavioural functions. These need to be persistent and interfere with the day-to-day life of that person.

Mind blindness	A state in which an individual has a poor theory of mind and is unable to attribute thoughts and behaviours correctly to themselves or others.
Modality	A type of behaviour or expression; a way of treating something.
Neuron	A basic nerve cell that builds the nervous system and transmits information around the body.
Neurotransmitter	Transmits the nerve impulses.
Olfactory	The sense of smell.
Parasuicide	Overdoses, or self-cutting behaviour of low medical lethality.
Pareidolia	A psychological phenomenon where individuals perceive random stimuli as significant. Common examples are seeing faces in clouds.
Pathology	Relates to the study and diagnosis of disease. It refers to the process of defining a condition.
Perpetuating factors	These are the factors which may lead the child to continue to self-harm.
Pervasive development disorder	Refers to a group of conditions characterised by delays in development of many of the basic skills. This includes the ability to socialise, communicate and use imagination. Come under the umbrella of autistic or autism spectrum disorders.
Pharmacological	Relating to the preparation and use of drugs/medications.
Phenomenon/ phenomena	Events or people that are observed; subjects or topics.
Precipitating factors	These are the things which cause the disorder or problem.
Predisposing factors	These are the things which make the young person at risk from a particular disorder. Often these are factors which increase stress on the child.
Prevalence	The average rate of something occurring.
Prodromal phase	An undetermined length of time prior to the onset of a psychotic episode sometimes seen in schizophrenia. It is associated with a progressive decline in overall functioning, socially, academically and emotionally.
Prognosis	A medical term which considers the likely outcomes of a particular illness.
Psychosis	A term applied to behaviours, thoughts and perceptions which are a consequence of an individual's disconnection with reality.
Resilience factors	Relates to the ability of the individual to cope with stress.
Risk-factors	The things which increase the risk of an individual developing a mental health problem.
Schizophrenia	A mental illness characterised by hallucinations, delusions, disorganised speech and thoughts. It is a form of psychosis.
Self-injury	Injuring oneself for the purposes of expressing an emotion.

Self-harm	Deliberately inflicting harm on oneself. An extreme form of this is suicide.
Sensory processing difficulties	A difficulty taking in, processing and responding to sensory information from the environment and from within one's own body.
Separation anxiety	Anxiety which a child experiences when separated from a carer. It is seen in normal child development.
Social model	A fundamental aspect of the social model relates to equality. It argues that changes are needed in society to help those with disabilities or mental health problems. It argues that attempts to 'fix' the patient, particularly if against their wishes, are discriminatory.
Social Story™	An activity to help the individual understand a concept or situation which breaks the activities down into manageable segments to promote engagement and understanding.
Somatic	Relates to the body or bodily sensations. Often used to describe the physical bodily symptoms in conditions such as anxiety and depression (e.g. headaches).
Stereotypies	These tend to be simple movements, such as body rocking, marching, crossing and uncrossing of the legs.
Stigma	A negative view of someone's reputation.
Stress	Physical or mental tension.
Suicide	The taking of one's own life with intent. To bring about death by one's own hand.
Talking therapy	Interventions for mental health problems whereby talking with the individual is the main modality of therapy. Although each of the talking therapies are different, this group of therapies allow the individual to talk through their problems with a professional in the field of mental health. Includes therapies such as psychodynamic therapy, Cognitive Behavioural Therapy and family therapy.
Theory of mind	Likened to the concept of empathy, theory of mind relates to an individual's ability to see the world from someone else's point of view.
Tics	A tic is an involuntary action which is sudden and repetitive. It can either be a movement or a vocal utterance.
Vestibular	A person's sense of balance.

REFERENCES

AllPsych Online: The Virtual Psychology Classroom (2012). *Psychology Dictionary*. Available at http://allpsych.com/dictionary/d.html, accessed on 18 January, 2012.

American Art Therapy Association (2012). *What is art therapy?* Available at www.americanarttherapyassociation.org/upload/whatisarttherapy.pdf, accessed on 10 October, 2012.

The American Heritage. (2007). *Medical Dictionary*. Boston: Houghton Mifflin Company.

Andersen, T. (1987). The reflecting team: Dialogue and meta-dialogue in clinical work. *Family Process, 26*(4) 415–428.

Anderson, S., and Morris, J. (2006). Cognitive behaviour therapy for people with Asperger syndrome. *Behavioural and Cognitive Psychotherapy, 34*(3) 293–303.

Ando, H., and Yoshimura, I. (1979). Effects of age on communication skill levels and prevalence of maladaptive behaviors in autistic and mentally retarded children. *Journal of Autism and Developmental Disorders, 9*(1) 83–93.

Asperger, H. (1944). *'Die Autistischen Psychopathen' im kindesalter* ['Autistic psychopaths' in childhood] (in German). *Archiv für Psychiatrie und Nervenkrankheiten, 117*, 76–136.

Asperger, H. (1991). Autistic psychopathy in childhood (U. Frith translation). In U. Frith (Ed.) *Autism and Asperger Syndrome* (pp. 37–92). Cambridge: Cambridge University Press.

Attwood, T. (1999). *Modifications to cognitive behaviour therapy to accommodate the cognitive profile of people with Aperger's syndrome.* Available at www.tonyattwood.com.au/paper2.htm – specifically – www.tonyattwood.com.au/index.php?option=com_content&view=article&id=81:modifications-to-cognitive-behaviour-therapy-to-accommodate-the-cognitive-profile&catid=45:archived-resource-papers&Itemid=181, accessed on 19 November 2012.

Attwood, T. (2007). *The Complete Guide to Asperger's Syndrome.* London: Jessica Kingsley Publishers.

Bakken, T., Helverschou, S., Eilertsen, D., Heggelund, T., Myrbakk, E., and Martinson, H. (2010). Psychiatric disorders in adolescents and adults with autism and intellectual disability: A representative study in one county in Norway. *Research in Developmental Disabilities, 31*(6), 1669–1677.

Baron-Cohen, S. (1989). The autistic child's theory of mind: A case of specific developmental delay. *Journal of Child Psychology and Psychiatry, 30*(2), 285–97.

Baron-Cohen, S., Leslie, A. M., and Frith, U. (1985). Does the autistic child have a 'theory of mind'? *Cognition, 21*(1), 37–46.

Baron-Cohen, S., Mortimore, C., Moriarty, J., Izaguirre, J., and Robertson, M. (1999). The prevalence of Gilles de la Tourettes's syndrome in children and adolescents with autism. *Journal of Child Psychology and Psychiatry, 40*(2), 213–218.

Bauermeister, J., Shrout, P., Chavez, L., Rubio-Stipec, M. *et al.* (2007). ADHD and gender: Are the risks and sequel of ADHD the same for boys and girls? *Journal of Child Psychology and Psychiatry, 48*(8), 831–839.

Beck, A. (1987). Cognitive models of depression. *Journal of Cognitive Psychotherapy, 1*(1), 5–37.

Beck, A. (1991). Cognitive therapy: A 30 year retrospective. *American Psychologist, 46*(4), 368–375.

Beebe, D. and Risi, S. (2003). Treatment of adolescents and young adults with high-functioning autism or Asperger syndrome. In M. Reinecke, F., Dattilio, and Freeman, A. (Eds) *Cognitive Therapy with Children and Adolescents: A Casebook for Clinical Practice.* (2nd Edition) (pp. 369–401). New York: Guilford Press.

Beersma, D., Dijk, D., Blok, C., and Everhardus, I. (1990). REM sleep deprivation during 5 hours leads to an immediate REM sleep rebound and to suppression of non-REM sleep intensity. *Electroencephalography and Clinical Neurophysiology, 76*(2)114–122.

Berg, F. M. (2001). *Children and Teens Afraid to Eat: Helping Youth in Today's Weight-Obsessed World.* Hettinger, ND: Healthy Weight Network.

Bettelheim, B. (1967). *The Empty Fortress: Infantile Atism and the Birth of the Self.* New York: The Free Press.

Bhugra, D. (2005). The global prevalence of Schizophrenia. *PLoS Medicine, 2*(5), e151–e152.

Birch, L. L., and Fisher, J. O. (1998). Development of eating behaviours among children and adolescents. *Pediatrics, 101*(3 Pt2) 539–549.

Bleuler, P. (1911, English edition 1950). *Dementia Praecox or the Group of Schizophrenias.* New York: International University Press.

Bloch, M., and Leckman, J. (2009). Clinical course of Tourette syndrome. *Journal of Psychosomatic Research, 67*(6) 497–501.

Bromley, J., Hare, D. J., Davison, K., and Emerson, E. (2004). Mothers supporting children with autistic spectrum disorders: Social support, mental health status and satisfaction with services. *Autism, 8*(4), 409–423.

Bruscia, K. (1982). Music in the assessment and treatment of echolalia. *Music Therapy, 2*(1), 25–41.

Burklow, K., Phelps, A., Schultz, J., McConnell, K., and Rudolf, C. (1998). Classifying complex pediatric feeding disorders. *Journal of Pediatric Gastroenterology and Nutrition, 27*(2) 143–147.

Campbell, J. (1975). Illness is a point of view: The development of children's concepts of illness. *Child Development, 46*(1) 92–100.

Canitano, R., and Vivanti, G. (2007). Tics and Tourette syndrome in autism spectrum disorders. *Autism, 11*(1), 19–28.

Cannon, W. B. (1929). *Bodily Changes in Pain, Hunger, Fear and Rage.* New York: Appleton-Century-Crofts.

Cantwell, D. (1996). Attention Deficit Disorder: A review of the past years. *Journal of the American Academy of Child and Adolescent Psychiatry, 35*(8), 978–987.

Carrington, S., Templeton, E., and Papinczak, T. (2003) Adolescents with Asperger Syndrome and Perceptions of Friendship. *Focus on Autism and Other Developmental Disabilities, 18*(4), 211–218.

Cattanach, A. (2003). *An Introduction to Play Therapy.* Hove: Brunner-Routledge.

Cederlund, M., Hagberg, B., and Gillberg, C. (2010). Asperger syndrome in adolescent and young adult males. Interview, self- and parent assessment of social, emotional, and cognitive problems. *Research in Developmental Disabilities, 31*(2), 287–298.

Centers for Disease Control and Prevention. (2000). Youth risk behavior surveillance: United States, 1999. *Morbidity and Mortality Weekly Report, 49*(SS05), 1–96.

Chan, R. C. K., Shum, D., Toulopoulou, T., and Chen, E. Y. H. (2008). Assessment of executive functions: Review of instruments and identification of critical issues. *Archives of Clinical Neuropsychology, 23*(2), 201–216.

Chandra, A., and Minkovitz, C. S. (2006). Stigma starts early: Gender differences in teen willingness to use mental health services. *Journal of Adolescent Health, 38*(6) 754.e1–754.e8.

Chorpita, B. F. (2007). *Modular Cognitive-Behavioral Therapy for Childhood Anxiety Disorders.* New York: Guilford Press.

Cole, D. J. (1992). The reversibility of death. *Journal of Medical Ethics, 18*(1), 26–30.

Colten, H., and Altevogt, B. (2006). *Sleep Disorders and Sleep Deprivation: An Unmet Public Health Problem.* Washington, DC: The National Academic Press.

Comings, D. (1994). Tourette syndrome: A hereditary neuropsychiatric disorder. *Annals of Clinical Psychiatry, 6*(4), 235–247.

Costello, E. J., Mustillo, S., Erkanli, A., Keeler, G., and Angold, A. (2003). Prevalence and development of psychiatric disorders in childhood and adolescence. *Archives of General Psychiatry, 60*(8) 837–844.

Damasio, A. R. (2001). Fundamental feelings. *Nature, 413*, 781.

Davis, T. E., III, and Ollendick, T. H. (2005). A critical review of empirically supported treatments for specific phobia in children: Do efficacious treatments address the components of a phobic response? *Clinical Psychology: Science and Practice, 12*, 144–160.

Dogra, N., Parkin A., Gale, F., and Frake, C. (2009). *A Multidisciplinary Handbook of Child and Adolescent Mental Health for Front-Line Professionals* (2nd Edition). London: Jessica Kingsley Publishers.

Drahota, A., Wood, J. J., Sze, K. M., and Van Dyke, M. (2011). Effects of cognitive behavioral therapy on daily living skills in children with high-functioning autism and concurrent anxiety disorders. *Journal of Autism and Developmental Disorders, 41*(3), 257–265.

Edwards, R., Williams, R., Dogra, N., O'Reilly, M., and Vostanis, P. (2008). Facilitating and limiting factors of training available to staff of Specialist CAMHS. *The Journal of Mental Health Training, Education and Practice, 3*(3), 22–31.

Escher, S., Romme, M., Buiks, A., Delespaul, P., and van Os, J. (2002). Formation of delusional ideation in adolescents hearing voices: A prospective study. *American Journal of Medical Genetics, 114*(8) 913–920.

Farrugia, D. (2009). Exploring stigma: Medical knowledge and the stigmatisation of parents of children diagnosed with autism spectrum disorder. *Sociology of Health and Illness, 31*(7), 1011–1027.

Fisher, M. (2003). The course and outcome of eating disorders in adults and in adolescents: A review. *Adolescent Medicine, 14*(1), 149–158.

Francis, L., Ventura, A., Marini, M., and Birch, L. (2012). Parent overweight predicts daughters' increase in BMI and disinhibited eating from 5 to 13 years. *Obesity, 15*(6), 1544–1554.

Frith, U., and Happé, F. (1994). Autism: beyond 'theory of mind'. *Cognition, 50*(1–3) 115–132.

Gaebel, W., Zaske, H., and Baumann, A. (2006). The relationship between mental illness severity and stigma. *Acta Psychiatrica Scandinavica, 113*(5429) 41–45.

Geller, D. (2006). Obsessive-compulsive and spectrum disorders in children and adolescents. *The Psychiatric Clinics of North America, 29*(2), 353–370.

Ghaziuddin, M. (2005). *Mental Health Aspects of Autism and Asperger Syndrome.* London: Jessica Kingsley Publishers.

Ghaziuddin, M., Tsai, L. Y., and Ghaziuddin, N. (1992). Comorbidity of autistic disorder in children and adolescents. *European Child and Adolescent Psychiatry, 1*(4), 209–213.

Gilberg, C. (2002). *A Guide to Asperger Syndrome.* Cambridge: Cambridge University Press.

Gillberg, C., and Råstam, M. (1992). Do some cases of anorexia nervosa reflect underlying autistic-like conditions? *Behavioural Neurology, 5*(1) 27–32.

Gold, C., Wigram, T., and Elefant, C. (2006). Music therapy for autistic spectrum disorder (Cochrane review). *Cochrane Database of Systematic Reviews Issue 2.*

Golnik, A. E., and Ireland, M. (2009). Complementary alternative medicine for children with autism: A physician survey. *Journal of Autism and Developmental Disorders, 39*(7) 996–1005.

Goodman, R., and Scott, S. (2005). *Child Psychiatry* (2nd Edition). Oxford: Blackwell Publishing.

Gray, C. (2002a). *My Social Stories Book.* London: Jessica Kingsley Publishers.

Gray, D. (2002b). 'Everybody just freezes. Everybody is just embarrassed': Felt and enacted stigma among parents of children with high functioning autism. *Sociology of Health and Illness, 24*(6), 734–749.

Green, H., McGinnity, A., Meltzer, H., Ford, T., and Goodman, R. (2004). *Mental health of children and young people in Great Britain, 2004.* London: Office for National Statistics (Department of Health).

Health Advisory Service (NHS). (1995). *Together we Stand: Commissioning, Role and Management of Child and Adolescent Mental Health Services.* London: HMSO.

Hossain, M. S. (2008). *Human Immortality: Death and Adjustment Hypotheses Elaborated.* South Carolina: Book Surge Publishing.

Idler, E. L. (1979). Definitions of health and illness and medical sociology. *Social Science and Medicine, 13A,* 723–731.

Kalvya, E. (2009) Comparison of eating attitudes between adolescent girls with and without Asperger syndrome. Daughters' and mothers' reports. *Journal of Autism and Developmental Disorders, 39*(3) 480–486.

Kanner, L. (1943). Autistic disturbances of affective contact. *Nervous Child, 2,* 217–250.

Kanner, L. (1949). Problems of nosology and psychodynamics in early childhood autism. *American Journal of Orthopsychiatry, 19*(3) 416–426.

Karim, K., Cook, L., and O'Reilly, M. (2012). Diagnosing autistic spectrum disorder in the age of austerity. *Child: Care, Health and Development,* doi:10.1111/j.1365–2214.2012.01410.x.

Kendall, P. C. (1993). Cognitive-behavioral therapies with youth: Guiding theory, current status, and emerging developments. *Journal of Consulting and Clinical Psychology, 61*(2), 235–247

Khalifa, N., and von Knorring, A.L. (2007). Tourette syndrome and other tic disorders in a total population of children: Clinical assessment and background. *Acta Paediatrica, 94*(11), 1608–1614.

King, R. A., Scahill, L., Findley, D., and Cohen, D. J. (1998). Psychosocial and behavioral treatments. In J. F. and D. J. Cohen (Eds) *Tourette's Syndrom: Tics, Obsessions, Compulsions: Developmental Psychopathology and Clinical Care* (pp. 338–359). New York: John Wiley and Sons.

Kjelsäs, E., Bjornstrom, C., and Gunnar, G. (2004). Prevalence of eating disorders in female and male adolescents. *Eating Behaviors, 5*(1), 13–25.

Klin, A., and Lemish, D. (2008). Mental disorders stigma in the media: Review of studies on production, content, and influences. *Journal of Health Communication, 13*(5) 434–449.

Kreitman, N., Greer, P.S. and Bagley, C.R. (1969). Parasuicide. *British Journal of Psychiatry, 115,* June, 746–747.

Lay, B., Blanz, B., Hartman, M., and Schmidt, M. (2000). The psychosocial outcome of adolescent-onset schizophrenia: A 12-year followup. *Schizophrenia Bulletin, 26*(4), 801–816.

LeBlanc, M., and Ritchie, M. (2001). A meta-analysis of play therapy outcomes. *Counselling Psychology Quarterly, 14*(2), 149–163.

Leckman, J. F., and Cohen, D. J. (2005). Tic disorders. In M. Rutter and E. Taylor (Eds). *Rutter's Child and Adolescent Psychiatry* (4th Edition) (pp. 593–611). Oxford: Blackwell Publishing.

Leckman, S. R., Nieto, C., Libby, S. J., Wing, L., and Gould, J. (2007). Describing the sensory abnormalities of children and adults with autism. *Journal of Autism and Developmental Disorders, 37*(5) 894–910.

Leckman, J. F., Walker, D. E., and Cohen, D. J. (1993). Premonitory urges in Tourette's syndrome. *American Journal of Psychiatry, 150*(1) 98–102.

Link, B. G., and Phelan, J. C. (2001). Conceptualizing stigma. *Annual Review of Sociology, 27,* 363–385.

Link, B. G., Phelan, J. C., Bresnahan, M., Stueve, A., and Pescosolido, B. A. (1999). Public conceptions of mental illness: Labels, causes, dangerousness, and social distance. *American Journal of Public Health, 89*(9), 1328–1333.

Lugnegard, T., Hallerback, M. U., and Gillberg, C. (2011). Psychiatric comorbidity in young adults with a clinical diagnosis of Asperger syndrome. *Research in Developmental Disabilities, 32*(5), 1910–1917.

MacHale, R., McEvoy, J., and Tierney, E. (2009). Caregiver perceptions of the understanding of death and need for bereavement support in adults with intellectual disabilities. *Journal of Applied Research in Intellectual Disabilities, 22*(6), 574–581.

Macklin, R. (1972). Mental health and mental illness: some problems of definition and concept formation. *Philosophy of Science, 39*(3) 341–365.

Manikam, R., and Perman, J. A. (2000). Pediatric feeding disorders. *Journal of Clinical Gastroenterology, 30*(1), 34–46.

Mayes, S. D., Calhoun, S. L., Murray, M. J., and Jahanara, Z. (2011). Variables associated with anxiety and depression in children with autism. *Journal of Developmental and Physical Disabilities, 23*(4), 325–337.

McDougle, C. J., Kresch, L. E., Goodman, W. K., Naylor, S. T., *et al.* (1995). A case–controlled study of repetitive thoughts and behavior in adults with autistic disorder and obsessive-compulsive disorder. *American Journal of Psychiatry, 152*(5) 772–777.

McKinstry, L. (2005). 'Not ill – just naughty: Leo McKinstry on the scandal of Attention Deficit Hyperactivity Disorder, whereby parents are paid to bring up their children badly.' *Spectator, 297*(9212) 18–24.

Mental Health Foundation (1999). *Bright Futures: Promoting Children and Young People's Mental Health*. London: MHF.

Metcalf, P., and Huntington, R. (1991). *Celebrations of Death: The Anthropology of Mortuary Ritual*. New York: Cambridge University Press.

Miguel, E., Rosario-Campos, M., Shavitt, R., Hounie, A., and Mercadente, M. (2001). The tic-related obsessive-compulsive disorder phenotype. In D. Cohen, C. Goetz, and J. Jankovic, (Eds). *Tourette Syndrome* (pp. 45–55). New York: Williams and Williams.

Millstein, S. G., Adler, N. E., and Irwin, C. E. (1981). Conceptions of illness in young adolescents. *Pediatrics, 68*(6), 834–839.

Morey, C., Corcoran, P., Arensman, E., and Perry, I. J. (2008). The prevalence of self-reported deliberate self-harm in Irish adolescents. *BMC Public Health, 8,* 79, doi:10.1186/1471-2458-8-79.

Moseley, D., Tonge, B., Brereton, A., and Einfeld, S. (2011). Psychiatric comorbidity in adolescents and young adults with autism. *Journal of Mental Health Research in Intellectual Disabilities, 4*(4), 229–243.

Muehlenkamp, J. J., Claes, L., Havertape, L., and Plener, P. L. (2012). International prevalence of adolescent non-suicidal self-injury and deliberate self-harm. *Child and Adolescent Psychiatry and Mental Health, 6,* 10: doi:10.1186/1753-2000-6-10.

Mukaddes, N. M., Herguner, S., and Tanidir, C. (2010). Psychiatric disorders in individuals with high-functioning autism and Asperger's disorder: Similarities and differences. *World Journal of Biological Psychiatry, 11*(8), 964–971.

Myant, K., and Williams, J. (2005). Children's concepts of health and illness: Understanding of contagious illnesses, non-contagious illnesses and injuries. *Journal of Health Psychology, 10*(6), 805-819.

National Autistic Society. (2012). *You need to know*. Available at www.autism.org.uk/global/content/search%20results.aspx?q=CAMHS, accessed 12 May 2013.

National Institute for Health and Clinical Excellence (NICE). (2008). *Attention deficit hyperactivity disorder: Diagnosis and management of ADHD in children, young people and adults*. Available at www.nice.org.uk/CG72, accessed on 12 May, 2013.

National Institute of Mental Health. (2012a). *Statistics: Any disorder among children*. Available at www.nimh.nih.gov/statistics/1ANYDIS_CHILD.shtml, accessed on 21 January, 2012.

National Institute of Mental Health (2012b) *Rate of bipolar symptoms among teens approaches that of adults*. Available at www.nimh.nih.gov/science-news/2012/rate-of-bipolar-symptoms-among-teens-approaches-that-of-adults.shtml, accessed on 13 May 2013.

National Mental Health Strategy; Australia. (updated: 2010). *What is mental illness?* Available at www.health.gov.au/internet/main/publishing.nsf/content/B7B7F48 65637BF8ECA2572ED001C4CB4/$File/whatmen.pdf, accessed on 21 January, 2012.

Nutt, D. (2002). The neuropharmacology of serotonin and noradrenaline in depression. *International Clinical Psychopharmocology, 17 Suppl 1:* S1–S12.

O'Reilly, M., and Parker, N. (2013). 'You can take a horse to water but you can't make it drink': Exploring children's engagement and resistance in family therapy. *Contemporary Family Therapy 35,* 3, 491–507.

O'Reilly, M., Cook, L., and Karim, K. (2012). Complementary or controversial care? The opinions of professionals on complementary and alternative interventions for autistic spectrum disorder. *Clinical Child Psychology and Psychiatry, 17*(4), 602–615.

O'Reilly, M., Ronzoni, P., and Dogra, N. (2013). *Research with Children: Theory and Practice.* London: SAGE.

O'Reilly, M., Taylor, H., and Vostanis, P. (2009). 'Nuts, schiz, psycho': An exploration of young homeless people's perceptions and dilemmas of defining mental health. *Social Science and Medicine, 68*(99), 1737–1744.

O'Reilly, M., Vostanis, P., Taylor, H., Day, C., Street, C., and Wolpert, M. (2012). Service user perspectives of multi-agency working: A qualitative study with parents and children with educational and mental health difficulties. *Child and Adolescent Mental Health,* doi:10.1111/j.1475-3588.2012.00674.x.

Parker, N., and O'Reilly, M. (2012). 'Gossiping' as a social action in family therapy: The pseudo-absence and pseudo-presence of children. *Discourse Studies, 14(4),* 1–19.

Parker, N., and O'Reilly, M. (2013). Reflections from behind the screen: Avoiding therapeutic rupture when utilising reflecting teams. *The Family Journal: Counseling for Couples and Families, 21(2),* 170–179.

Polanczyk, G., de Lima, M. S., Horta, B., Biederman, J., and Rohde, L. (2007). The worldwide prevalence of ADHD: A systematic review and metaregression analysis. *American Journal of Psychiatry, 164*(6), 942–948.

Price, R., Kidd, K., Cohen, D., Pauls, D., and Leckman, J. (1985). A twin study of Tourette syndrome. *Archives of General Psychiatry, 42*(8), 815–820.

Puleo, C. M., and Kendall, P. C. (2011). Anxiety disorders in typically developing youth: Autism spectrum symptoms as a predictor of cognitive-behavioral treatment. *Journal of Autism and Developmental Disorders, 41*(3), 275–286.

Råstam, M. (2008). Eating disturbances in autism spectrum disorders with focus on adolescent and adult years. *Clinical Neuropsychiatry – Journal of Treatment Evaluation, 5*(1), 31–42.

Reisenzein, R. (2007). What is a definition of emotion? And are emotions mental-behavioral processes? *Social Science Information, 46*(3), 424–428.

Rimland, B. (1964). *Infantile Autism: The Syndrome and its Implications for a Neural Theory of Behavior.* New York: Appleton-Century-Crofts.

Robinson, R. (1998). Obsessive-compulsive disorder in children and adolescents. *Bulletin of the Menninger Clinic, 62*(4), A49–A64.

Rotter, J. B. (1954). *Social Learning and Clinical Psychology.* Michigan: Prentice-Hall.

Royal College of Psychiatrists. (2012). *Self-harm: Key facts.* London: Royal College of Psychiatrists. Available at www.rcpsych.ac.uk/expertadvice/problemsdisorders/self-harm/self-harm-keyfacts.aspx, accessed 19 August 2013.

Schreck, K., and Williams, K. (2006). Food preferences and factors influencing food selectivity for children with autism spectrum disorders. *Research in Developmental Disabilities, 27*(4), 353–363.

Scottish Needs Assessment Programme. (2005). *The mental health of children and young people: A framework for promotion, prevention and care.* Available at www.scotland.gov.uk/Publications/2005/10/2191333/13341, accessed on 21 January, 2012.

Sharpe, D., and Baker, D. (2007). Financial issues associated with having a child with autism. *Journal of Family and Economic Issues, 28,* (2) 247–264.

Sheldon, S., Ferber, R., and Kryger, M. (Eds). (2005). *Principles and Practice of Pediatric Sleep Medicine*. Philadelphia, PN: Elsevier Saunders.

Siegel, J. (2001). The REM sleep-memory consolidation hypothesis. *Science, 294,*(5544), 1058–1063.

Silva, R. R., Munoz, D. M., Barickman, J., and Friedhoff, A. J. (1995). Environmental factors and related fluctuation of symptoms in children and adolescents with Tourette's disorder. *Journal of Child Psychology and Psychiatry, 36*(2), 305–312.

Simonoff, E., Pickles, A., Charman, T., Chandler, S., Loucas, T., and Baird, G. (2008). Psychiatric disorders in children with autism spectrum disorders: Prevalence, comorbidity, and associated factors in a population-derived sample. *Journal of the American Academy of Child and Adolescent Psychiatry, 47*(8), 921–929.

Sims, A. (1995). *Symptoms in the Mind*. London: W.B. Saunders.

Slaughter, V. (2005). Young children's understanding of death. *Australian Psychologist, 40,*(3), 179–186.

Smith, T., Magyar, C., and Arnold-Saritepe, A. (2002). Autism spectrum disorder. In: D.T. Marsh and M. A. Fristad (Eds), *Handbook of Serious Emotional Disturbance in Children and Adolescents* (pp. 131–148). New York: John Wiley and Sons, Inc.

Sobanski, E., Marcus, A., Henninghausen, K., Hebebrand, J., and Schmidt, M. H. (1999). Further evidence for a low body weight in male children and adolescents with Asperger's disorder. *European Child and Adolescent Psychiatry, 8*(4), 312–314.

Speece, M., and Brent, S. (1984). Children's understanding of death: A review of three components of a death concept. *Child Development, 55*(5), 1671–1686.

Steinhausen, H.-C. (2002). The outcome of anorexia nervosa in the 20th Century. *American Journal of Psychiatry, 159*(8), 1284–1293.

Stratton, P. (2010). *The Evidence Base of Systematic Family and Couples Therapies*. London: The Association for Family Therapy, UK.

Sullivan, P., Neale, M., and Kendler, K. (2000). Genetic epidemiology of major depression: Review and meta-analysis. *American Journal of Psychiatry, 157*(10), 1552–1562.

Thompson, E. A., Mazza, J., Herting, J. R., Randell, B. P., and Eggert, L. L. (2005). The mediating roles of anxiety, depression, and hopelessness on adolescent suicidal behaviors. *Suicide and Life Threatening Behavior, 35*(1), 14–34.

Tillman, R. and Geller, B. (2003). Definitions of rapid, ultrarapid, and ultradian cycling and of episode duration in pediatric and adult bipolar disorders: A proposal to distinguish episodes from cycles. *Journal of Child and Adolescent Psychopharmacology, 13*(3), 267–271.

van Steensel, F. J. A., Bogels, S. M., and Perrin, S. (2011). Anxiety disorders in children and adolescents with autistic spectrum disorders: A meta-analysis. *Clinical Child and Family Psychology Review, 14*(3), 302–317.

Vostanis, P., O'Reilly, M., Taylor, H., Day, C., *et al.* (2012). What can education teach child mental health services? Practitioners' perceptions of training and joint working. *Emotional and Behavioural Difficulties, 17*(2), 109–124.

Walkup, J., Albano, A., Piacentini, J., Birmaher, B., *et al.* (2008). Cognitive behavioral therapy, Sertraline, or a combination in childhood anxiety. *New England Journal of Medicine, 359*, 2753–2766.

Wasserman, D., Cheng, Q., and Jiang, G. X. (2005). Global suicide rates among young people aged 15–19. *World Psychiatry, 4*(2), 114–120.

Westbrook, D., Kennerley, H., and Kirk, J. (2011). *An Introduction to Cognitive Behaviour Therapy: Skills and Applications* (2nd Edition). London: Sage.

White, S. W., Oswald, D., Ollendick, T., and Scahill, L. (2009). Anxiety in children and adolescents with autism spectrum disorders. *Clinical Psychology Review, 29*(3), 216–229.

Wiggs, L., and Stores, G. (2004). Sleep patterns and sleep disorders in children with autistic spectrum disorders: Insights using parent report and actigraphy. *Developmental Medicine and Child Neurology, 46,* 372–380.

Wilbarger, P. (1995). The Sensory Diet: Activity programs based on sensory processing theory. *Sensory Integration Special Interest Section Newsletter, 18*(2), 1–4.

Wing, L. (1981a). Language, social and cognitive impairments in autism and severe mental retardation. *Journal of Autism and Developmental Disorders, 11*(1), 31–44.

Wing, L. (1981b). Asperger's syndrome: A clinical account. *Psychological Medicine, 11*(1), 115–129.

Wing, L. (1996). *The Autistic Spectrum.* London: Constable and Company Ltd.

Wing, L., and Gould, J. (1979). Severe impairments of social interaction and associated abnormalities in children: Epidemiology and classification. *Journal of Autism and Developmental Disorders, 9*(1), 11–29.

WHO (World Health Organization) (2010a). *Mental health: Strengthening our response: Fact sheet.* Available at www.who.int/mediacentre/factsheets/fs220/en/, accessed on 21 August 2012.

WHO (World Health Organization) (2010b). *The ICD-10 for mental and behavioural disorders: Clinical descriptions and diagnostic guidelines.* Available at www.who.int/classifications/icd/en/bluebook.pdf, accessed on 29 January, 2012.

WHO (World Health Organization) (2011). *Mental health: A state of well-being.* Available at www.who.int/features/factfiles/mental_health/en/, accessed on 18 January, 2012.

Yadav, V., O'Reilly, M., and Karim, K. (2010). Secondary school transition: Does mentoring help 'at risk' children? *Community Practitioner, 83*(4), 24–28.

Zohar, A. H. (1999). The epidemiology of obsessive-compulsive disorder in children and adolescents. *Child and Adolescent Psychiatric Clinic of North America, 8*(3), 445–460.

SUBJECT INDEX

AUTHOR INDEX